classic
motorcycles

MILLER'S

2002

MILLER'S CLASSIC MOTORCYCLES YEARBOOK & PRICE GUIDE 2002

Created and designed by
Miller's Publications
The Cellars, High Street
Tenterden, Kent TN30 6BN
Telephone: 01580 766411
Fax: 01580 766100

General Editor: Mick Walker
Production Co-ordinator: Philip Hannath
Editorial Assistants: Rosemary Cooke, Maureen Horner, Lalage Johnstone, Deborah Wanstall
Designer: Kari Reeves
Advertisement Designer: Simon Cook
Jacket Design: Colin Goody
Advertising Executive: Jo Hill
Advertising Assistant: Melinda Williams
Production Assistants: Caroline Bugeja, Ethne Tragett
Additional Photography: David Hawtin, Robin Saker
Indexer: Hilary Bird

First published in Great Britain in 2001
by Miller's, a division of Mitchell Beazley,
imprints of Octopus Publishing Group Ltd,
2–4 Heron Quays, London E14 4JP

© 2001 Octopus Publishing Group Ltd

A CIP catalogue record for this book is
available from the British Library

ISBN 1 84000 441 X

While every care has been exercised in the
compilation of this guide, neither the
authors nor publishers accept any liability
for any financial or other loss incurred
by reliance placed on the information contained in
Miller's Classic Motorcycles Yearbook & Price Guide

Illustrations and film output by CK Litho, Whitstable, Kent
Printed and bound by Toppan Printing Co (HK) Ltd, China

Front cover illustration:

1960 World Champion MV 125 dohc single,
£90,000–110,000 / $130,500–159,500 ⊞ **MW**

classic
motorcycles

GENERAL EDITOR
Mick Walker

FOREWORD
Colin Seeley

MILLER'S

2002

Contents

Acknowledgements. 6
Foreword 7
How to use this book 8
The MOT - A Testing Time 9
The Motorcycle Market. 10

Aermacchi 11
AJS 12
Ambassador 15
Ariel 16
BD 19
Beardmore-Precision. 20
Benelli 20
Berneg 21
Bimota 22
BM 22
BMW 22
Bradbury. 24
Brough-Superior 25
BSA. 26
Cagiva 33
Capriolo 33
Chater-Lea 34
Cimatti. 34
Comet 35
Coventry Eagle 35
DKW 36
Douglas 36
Ducati. 37
Dunelt 44
Excelsior. 44
FN 44
Francis-Barnett 45
Gilera 45
Henderson 46
Hesketh 46
Honda 47
Colour Review. 49–56
Indian 57
Iso 57
Itom 58
James 58
Kawasaki. 59
Laverda 61
Levis 62
Lincoln. 62
Malanca 62
Maserati 63
Matchless 63
Mi-Val 65
MM 65
Mondial 65
Motobi 66

Moto Guzzi. 66
Motom 70
Moto Morini. 70
Moto Reve 73
MV Agusta 73
MZ 75
Neracar. 76
New Hudson. 76
New Imperial 76
Norton 77
OEC 82
Panther 83
Parilla 84
Peugeot. 84
Premier. 85
Quadrant 85
Raleigh 86
Rickman 87
Rover 87
Royal Enfield 88
Rudge 90
Rumi 91
Scott. 92
Sertum 93
Sun. 93
Sunbeam 94
Suzuki. 98
Triumph. 99
TWN. 112
Velocette 112
Vincent-HRD 117
Werner 119
Yamaha 120
Colour Review. 121–128
Dirt Bikes 129
Military Bikes 134
Monkey Bikes 136
Mopeds. 137
Police Bikes. 138
Racing Bikes 139
Scooters 150
Sidecars. 153
Specials. 157
Memorabilia 162

Key to Illustrations 167
Glossary 169
Index to Advertisers. 170
Bibliography 170
Directory of Museums 171
Directory of Motorcycle Clubs 172
Index 174

Acknowledgements

The publishers would like to acknowledge the great assistance given by our consultants:

Malcolm Barber	81 Westside, London SW4 9AY Tel: 0207 228 8000
Rob Carrick	5 Tinkers Lane, Wimbotsham, King's Lynn, Norfolk PE34 3QE Tel: 01366 388801
David Hawkins	81 Westside, London SW4 9AY Tel: 0207 228 8000
Michael Jackson	Sotheby's, 34–35 New Bond Street, London SW1A 2AA Tel: 0207 493 8080
Brian Verrall	Caffyns Row, High Street, Handcross, Nr Haywards Heath, West Sussex RH17 6BJ Tel: 01444 400678
Rick Walker	R&M Walker, 45 Caves Close, Terrington St Clement, King's Lynn, Norfolk Tel: 01553 829141

We would like to extend our thanks to all auction houses, their press offices, and dealers who have assisted us in the production of this book, along with the organisers and press offices of the following events:

The International Classic Motor Cycle Show

Louis Vuitton Classic

Foreword

I have pleasure in being asked to write this foreword for the 2002 edition of *Miller's Classic Motorcycle Yearbook and Price Guide*. Now at retirement age I cannot believe that I have had fifty years involvement with the motorcycle sport and industry.

Keen to enter the motorcycle arena at fourteen years of age then leaving school at fifteen, I forfeited an engineering career to join the Dartford dealership of Schwieso Brothers, as a young mechanic. Harold and Les Schwieso being past grass track stars at Brands Hatch.

Nineteen-fifty-four at the age of eighteen years saw the start of my own motorcycle repair business in Belvedere. Followed two years later by the opening of my first motorcycle retail shop and also being appointed main agent for AJS and Matchless motorcycles. This started my long association with the AMC factory. Other agencies soon followed: Velocette, Frances-Barnett, NSU, Ariel, Greeves with Canterbury, Busmar, Wessex and Watsonian sidecars.

Eleven years of retailing followed during which time my racing career had started. In 1954 riding a Triumph Trophy in scrambles, sprints, hill climbs and grass track events. With Colin Seeley the rider agent painted on our pick-up van I turned to Greeves, riding at Canada Heights at Swanley, Kent, at the opening of that venue.

From my early childhood motorcycles were in the family and I learned to ride my father's Vincent Rapide sidecar outfit at fourteen. Then passing my road test at sixteen, sidecar outfits were in my blood with Ted Davis the Vincent factory rider and George Brown my heroes.

Nineteen-sixty-one proved to be the turning point riding the first Matchless G50 fitted with a Canterbury racing sidecar and I finished sixth in my first Isle of Man TT, what a proud moment for me, my passenger, the late Wally Rawlings and the AMC factory. Two more silver IOM replicas were to follow on the Matchless with third and sixth places respectively in 1962 and 1963. Then I turned to BMW and the world stage.

Meantime, 1966 saw the emergence of the first Seeley-AJS and Seeley-Matchless racing solo machines ridden by Derek Minter and John Blanchard that season.

With the AMC factory going into liquidation later that year a full take over of all racing assets by Colin Seeley Racing Developments took place and manufacturing carried on with success achieving wins in the 1968 and 1969 British 500 Championship and runners up in 1970 and 1971. As the expansion of the Seeley design and frame manufacturing a total of 25 different models were produced.

So it is a great privilege that in a period of some 20 to 35 years later the Seeley name is held in such high esteem. Classics in their own right alongside the greats of our past industry as depicted in the *Miller's Classic Motorcycle Yearbook and Price Guide*.

For me it has been a most enjoyable career combined at times with a few tears. Having now gone full circle I act as a consultant with Bonhams and Brooks the auctioneers. I look forward to this latest edition of the excellent *Miller's Classic Motorcycle Yearbook and Price Guide* from which I am sure I can still learn!

How to use this book

It is our aim to make this Guide easy to use. Motorcycle marques are listed alphabetically and then chronologically. Dirt Bikes, Military Bikes, Monkey Bikes, Mopeds, Racing Bikes, Scooters, Sidecars and Specials are located after the marques, towards the end of the book. In the Memorabilia section objects are grouped by type. If you cannot find what you are looking for, please consult the index which starts on page 174.

Ariel (British 1902–70)

Ariel was one of the true pioneers of the British cycle and motorcycle industries. However, it could trace its origins as far back as 1847, when the name was used for a wheel, then later in 1871 for a penny-farthing cycle. It appeared on a variety of bicycles over the following quarter of a century, before the Ariel Cycle Company was incorporated during 1897. This company was owned by the Birmingham based Dunlop Rubber Company, and had come into being because of a rift between the tyre manufacturer

and other cycle companies, who objected to the Dunlop name adorning bicycles. One has to remember that in those days Dunlop had a virtual monopoly on the supply of tyres to the cycle trade.

Then, in 1896, another firm that made parts for the industry, Cycle Components, appointed Charles Sangster to their board. Later, his family played a major role in the development of the British motorcycle industry during the first half of the 20th Century.

1932 Ariel Square Four, 498cc overhead-camshaft 4-cylinder engine, partly dismantled restoration project, comprising complete rolling chassis, petrol tank, gearbox, clutch, mudguards, chainguard, tank-top instrument panel, headlamp shell and lens, rear light/mounting bracket, crankcases with crankshafts and con-rods, cylinder head with valve gear, timing cover and cam cover.
£2,300–2,700
$3,300–4,000 ⚒ BKS

1938 Ariel VB, 597cc side-valve single, 86.4 x 102mm bore and stroke, valenced front mudguard, 'Brooklands can' exhaust, chrome tank.
£2,000+
$2,900+ ⚙ AOC/AOM

BMW (German 1923–)

1938 BMW R51, 494cc overhead-valve flat-twin, 68 x 68mm stroke and bore, 24bhp at 5,600rpm.
£6,500–7,800
$9,500–11,500 ⚒ BKS
This model's performance and reliability were such that it was quickly adopted by the German traffic police.

c1939 BMW R35, 342cc overhead-valve single, 72 x 84mm bore and stroke, 14bhp at 4,500rpm, hand gear-change, shaft final drive.
£8,000–9,000
$11,600–13,000 ⊞ AtMC

Miller's Motorcycle Milestones

BMW R90S 898cc (German 1973)
Price range: £2,500–3,500 / $3,600–5,000
The press called the R90S Germany's sexiest superbike, which was an apt description of what became probably BMW's best-loved street bike of the post-war era.
The R90S was launched in a blaze of publicity on 2 October, 1973, at the Paris salon. This setting was fortunate, as it was there, 50 years before, that BMW had presented its very first motorcycle, the Max Friz-designed R32.
Paris in 1973 also marked the arrival of the Stroke 6 range, of which the R90S was the glamour model; the machine that hurled BMW to the very top of the Superbike stakes.

The R90S employed an 898cc (90 x 70.6mm) version of the famous flat-twin engine and, as with all the Stroke 6 models, saw a switch from a four- to five-speed gearbox.
Compared to the standard R90, the 'S' variant put out an additional 7bhp (67bhp). Weighing 200kg (441lb) dry, the R90S could top 125mph.
But it was in its styling that the R90S really represented a major milestone in BMW's history, featuring as it did a dual racing-style seat, fairing cowl, twin hydraulically-operated front disc brakes and an exquisite airbrushed custom paint job in smoked silver-grey (later also in orange) for the bodywork, which meant that no two machines were ever absolutely identical.

Marque Introduction
provides an overview of the marque including factory changes and in some instances the history of a particular model. Introductions change from year to year and not every section will begin with an introduction.

Caption
provides a brief description of the motorcycle or item, and could include comments on its history, mileage, any restoration work carried out and current condition.

Price Guide
these are based on actual prices realised shown in £sterling and a US$ conversion. Remember that Miller's is a PRICE GUIDE not a PRICE LIST and prices are affected by many variables such as location, condition, desirability and so on. Don't forget that if you are selling it is quite likely you will be offered less than the price range. Price ranges for items sold at auction include the buyer's premium.

Source Code
refers to the 'Key to Illustrations' on page 167 that lists the details of where the item was sourced. Advertisers are also indicated on this page.
The ⚒ icon indicates the item was sold at auction.
The ⊞ icon indicates the item originated from a dealer.
The ⚙ icon indicates the item belonged to a member of a motorcycle club, see Directory of Motorcycle Clubs on page 172.

Bold Footnote
covers relevant additional information about a motorcycle's restoration and/or racing history, designer, riders and special events in which it may have participated.

Miller's Motorcycle Milestones
highlights important historic motorcycle events and the effect they have had on the motorcycle industry.

The MOT - A Testing Time

It was on 30 April, 1963 that the Ministry of Transport instituted a mandatory roadworthiness test for all motor vehicles over five years old, this was soon reduced to encompass all machines over three years old, and remains much the same today as it was then, although now administered by the Department of Transport.

Despite a name change of the administrative authority, the test is still known officially as the MOT test. This annual inspection was introduced as a measure to ensure that all road vehicles were in a safe and roadworthy condition, as earlier research had highlighted the fact that some owners just did not bother to maintain their means of transport, through false economy or sheer ignorance. The test is quite straightforward and should present the average owner with no real problems, for it is a very BASIC common sense safety check. In fact the acceptable inspection standards are woefully low and, in the mind of the author and many other reputable testers, do not go far enough to ensure the machine and owner's safety.

The Department of Transport deems it not practical to lay down limits of wear for all components of every motorcycle, and leaves this to the tester's experience. There are only five measurable items on the inspection that are given a finite figure to work to, and these are:

1) The winker flash rate, which must be within 60 – 120 flashes per minute.
2) A minimum tyre tread depth of 1mm over 75% breadth.
3) A minimum brake efficiency figure of 30 and 25%.
4) A minimum of 1.5mm for brake pads or shoe linings.
5) A maximum wheel rim distortion of 4mm lateral run-out (2mm on alloy rims) and 3mm eccentricity.

All other items are checked at the tester's discretion, and within this grey area the tester must apply his own standards of serviceability.

When checking the brakes of a classic or vintage machine, the systems only have to be tested to just past the minimum efficiency figure, which is a percentage requirement of the all-up weight of the bike plus its rider. All machines have to achieve this standard, which is 30% on the main brake and 25% on the secondary brake; this is the requirement for mopeds and less powerful machinery. Veteran machines have different rules, in that only one braking system is required if the machine was first registered for use before 1 January, 1927. On modern machines the main brake is the front one, but on older bikes with equal-sized drum brakes the main brake may well be at the rear, as more pressure can be applied by the foot than the hand.

The minimum testing requirements for brakes and tyres are an insult to the rider who has any sense of self preservation, and any common sense motorcyclist would never let them wear down to this level. On the other hand there are other regulations that have to be adhered to that were never in force during the classic and vintage periods. These are retrospective rules that have been introduced to enhance the safety of the older machine, and mainly affect the lighting system. The rules state that all machines used after 1936 must be equipped with a stop lamp, even though we know that many never were, the stop lamp being offered as an optional extra on some bikes only. When the 98cc Autocycle became popular transport in the 1940s and 1950s it was fitted with what was basically a push-bike 'add-on' lighting system, which used a single-beam headlamp. The rules now require that motorcycles (and the 98cc Autocycle is classed as a motorcycle) must be fitted with a high- and low-beam headlamp. There are ways around these two retrospective rules, for the MOT regulations state that if the lamps are masked, painted over or permanently disconnected then they need not be tested. In this respect, if the machine does not conform to the requirements, the simple answer is to cover the front and rear lamps with masking tape prior to the test. All motorcycles require a front lamp that has both a main and dipped beam, except the 25mph moped or a moped first used before 1 January, 1972, which was equipped only with a dipped beam. A motorcycle made before January 1931 does not require a headlamp at all.

The horn is another testable item, which should be capable of giving an audible warning and being heard by other road users, its sound being neither harsh nor grating. Most machines of the classic period were equipped with an electric horn that was adversely affected by low battery voltage, and was often replaced by a 'squeaky' bulb horn. This replacement is perfectly acceptable provided that the machine was registered for use before 1973.

Remember the MOT test is a mandatory inspection, formulated to ensure your safety; and the MOT certificate only relates to the testable items and should not be regarded as evidence of general mechanical condition, as so many vendors think when it comes to selling the machine. The test does not cover all the points listed in the Construction and Use or Type Approval regulations, so it is possible that your bike may be MOT roadworthy, but still be illegal for use on the road in the eyes of the law. Compliance with the Construction and Use Regulations is the rider's responsibility – and ignorance of the law is no defence, but your local friendly traffic policeman is always at hand (when you least require his services) to give his 'own' ideas as to the rules laid down in this rather weighty publication.

Rob Carrick

The Motorcycle Market

The last twelve months have seen considerable upheavals in the auction world, but with the final withdrawal of Sotheby's from the automobilia market, its last link with motoring and motorcycling sales was severed. In October, Brooks took over the fine art auction house of Bonham's to become Bonham's & Brooks, and as we close for press, it has announced that it is merging with the UK operation of Phillips. The new company will be known as Bonham's. H & H, which boldly entered the motorcycle auction fray late in 1999, has since advertised for a suitable venue where it could hold more, but no sales have been announced. BCA (formerly ADT) recently held its first sale, planning to offer 25 machines, but this was disappointing following the with-drawal of 20 of them because of a legal dispute. BCA is planning a sale of some 22 bikes as we go to press, and indicated that it hopes to schedule two sales a year, initially as an experiment.

Cheffins, Grain and Comins has held a number of vehicle sales, some of which have included motorcycles, and Lambert & Foster in Kent, recently returned to the vehicle auction scene after being absent for a while, also sells the odd two-wheeler. The only provincial house remaining wholly committed to motorcycle-only sales, however, continues to be Palmer Snell, which was back at Shepton Mallett in October. Some 81 machines were offered, of which 45 found new homes, but top price was £2,900 ($4,200) for a 1961 Triumph Thunderbird 6T and, as in previous years, most of the machines and prices were in the lower range.

In fact, October was dominated by the Brooks Stafford sale on the 15th, which was very successful, producing some really excellent prices. The highest price achieved went to a Brough-Superior, in this case a 1938 SS100 sold for £38,900 ($55,500), but other good prices included £12,363 ($18,000) for a 1955 Vincent Black Knight, £12,420 ($18,100) for a 1943 BMW R75 Sahara combination with military accessories (Axis forces combinations are doing very well at present), £12,075 ($17,500) for a 1953 Vincent Black Shadow, and £9,200 ($13,400) for a 1960 AJS 350cc 7R. Novelty machines like Honda Monkey Bikes and motor-assisted tandems, Cyclemaster trade bikes, etc continue to do well, with Monkey Bikes invariably nudging £1,000 ($1,500). There appears to be a softening of the market in two-stroke veterans, low-capacity Pioneers and two-stroke flat-tankers.

Multi-cylinder Pioneers and vintage machines continue to do well, however, and the £7,475 ($10,800) for a 1929 BMW 750cc R62 twin at Stafford in October is typical. While the two Stafford sales held by Brooks continued to be the market barometers, this company does not confine itself to bikes-only sales. At Beaulieu, Harrogate and Olympia, motorcycles were sold successfully alongside cars and automobilia – 39 found new homes at Harrogate, for example, with a 1912 FN bringing £4,370 ($6,350), and a 1951 Vincent Rapide exceeding low estimate

to make £10,005 ($14,500). By the end of 2000, Bonham's & Brooks motorcycle sales totalled over £2 million ($3 million) for the year.

All eyes, naturally, were turned to the traditional April sale held at the Stafford County Showground by Bonham's & Brooks, but sadly the crisis caused by foot-and-mouth disease forced postponement of this important sale until 8 July 2001. By that time, the company's June sale at Harrogate had taken place. Among the motorcycles sold were an unrestored 1923 Triumph Model H at £2,645 ($3,850) and a 1935 Rudge Special at £4,025 ($5,850). Despite the delayed date, however, Stafford lived up to expectations, totalling well over £600,000 ($870,000).

Top price of £58,700 ($85,100) was paid for the ex-Geoff Duke 1953 NSU R22 Rennmax 248cc racer used in the Austrian GP, and other famous races, while an immaculate low-mileage 1974 MV Agusta 750S brought £16,100 ($23,500). A 1929 BMW 750cc R63 realised £12,880 ($18,800), a 1952 Vincent Black Shadow was bid to £11,270 ($16,200), and a 1926 Sunbeam 500 Sprint Special went all the way to £11,500 ($16,700). A two-owner 1925 Indian Scout V-twin in original condition realised £6,900 ($10,000), and a 1934 Sunbeam 95R racer reached £8,050 ($11,650).

A 1950 Norton 490cc International found a new home at £4,830 ($7,050), and a 1931 Rudge Ulster was not far behind at £4,200 ($6,100). Despite being unrestored, a 1922 Henderson four-cylinder combination made £9,775 ($14,000), reflecting high interest at present in American multi-cylinder machines, but racing machines – particularly Japanese and non-British makes – are still a very specialist market when not associated with household British names. Unrestored, the ex-Bill Lacey 1926 Grindlay-Peerless racer brought £4,370 ($6,350), underlining interest in all Brooklands-related machines, while the ex-J D Potts 1929 'Hundred' model from the same maker went as high as £12,650 ($18,200). More modest machines also have their following, with good D1 Bantams making £500 ($720) plus, and Cyclemaster-assisted pedal cycles in top condition achieving the same levels. Demand still points to rare machines, and those with provenance and, in some cases, an exceptional restoration (even on a fairly everyday classic) will see an above-average price. This may not always reflect the cost of the restoration.

The market continues to be enthusiast-driven, and despite the strength of the pound, foreign buyers were still prominent. The strengthening dollar has encouraged American bidders back into the market, however, and Stafford continues to have an international atmosphere, Europe always being represented by bidders from Holland, Germany and Switzerland in particular, not to forget the enthusiasts from Spain and Austria, who nearly always come away as successful buyers. So, it is fair to say that the future can be faced with confidence.

Malcolm Barber

Aermacchi *(Italian 1950–78)*

1961 Aermacchi 250 Ala Verde, 246.2cc overhead-valve single-cylinder engine, 66 x 72mm bore and stroke, 25bhp, 4-speed gearbox, wet clutch, 84mph top speed.
£2,000–2,200
$2,900–3,200 ⊞ MW
The original Aermacchi single featured long-stroke bore-and-stroke dimensions.

1961 Aermacchi Ala Azzurra, 246.2cc overhead-valve horizontal single, 4-speed gearbox, full-width drum brakes.
£1,800–2,000
$2,600–2,900 ⊞ VICO
The Ala Azzurra was a detuned version of the Ala Verde, offering a 75mph top speed.

1965 Aermacchi 250 Sprint H, overhead-valve horizontal single-cylinder engine, wet clutch, Silentium silencer, offside side-stand, standard US specification apart from rear dampers, mirrors and indicators.
£1,800–2,000
$2,600–2,900 ⊞ MW

1971 Aermacchi 350 Sprint SG, 344cc overhead-valve single-cylinder engine, 74 x 80mm bore and stroke, dry clutch, open frame, 92mph top speed, twin-pipe exhaust with twin silencers, original apart from paintwork.
£1,800–2,000
$2,600–2,900 ⊞ MW

1966 Aermacchi Sprint, 246.2cc overhead-valve horizontal single-cylinder engine, wet clutch, 5-speed gearbox.
£2,000–2,200
$2,900–3,200 ⊞ NLM

1973 Aermacchi SS350, 344cc ohv horizontal single, 5-speed gearbox, dry clutch, full loop frame, twin-leading-shoe front brake, electric start, non-standard silencers.
£2,000–2,200
$2,900–3,200 ⊞ NLM
This model was sold under the Harley-Davidson banner, as the American company had gained total control of Aermacchi in 1972.

1974 Aermacchi SS350, 344cc overhead-valve horizontal single, dry clutch, 12 volt electrics, electric start, 5-speed gearbox, twin-leading-shoe front brake, full cradle frame, direction indicators, non-standard silencers.
£1,600–2,000
$2,300–2,900 ⊞ MW

AJS (British 1909–66)

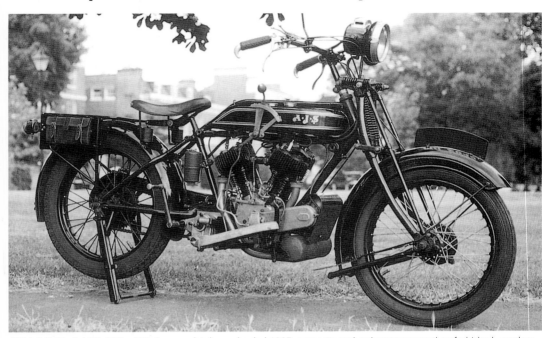

1924 AJS Model D1, 799cc V-twin, completely overhauled 1997, magneto and carburettor recently refurbished, gearbox serviced, front brake uprated.
£5,400–6,000
$7,800–8,700 ⚒ BKS
The D-series side-valve V-twins were an established feature in the AJS catalogue from 1912. In its earliest form, the engine displaced 631cc with two speeds, increased to 696cc with three speeds for 1913, followed by 748cc for 1914. The model continued in production, largely unaltered, during WWI, a number being supplied to the Russians. After the war, the Model D sustained AJS, receiving an increase in displacement to 799cc in 1921, together with new valves and detachable cylinder heads. The next major change occurred for 1924, when the Model D was joined by the D1. The new model featured lighter mudguards and a simpler electrical system, resulting in a lower price. It was always offered as a combination with an AJS-built sidecar, but a number of machines subsequently lost their appendages and proved just as suitable for solo use.

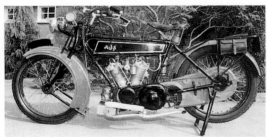

1915 AJS Model D, 799cc V-twin.
£4,000–4,400
$5,800–6,500 ⚒ BKS

Miller's is a price GUIDE not a price LIST

1926 AJS Big Port, 348cc overhead-valve single, 74 x 81mm bore and stroke, forward-mounted magneto, hand-change gearbox, kickstart, chain final drive.
£4,000–4,300
$5,800–6,250 ⊞ YEST
The famous Big Port was one of the AJS factory's biggest sellers during the Wolverhampton years.

1927 AJS V-twin, 799cc narrow-angle V-twin engine, rigid frame, hand-change gearbox, 'coffin' fuel tank, some parts including chainguards and lighting equipment missing.
£5,000–6,000
$7,250–8,700 ⚒ TEN

1927 AJS Big Port, 498cc inlet-over-exhaust single, 3-speed hand-change gearbox, pillion pad, unrestored, complete and original.
£4,250–4,500
$6,100–6,500 ⊞ PM

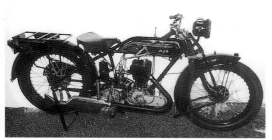

1928 AJS 500, 498cc inlet-over-exhaust single, hand-change gearbox, complete with lighting equipment and rear parcel carrier.
£3,500–4,000
$5,000–5,800 ⊞ YEST

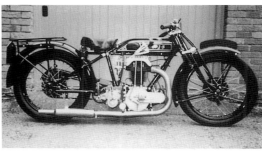

1928 AJS Big Port, 498cc overhead-valve vertical single, 84 x 90mm bore and stroke, fully restored.
£4,500–5,500
$6,500–8,000 ⚒ BKS

1930 AJS Model 9, 498cc side-valve single, forward-mounted magneto, dry-sump lubrication, hand-change gearbox, saddle tank, chain final drive.
£2,600–2,900
$3,800–4,300 ⊞ BLM

1936 AJS Model 22, 245cc overhead-valve single, 62.5 x 80mm bore and stroke, foot-change gearbox, assembled from spare parts.
£2,250–2,500
$3,250–3,650 ⚲ NAC
The Model 22 was in production from 1935 until 1940. The original version, such as the example shown here, featured magneto ignition; from 1938, a switch was made to coil ignition.

1947 AJS Model 16M, 348cc overhead-valve pre-unit single, 16bhp at 5,600rpm.
£2,250–2,750
$3,200–4,000 ⊞ BLM
The Model 16M was basically the AJS version of the better-known Matchless G3L. It remained in production from 1945 until 1955.

▶ **1951 AJS Model 18S,** 497cc overhead-valve pre-unit single, 82.5 x 93mm bore and stroke, 23bhp at 5,400rpm, fully restored.
£2,500–2,800
$3,600–4,000 ⊞ BLM
This was the first year in which the 18S received 'Jampot' rear suspension units, new fork internals and an aluminium cylinder head.

1958 AJS Model 16MS, 348cc overhead-valve pre-unit single, 16bhp at 5,600rpm.
£1,500–2,500
$2,200–3,600 ⊞ BLM
Coil ignition replaced the old magneto on the 16MS from 1958 onward, making the engine bottom-end look a lot smaller. Also new (from 1957) was the AMC gearbox, which superseded the original Burman unit.

1959 AJS Model 16MS, 348cc overhead-valve single, coil ignition, AMC gearbox, full-width hubs, dualseat, restored to original specification.
£1,500–2,000
$2,200–2,900 ⊞ BLM

1959 AJS Model 16, 348cc overhead-valve single, coil ignition, centre and side stands, mirrors, unrestored.
£1,650–1,950
$2,400–2,800 ⚒ PS

◄ **1960 AJS Model 31,** 646cc overhead-valve parallel twin, alloy head, iron barrel, dry-sump lubrication, 4-speed foot-change gearbox, duplex frame.
£2,500–2,800
$3,600–4,000 ⊞ BB
From 1960, the Model 31 was uprated with a new cylinder head, reduced valve angle, double-rate valve springs and a modular iron crankshaft. It also had closer gear ratios, a smaller headlamp shell and a two-level dualseat.

▶ **1960 AJS Model 20,** 498cc overhead-valve twin, 66 x 72.8mm bore and stroke, 30.5bhp at 6,800rpm, coil ignition, full-width hubs, original specification.
£2,500–3,000
$3,600–4,400 ⊞ OBMS
The Model 20 was built from 1949 until 1961.

1960 AJS Model 31, overhead-valve parallel twin, 72 x 79.3mm bore and stroke, AMC 4-speed gearbox, magneto/dynamo, full-width hubs, engine rebuilt to CSR specification, CSR siamesed exhaust.
£2,500–3,000
$3,600–4,400 ⊞ BLM

▶ **1960 AJS Model 31,** 646cc overhead-valve twin, 7.5:1 compression ratio, non-standard dualseat.
£2,000–2,500
$4,400–3,600 ⊞ BLM
This was the first year of coil ignition on the Model 31. It also had an alternator charging system.

1966 AJS Model 14 CSR, 248.5cc overhead-valve unit single, 69.85 x 64.85mm bore and stroke, 18bhp, 80mph top speed, restored to non-standard specification with alloy mudguards, Japanese front brake, flat handlebars and upswept silencer.
£500–550
$720–800 ⊗ NAC

Ambassador *(British 1947–64)*

> A known continuous history can add value to and enhance the enjoyment of a motorcycle.

◀ **1958 Ambassador Supreme 2T,** 249cc 2-stroke twin, 50 x 63.5mm bore and stroke, 4-speed gearbox, 17in wheels, 6in brakes, telescopic forks, swinging-arm suspension.
£1,250–1,500
$1,800–2,200 ⌁ H&H
The Supreme, with Villiers 2T twin-cylinder engine, was built between 1956 and 1958.

Ariel *(British 1902–70)*

Ariel was one of the true pioneers of the British cycle and motorcycle industries. However, it could trace its origins as far back as 1847, when the name was used for a wheel, then later in 1871 for a penny-farthing cycle. It appeared on a variety of bicycles over the following quarter of a century, before the Ariel Cycle Company was incorporated during 1897. This company was owned by the Birmingham based Dunlop Rubber Company, and had come into being because of a rift between the tyre manufacturer and other cycle companies, who objected to the Dunlop name adorning bicycles. One has to remember that in those days Dunlop had a virtual monopoly on the supply of tyres to the cycle trade.

Then, in 1895, another firm that made parts for the industry, Cycle Components, appointed Charles Sangster to their board. Later, his family played a major role in the development of the British motorcycle industry during the first half of the 20th Century.

In late 1897, Cycle Components purchased the Ariel firm, and in the following year used the brandname for a powered tricycle. As with many pedal cycle firms, interest in the internal-combustion engine had begun to grow, and Sangster and his fellow director, S. F. Edge, were keen to move into this new field. Like many similar devices at the time, the Ariel tricycle was powered by a licence-built French De Dion engine.

In 1900, Ariel constructed a quadricycle. Essentially, this was the tricycle equipped with twin front wheels (the earlier model had a single wheel at the front). The following year saw the arrival of a full motor car, while the tricycle and quadricycle continued to be made. In the same year the prototype Ariel motorcycle appeared. It employed a Belgian Minerva power unit with belt final drive and was equipped with pedals to assist climbing hills and starting.

Then, in 1902, the name of the parts company was changed to Components Ltd, with Charles Sangster as managing director. At the same time, the cycle and motorcycle business was split into two. The first production Ariel motorcycle left the Birmingham factory that year.

1932 Ariel Square Four, 498cc overhead-camshaft 4-cylinder engine, partly dismantled restoration project, comprising complete rolling chassis, petrol tank, gearbox, clutch, mudguards, chainguard, tank-top instrument panel, headlamp shell and lens, rear light/mounting bracket, crankcases with crankshafts and con-rods, cylinder head with valve gear, timing cover and cam cover.
£2,300–2,700
$3,300–4,000 ⚒ BKS

1938 Ariel VB, 597cc side-valve single, 86.4 x 102mm bore and stroke, valenced front mudguard, 'Brooklands can' exhaust, chrome tank.
£2,000+
$2,900+ ᪅ AOC/AOM

1951 Ariel NH Red Hunter, 499cc overhead-valve single, 81.8 x 95mm bore and stroke, one of last examples built with rigid frame.
£2,500–3,000
$3,600–4,300 ⊞ BLM

1951 Ariel VH350 Red Hunter, 346cc overhead-valve single, iron head and barrel, 72 x 85mm bore and stroke, 2-port head, 19.4bhp at 5,800rpm, fitted with optional high-level exhaust.
£2,500–3,000
$3,600–4,300 ⚒ PS

1952 Ariel KH, 499cc overhead-valve twin, 63 x 80mm bore and stroke, iron head and barrels, 26bhp at 6,500rpm, plunger rear suspension, concours condition.
£2,400–2,900
$3,500–4,200 ⚒ BKS
The KH was built from 1948 until 1957.

1953 Ariel NH350 Red Hunter, 346cc overhead-valve single, 72 x 85mm bore and stroke, iron head and barrel, 4-speed foot-change gearbox, telescopic forks, link plunger rear suspension, single seat and pillion pad, original apart from Avon handlebar fairing, unrestored.
£1,150–1,250
$1,500–1,800 ⊞ BB
The NH was in production from 1945 until 1959.

1953 Ariel Square Four 4G Mk II, 995cc overhead-valve 4-cylinder engine, 65 x 75mm bore and stroke, 4-pipe exhaust, dualseat, original, unrestored.
£3,500–4,000
$5,000–5,800 ⚒ BKS
The 4G Mk II model was introduced in 1953.

1954 Ariel VH Red Hunter, 499cc overhead-valve single, 81.8 x 95mm bore and stroke, alloy head, iron barrel, 26hp at 6,000rpm, original specification, very good condition.
£3,400–3,800
$5,000–5,500 ⊞ BB
Developed for off-road use, the swinging-arm frame appeared on the VH Red Hunter for 1954.

1954 Ariel NH350 Red Hunter, 346cc overhead-valve single, alloy cylinder head, 4-speed foot-change gearbox, restored.
£2,700–3,200
$3,900–4,600 ⊞ BLM
For 1954, the NH Red Hunter was given the swinging-arm frame, a four-gallon fluted tank, and a new toolbox, oil tank and air filter.

c1954 Ariel 4G Mk II Square Four, 998cc overhead-valve 4-cylinder engine, 4-pipe exhaust with twin silencers, chrome fluted tank, plunger frame, dualseat, concours condition.
£4,450–5,000
$6,500–7,250 ⊞ AtMC

1950s Ariel Square Four, 995cc overhead-valve 4-cylinder engine, 65 x 75mm bore and stroke, 4-speed foot-change gearbox, plunger rear suspension.
£3,500–4,000
$5,000–5,800 ⊞ PMo
This machine was assembled from a 1952 twin-pipe 4G Mk I engine and a later frame with an enlarged oil tank, and earlier-style tank and front brake.

1957 Ariel NH, 346cc overhead-valve single, 72 x 85mm bore and stroke, alloy head, iron barrel with integral pushrod tunnels, full-width brake hubs, swinging-arm frame, fluted tank, headlamp nacelle, dualseat.
£1,100–1,300
$1,600–1,900 ⊞ PM

► **1958 Ariel Leader,** 247cc piston-port 2-stroke twin, 54 x 54mm bore and stroke, fitted with all accessories including indicators and 8-day clock.
£1,150–1,300
$1,650–1,850 ⊞ BB
The Leader was announced in July 1958, and it created an instant sensation. Designed by Val Page, it was the first British bike to make substantial use of pressings, die-castings and plastics. It offered full enclosure with built-in legshields and screen, a pressed-steel frame and many unique features. This bike was one of the first built.

1956 Ariel VB, 598cc side-valve single, 86.4 x 102mm bore and stroke, 17bhp at 4,400rpm, swinging-arm rear suspension, headlamp nacelle, fluted tank, in need of cosmetic restoration.
£800–1,200
$1,150–1,750 ⊞ BLM
The VB was in production from 1945 until 1958.

1957 Ariel LH Colt, 198cc overhead-valve single, 60 x 70mm bore and stroke, 10bhp at 5,600rpm, plunger rear suspension.
£700–1,000
$1,000–1,500 ⊞ BLM
The Colt was in production from 1954 until late 1959, the engine being based on the BSA C11G unit, but with a smaller displacement.

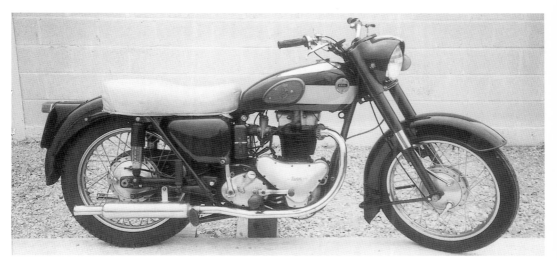

1958 Ariel FH Huntmaster, 647cc overhead-valve parallel twin, 70 x 84mm bore and stroke, iron head and barrels, 35bhp at 5,750rpm, full-width alloy hubs, swinging-arm rear suspension.
£2,000–2,500
$2,900–3,600 ⊞ **BLM**
The FH was produced between 1954 and 1959.

1964 Ariel Arrow 200, 199.5cc piston-port 2-stroke twin, 48.5 x 54mm bore and stroke, 14bhp at 6,250rpm, extensively restored, engine and gearbox rebuilt.
£1,200–1,400
$1,750–2,000 ⚹ **CGC**
The final descendent of the Leader was the Arrow 200.

1961 Ariel Golden Arrow Replica, 247cc piston-port 2-stroke twin, alloy heads, iron barrels.
£1,750–1,950
$2,500–2,900 ⊞ **PMo**
Ariel's Super Sports Arrow was better-known as the Golden Arrow. This particular machine was converted from a standard Arrow.

BD *(Czechoslovakian 1927–29)*

1928 BD 500 Single, 490cc bevel-driven double-overhead-camshaft unit-construction single, hand-change gearbox, chain final drive.
£6,300–7,000
$9,000–10,200 ⊞ **AtMC**
Based in Prague, BD (Breitfeld-Danëk) built high-quality 350cc and 490cc singles. Production continued after 1929 under the Praga name, the machines receiving shaft final drive.

Beardmore-Precision
(British 1906–23)

1923 Beardmore-Precision Model D, 349cc side-valve vertical single, iron head and barrel.
£4,300–4,800
$6,000–7,000 ⊞ YEST

Benelli (Italian 1911–89)

1934 Benelli Roadster, 220cc overhead-camshaft twin-port single, iron head and barrel, rigid frame, small-diameter brakes.
£2,800–3,200
$4,000–4,600 ⊞ MW
Only the rigid-frame models had high-level exhausts.

1946 Benelli 250 Sport, 247cc overhead-camshaft twin-port single, 67 x 70mm bore and stroke, girder forks, swinging-arm frame, rear light missing, in need of restoration.
£1,500–1,800
$2,200–2,600 ⊞ MW

▶ **1954 Benelli 125 Leoncino 2T,** 124cc 2-stroke single, 4-speed gearbox, telescopic front forks, swinging-arm rear suspension.
£1,800–1,900
$2,600–2,800 ⊞ MW
Benelli's 125 Leoncino was produced in both 2T (two-stroke) and 4T (four-stroke) versions. Leon Tartarini used one to win his class in the 1953 Giro d'Italia.

1975 Benelli 750 SE1, 747.7cc overhead-camshaft across-the-frame 6-cylinder engine, 56 x 56.6mm, 3 Dell'Orto 24mm carburettors, chain-drive, standard specification apart from crashbars and mirrors.
£2,800–3,000
$4,000–4,400 ⊞ MW
The 750 SE1 was the world's first production six-cylinder superbike.

1976 Benelli 500 Quattro, 498cc overhead-camshaft 4-cylinder engine, 5-speed gearbox, standard specification apart from rubber front fork gaiters.
£2,400–2,500
$3,500–3,650 ⊞ CotC

1977 Benelli 500 Quattro, 498cc overhead-camshaft 4-cylinder engine, 56 x 50.6mm bore and stroke, 4 Dell'Orto 22mm carburettors, 47bhp at 9,250rpm, 4-pipe exhaust, Brembo front disc brake, Grimeca drum rear brake, 18in wheels, standard specification, concours condition.
£2,800–3,200
$4,000–4,600 ⊞ MW
This model was generally thought of as an Italian copy of the Honda CB500 four.

Berneg *(Italian 1955–61)*

1955 Berneg 150 Twin, 158cc overhead-camshaft parallel twin, head-mounted distributor, 4-speed foot-change gearbox, full loop frame, swinging-arm rear suspension, 62mph top speed, original specification, unrestored.
£1,800–2,000
$2,600–2,900 ⊞ AtMC
The Berneg name came from Paride Bernardi and Corrado Negrini, who joined forces in Bologna during the early 1950s. The machine was designed by Alfonso Druisiani.

Bimota *(Italian 1975–)*

◄ **2000 Bimota SB8/R,** 996cc double-overhead-camshaft Suzuki TL1000 V-twin engine, Bimota chassis, specification includes many titanium and carbon fibre components, 1 of only 20 made, 4,700km from new.
£13,000–15,500
$18,850–22,450 ⊞ NLM

BM *(Italian 1952–72)*

1958 BM Bonvicini B0, 49cc 2-stroke single, alloy head, iron barrel, full-width brake hubs, Ceriani front forks, swinging-arm rear suspension, 'jelly-mould' fuel tank, original, unrestored.
£600–900
$870–1,300 ⊞ VICO

BMW *(German 1923–)*

◄ **1929 BMW R62,** 745cc side-valve flat-twin, 78 x 78mm bore and stroke, 18bhp at 3,400rpm, restored 1986, non-standard chrome rims, used daily from 1987 until spring 2000.
£7,500–9,000
$10,800–13,000 ⚡ BKS
Following the collapse of its aero engine business after WWI, BMW turned to other areas of manufacture, motorcycles among them. Its first two models, marketed as the Frink and Helios, were failures, but a successful proprietary engine was supplied to other manufacturers, such as Victoria. Designed by Max Friz and launched in 1923, the first motorcycle to be sold as a BMW was powered by a 493cc side-valve twin with horizontally-opposed cylinders; this flat-twin layout would forever be associated with the marque.

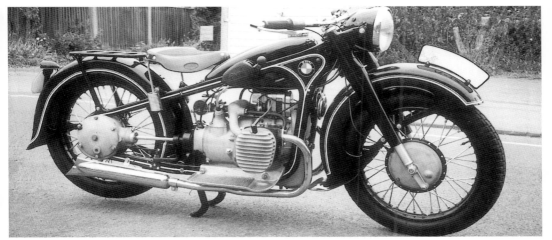

1936 BMW R12, 745cc side-valve flat-twin, shaft final drive, concours condition.
£13,500–15,000
$19,500–21,750 ⊞ AtMC
The R12 was essentially the earlier R11 model with telescopic forks and a four-speed gearbox. In all, 36,008 R12s were built between 1935 and 1942.

1938 BMW R51, 494cc overhead-valve flat-twin, 68 x 68mm stroke and bore, 24bhp at 5,600rpm.
£6,500–7,800
$9,500–11,500 ⤳ BKS
Introduced in 1938, the R51 incorporated a number of features that would become commonplace on post-war motorcycles. It had telescopic front forks together with plunger rear suspension, affording the rider a high level of comfort. A four-speed gearbox with foot operation was standard, and purchasers had the option of an Amal carburettor or a Bing instrument. The model's performance and reliability were such that it was quickly adopted by the German traffic police.

c1939 BMW R35, 342cc overhead-valve single, 72 x 84mm bore and stroke, 14bhp at 4,500rpm, hand gear-change, shaft final drive.
£8,000–9,000
$11,600–13,000 ⊞ AtMC

1960 BMW R50, 494cc overhead-valve flat-twin, original specification.
£3,200–3,500
$4,600–5,000 ⊞ PMo
The R50 superseded the R51/3. It was notable for its luxurious specification, which included full-width brake hubs, Earles front forks and swinging-arm rear suspension. This example has the optional Denfeld dualseat and rear carrier.

1953 BMW R51/3, 494cc overhead-valve flat-twin, 68 x 68mm bore and stroke, 24bhp at 5,800 rpm, telescopic front forks, plunger rear suspension, sprung single saddle, original specification.
£5,800–6,500
$8,400–9,400 ⊞ PMo
The R51/3 was built between 1951 and 1954.

▶ **1960 BMW R60/2,** 594cc overhead-valve flat-twin, 72 x 73mm bore and stroke, 30bhp at 5,800rpm, standard specification apart from optional rear carrier.
£3,800–4,500
$5,500–6,500 ⊞ MW
The R60/2 was produced between 1960 and 1969; 17,306 were built.

Miller's Motorcycle Milestones

BMW R90S 898cc (German 1973)
Price range: £2,500–3,500 / $3,600–5,000

The press called the R90S Germany's sexiest superbike, which was an apt description of what became probably BMW's best-loved street bike of the post-war era.

The R90S was launched in a blaze of publicity on 2 October, 1973, at the Paris salon. This setting was fortunate, as it was there, 50 years before, that BMW had presented its very first motorcycle, the Max Friz-designed R32.

Paris in 1973 also marked the arrival of the Stroke 6 range, of which the R90S was the glamour model; the machine that hurled BMW to the very top of the Superbike stakes.

The R90S employed an 898cc (90 x 70.6mm) version of the famous flat-twin engine and, as with all the Stroke 6 models, saw a switch from a four- to five-speed gearbox.

Compared to the standard R90, the 'S' variant put out an additional 7bhp (67bhp). Weighing 200kg (441lb) dry, the R90S could top 125mph.

But it was in its styling that the R90S really represented a major milestone in BMW's history, featuring as it did a dual racing-style seat, fairing cowl, twin hydraulically-operated front disc brakes and an exquisite airbrushed custom paint job in smoked silver-grey (later also in orange) for the bodywork, which meant that no two machines were ever absolutely identical.

The small fairing not only provided a surprising degree of protection for the rider, but also housed a voltmeter and electric clock. And for the first time BMW had employed a stylist, Hans Muth, for one of its motorcycles.

During its three-year lifespan (production ended in 1976), there were almost no changes, and the success of the R90S led BMW to build the fully-faired R100RS, which was a bestseller for well over a decade.

The R90S also proved popular in sports production racing events, gaining victories in the Isle of Man TT and at Daytona. The American importers for BMW at the time, the New York based Butler & Smith Company, even went as far as constructing a one-off racer based on the roadster.

Today, the machines that survive are eagerly sought by collectors, since they represent the nearest BMW have ever come to building a real sports bike.

◄ **1981 BMW R100CS,** 980cc overhead-valve flat-twin, 94 x 70.6mm bore and stroke, 5-speed gearbox, shaft final drive, BMW panniers, carrier and mirrors, concours condition.
£3,000–3,200
$4,350–4,650 ⊞ MW
The R100CS was sold between 1980 and 1984; 6,141 were built.

Bradbury *(British 1901–25)*

1913 Bradbury, 554cc side-valve long-stroke single, variable gearing, acetylene lighting, horn, footboards, built-in carrier.
£6,000–7,000
$8,700–10,200 ⊞ VER

Brough-Superior
(British 1902–39)

Although today George Brough is largely credited for the Brough-Superior marque, it was his father William Brough who had the foresight and enthusiasm that led to the formation of the famous Nottingham based company.

The first all-Brough engineered motorcycle arrived in 1902, and thanks to its outstanding performance and handling, several examples were entered in the reliability trials of the time, soon proving themselves to be winners in the world of motorcycle sport. And it was in this arena that William's son, George, first came to prominence, riding many of the company's bikes to success. This was also the cause of a disagreement between father and son in respect of the engine configuration to be used. In 1913, George had been pictured aboard a V-twin, which thereafter he favoured; whereas William Brough preferred the flat-twin (like Douglas and later BMW). In the early days, William's opinion ruled, resulting in flat-twin Broughs…but things were set to change.

In 1906, at the tender age of 16, George completed his first John O'Groats-to-Lands End trial, on a machine constructed by his father. Later, he would recall that this marathon was a miserable affair, not helped by poor weather and a supremely uncomfortable ride provided by the bike. It had the effect of giving him a vision for a more modern design of machine. This desire to improve things constantly brought him into conflict with his father over future developments. So, by 1919, he had set up business on his own account under the brandname of Brough-Superior (quite what his father thought of this is best left unrecorded!).

George Brough's idea was to use the very best components and technology available at the time. The results of this ethos were some of the best respected motorcycles ever built. His creations were not only reliable and fast, but also good looking and of high quality, thanks to fitments such as the famous Brough nickel-plated fuel tank. The term 'Rolls-Royce of Motorcycles' soon became synonymous with the name Brough-Superior.

In 1924, George Brough produced his most well-known model, the legendary SS100; each example was accompanied by a certificate to confirm that it had reached 100mph on the test track. To this day, the SS100 remains the most respected Brough of all. Some 3,000 Brough motorcycles, of all models, had been built by the time production ceased in 1939.

1924 Brough-Superior SS80, 998cc side-valve JAP engine, foot-change gearbox, nickel tank, excellent condition.
£28,500–29,500
$41,000–43,000 ⊞ VER

1938 Brough-Superior SS100, 990cc Matchless V-twin engine, fully restored, concours condition.
£38,900–46,600
$56,000–67,000 ⚲ BKS
The first SS100 was manufactured in 1924 and utilised a JAP engine. During 1936, the SS100 followed its smaller cousins by adopting a Matchless powerplant, which was equipped with hairpin valve springs. The machine was fitted with Castle forks as standard. Approximately 3,000 examples were built before WWII brought a halt to production.

1935 Brough-Superior SS80, 990cc side-valve Matchless 50° V-twin, foot-change gearbox, not to original specification.
£6,900–8,300
$9,900–12,000 ⚲ BKS
William Brough died on 11 September, 1934, in his 73rd year. His son, George, inherited the original Vernon Road works and, from 1935, began moving production from Haydn Road, Nottingham, to his father's original premises. Thus Brough-Superiors were made where, many years before, the Brough legend had begun.

> A known continuous history can add value to and enhance the enjoyment of a motorcycle.

BSA *(British 1906–71, late 70s–)*

1934 BSA J12, 499cc V-twin, girder forks, restored.
£6,000–7,000
$8,700–10,100 ↗ BKS
The J12 was announced for the civilian market in 1934, having been in production for the military for over a year. A four-cam, 45-degree, overhead-valve V-twin, the design was attractive, even though it was axed from BSA's line-up at the end of 1936.

1939 BSA G14, 985cc side-valve V-twin, 80 x 98mm bore and stroke, iron heads and barrels, restoration project.
£1,200–1,450
$1,700–2,000 ↗ BKS
The Model G14 was the last of BSA's 1000cc-class bikes.

◀ **1937 BSA B20,** 249cc side-valve single, 63 x 80mm bore and stroke, iron heads and barrel, hand-change gearbox, rigid frame, girder forks, fully restored.
£2,100–2,600
$3,000–3,700 ⊞ CotC
The B20 was only built in 1937 and 1938.

1946 BSA B31, 348cc overhead-valve single, 71 x 88mm bore and stroke, iron heads and barrel, 17bhp at 5,500rpm, 4-speed foot-change gearbox.
£1,200–2,000
$1,700–2,900 ⊞ BLM
The B31 was introduced in 1945 as a new model, with M-type crankcases, telescopic front forks and rigid frame, and the speedometer mounted in the tank.

1948 BSA M20, 496cc side-valve single, 82 x 94mm bore and stroke, 4-speed foot-change gearbox, telescopic forks, rigid frame.
£1,500–2,000
$2,100–2,900 ⊞ BLM
The M20 was built from 1937 until 1955; 1948 was the first year in which it was fitted with telescopic front forks in place of the original girders.

◀ **1948 BSA Bantam D1,** 123cc unit-construction piston-port 2-stroke single, 3-speed foot-change gearbox, restored to original specification, only 45 miles recorded since.
£1,100–1,300
$1,500–1,800 ⊞ BB
This is one of the original D1s with 'shovel' mudguard, flat silencer and rigid frame. It was a development of the 1939 DKW RT125, a German design considered war 'booty' by the Allies.

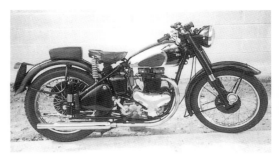

1948 BSA A7 Star Twin, 495cc overhead-valve pre-unit twin, 62 x 82mm bore and stroke, modified with later plunger frame, dualseat, Avonaire fairing, pannier boxes, unrestored.
£1,200–1,400
$1,700–2,000 🔧 H&H

1949 BSA A7 Twin, 495cc overhead-valve parallel twin, iron heads and barrel, chrome tank, telescopic forks, full loop frame, pillion pad.
£2,500–2,800
$3,600–4,000 ⊞ BLM
During 1949 and 1950, plunger rear suspension (fitted to this bike) was offered as an optional extra.

▶ **1951 BSA A10 Golden Flash,** 646cc overhead-valve pre-unit parallel twin, 70 x 84mm bore and stroke, 4-speed foot-change gearbox, telescopic front forks, plunger rear suspension, dualseat, good original condition.
£2,500–2,800
$3,600–4,000 ⊞ BLM
The A10 made its debut in 1950 and continued in production, with various changes, until late 1961.

1951 BSA B34, 499cc overhead-valve pre-unit single, 85 x 88mm bore and stroke, alloy engine, telescopic forks, plunger frame.
£3,500–4,000
$5,000–5,800 ⊞ BLM

1954 BSA B31, 348cc overhead-valve single, 71 x 88mm bore and stroke, 6.5:1 compression ratio, 17bhp at 5,500rpm, 4-speed gearbox, original and unrestored.
£1,600–1,800
$2,300–2,600 ⊞ BB
The B31 was sold between 1945 and 1959, and was one of the best of the heavyweight 350cc-class British singles. This example was built in the first year of the swinging-arm frame.

1955 BSA A10 Golden Flash, 646cc overhead-valve pre-unit parallel twin, swinging-arm frame, 8in front brake, headlamp nacelle.
£1,500–1,800
$2,100–2,600 🔧 COYS
The A10 was suitable for both solo and sidecar use. Even with a chair attached, it could cruise at 70mph, while in solo guise it could top 100mph.

◀ **1955 BSA A7 Shooting Star,** 497cc overhead-valve pre-unit twin, alloy cylinder head, 32bhp at 6,250rpm, 93mph top speed, concours condition.
£4,400–4,900
$6,200–7,000 ⊞ PMo
The Shooting Star and Road Rocket (high-performance version of the 646cc A10) were the sporting twins of BSA's mid-1950s range.

1955 BSA A7 Shooting Star, 497cc overhead-valve twin, 66 x 72.6mm bore and stroke, telescopic forks, swinging-arm frame, original specification, in need of restoration.
£1,800–2,400
$2,600–3,400 ⊞ BLM
BSA introduced the Shooting Star sports version of the A7 in 1955. In the same year, the company began fitting the new Amal Monobloc carburettor.

1955 BSA A7, 497cc overhead-valve pre-unit parallel twin, 62 x 72.6mm bore and stroke, iron heads and barrel, Burgess-type silencers, Ariel brakes, all original tinware, valanced mudguards, speedometer in headlamp.
£2,600–2,900
$8,000–4,200 ⊞ PMo

1955 BSA M21, 591cc side-valve single, 82 x 112mm bore and stroke, telescopic forks, plunger rear suspension, dualseat, original specification, concours condition.
£1,500–1,800
$2,100–2,600 ⊞ BLM
The M21 was a long-stroke slogger, making it an ideal sidecar tug.

▶ **1956 BSA C12,** 249cc overhead-valve single, 63 x 80mm bore and stroke, coil ignition, 11bhp at 5,200rpm, full-width hubs.
£500–800
$725–1,100 ⊞ BLM
The C12 entered its final form in 1956. It was the last of the BSA 250s before the introduction of the unit-construction C15 in 1958.

1956 BSA C11G, 249cc overhead-valve single, iron head and barrel, 4-speed gearbox, swinging-arm frame.
£700–800
$1,000–1,100 🔧 PS

1960 BSA A7 Shooting Star, 497cc overhead-valve pre-unit twin, several non-standard parts including mudguard, headlamp and front fork assembly, all from a later model.
£2,600–2,900
$3,700–4,200 ⊞ PMo

1961 BSA A10 Golden Flash, 646cc overhead-valve parallel twin, original apart from headlamp, excellent condition.
£2,200–2,500
$3,100–3,600 🔧 CGC

1962 BSA B40, 343cc overhead-valve single, 79 x 70mm bore and stroke, 21bhp at 7,000rpm.
£700–1,000
$1,000–1,400 ⊞ BLM
The B40 arrived in 1960 and continued in production until 1965. Compared to its smaller brother, the C15, the B40 not only featured a larger displacement, but also had 18in instead of 17in wheels and a larger 7in (as opposed to 6in) front brake.

1962 BSA C15 Star, 247cc overhead-valve single, distributor ignition, 17in wheels, full-width hubs.
£1,800–2,000
$2,600–2,900 ⊞ BLM
The C15 made its debut in 1958 and continued in production until 1967.

1962 BSA Rocket Gold Star, 646cc overhead-valve pre-unit twin.
£6,000–10,000
$8,700–14,500 ⊞ PMo
The most collectable of BSA's many pre-unit twin-cylinder models, the Rocket Gold Star was produced for only a few months, before being axed in favour of the new A65 unit-construction series. Only 1,800 examples were built. In performance terms, it was one of the fastest British production roadsters of its day, 50bhp being available by fitting a special silencer.

1962 BSA Rocket Gold Star, 646cc overhead-valve pre-unit twin, 70 x 84mm bore and stroke, 2-into-1 exhaust, Amal GP carburettor, magneto/dynamo, fitted with many aftermarket accessories including Lyta alloy tank, twin-leading-shoe front brake and several Taylor Dow components.
£6,500+
$9,500+ ⬚ **GSO**

1965 BSA C15, 247cc overhead-valve unit single, all original tinware, unrestored.
£750–900
$1,000–1,300 ⊞ **MAY**
BSA moved the C15's points to the timing cover for 1965; that year also saw an improved gearbox.

1965 BSA A65 Star, 654cc overhead-valve unit twin, 75 x 74mm bore and stroke, dry-sump lubrication, 38bhp at 5,800rpm.
£2,000–2,200
$2,900–3,100 ⊞ **BLM**
Introduced in 1962, the A65 and its smaller brother, the 500 A50, were BSA's first unit-construction twins.

▶ **1966 BSA Bantam D7,** 172cc piston-port 2-stroke single, 61.5 x 58mm bore and stroke, alloy head, iron barrel, 7.4bhp at 4,750rpm, 3-speed gearbox, unrestored.
£750–900
$1,000–1,300 ⊞ **OBMS**
The D7 was produced from 1959 until 1966.

1963 BSA Beagle, 74.7cc overhead-valve unit single, 47.6 x 42mm bore and stroke, flywheel-magneto ignition, 4-speed gearbox, spine frame, leading-link forks, dualseat, fully restored, concours condition.
£1,400–1,600
$2,000–2,300 ⊞ **CotC**
Introduced in 1963, the Beagle proved a poor seller, and production ceased in 1965.

1965 BSA A65 Lightning, 654cc overhead-valve unit-construction twin, twin-leading-shoe front brake, 106mph top speed, restored, engine mildly tuned with high-lift camshafts, improved oil system, electronic ignition, 12 volt electrical system.
£2,100–2,600
$3,000–3,700 ⬈ **BKS**

Miller's
Motorcycle Milestones

BSA A50/A65 499/654cc (British 1962)
Price range: £800–4,000 / $1,150–5,800

Some 70,000 BSA A50/A65 unit-construction overhead-valve twins were built over a ten-year period; the vast majority being the A65. The reason for this is that by the time of their introduction, at the beginning of the 1960s, the 500cc category was quickly going out of fashion, in favour of ever-larger engines.

The larger engine displaced 654cc with near-square bore and stroke dimensions of 75 x 74mm, whereas the smaller-engined 499cc A50 was a long-stroke with dimensions of 65.5 x 74mm.

At first, only 'cooking' touring models of the A50/A65 were offered, and it was not until 1964 that a more sporting model appeared, in the shape of the A65R Rocket. Still with a single carburettor, but with a higher compression ratio (9:1), fiercer cams, strengthened valve springs and a beefed-up clutch, the Rocket provided a top speed of over 105mph.

After this came a whole host of hotter models still, including the A65L Lightning and A50C Cyclone models. Both were also offered in A50CC and A65LC Clubman racing versions. The engines in the Clubman models were individually bench-tested, and the machines came equipped with a racing seat and handlebars, rearsets and close-ratio gear clusters.

The Clubman bikes, and the Lightning and Cyclone, also benefited from twin carburettors as standard.

Later still came the A65 Spitfire, A50 Hornet, A65T Thunderbolt, A50 Royal Star, A65F Firebird and finally, in 1972, the A70 Lightning.

1967 BSA A65 Lightning, 654cc unit-construction twin, export model with high bars.
£2,800–3,000
$4,000–4,300 ⊞ BLM
Early Lightnings came with twin carburettors, a rev-counter and a humped-back seat. Later models had a single carburettor to provide smoother running.

1967 BSA A65T Thunderbolt, 654cc overhead-valve twin.
£2,000–2,500
$2,900–3,600 ⊞ BLM
Compared to the Spitfire and Lightning, the single-carburettor Thunderbolt was not only less highly tuned, but also smoother to ride.

1967 BSA D10 Supreme, 172cc piston-port 2-stroke single, 4-speed gearbox, chrome tank.
£400–500
$580–725 ⊞ BLM
The D10 was introduced in 1966. It featured a contact-breaker on the outside of the primary chaincase, a larger alternator, four-plate clutch, larger carburettor and oval connecting rod.

▶ **1968 BSA D14/4,** 172cc piston-port 2-stroke single, 4-speed gearbox, unrestored.
£400–500
$580–725 ✦ PS

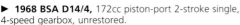

1969 BSA B25, 247cc overhead-valve unit single, 4-speed gearbox, twin-leading-shoe front brake, original, unrestored.
£500–700
$725–1,100 ⊞ MAY

1969 BSA B44 Shooting Star, 441cc overhead-valve unit single, 79 x 90mm bore and stroke, 4-speed gearbox, twin-leading-shoe front brake.
£1,700–1,900
$2,500–2,700 ⊞ BLM
The 441cc unit-construction engine was originally developed for Jeff Smith's motocrosser and was an enlarged version of the earlier C15 and B40 units.

c1971 BSA Firebird, 654cc overhead-valve twin, 75 x 75mm bore and stroke, high-level exhaust, oil-in-frame model, fully rebuilt to concours condition.
£5,350–5,950
$7,750–8,750 ⊞ AtMC
Built for the US market only, the Firebird was essentially a Lightning with street-scrambler styling.

1971 BSA B50 Gold Star, 498cc overhead-valve unit single, 84 x 90mm bore and stroke.
£1,900–2,000
$2,700–2,900 ⊞ BLM
Mainly intended for export, particularly to the USA, the B50 Gold Star was announced just as the company was on its last legs. It was only offered for a few months in 1971 and 1972. A similarly-styled 250 version was also available.

1969 BSA Starfire, 247cc overhead-valve unit single, 67 x 70mm bore and stroke, 4-speed gearbox, twin-leading-shoe front brake, high bars, fork gaiters, non-standard silencer.
£1,000–1,200
$1,450–1,740 ⊞ MAY
This was the first year that the Starfire received the twin-leading-shoe front brake.

1970 BSA A50 Royal Star, 499cc overhead-valve unit twin, single carburettor, rev-counter, good condition.
£2,300–2,600
$3,300–3,700 ⊞ PMo
Introduced in September 1965, the 500 Royal Star was a very underrated performer, and was much smoother than the A65 series.

1971 BSA Starfire, 247cc overhead-valve unit single, 10:1 compression ratio, 25bhp at 8,000rpm, 4-speed gearbox, 80mph top speed.
£900–1,000
$1,300–1,400 ⊞ PM

1971 BSA Thunderbolt, 654cc, fully restored to original specification, concours condition.
£3,100–3,500
$4,500–5,000 ⊞ PMo
The 1971 oil-in-frame range of BSA twins was designed at Umberslade Hall and launched at a massive trade and press party in London during November 1970.

Cagiva *(Italian 1978–)*

1986 Cagiva 650GT Alazzura, 649cc overhead-camshaft V-twin Ducati engine, 82 x 61.5mm bore and stroke, 66bhp at 9,000rpm, 109mph top speed, original, unrestored.
£1,900–2,000
$2,700–2,900 ⊞ NLM

Capriolo *(Italian 1946–64)*

◄ **1953 Capriolo 75 Sport,** 74cc overhead-valve unit single, pressed-steel frame, telescopic front forks, alloy rims, dualseat, original specification.
£1,800–2,100
$2,600–3,000 ⊞ VICO
Based in Trento in the north-east of Italy, Capriolo was owned by the massive Caproni organisation, which was famous in the first half of the 20th century for its various aircraft designs.

1955 Capriolo Cento 50, 149cc overhead-valve horizontal twin, chain final drive, telescopic forks, pressed-steel swinging-arm frame, full-width front brake hub.
£4,500–5,000
$6,500–7,200 ⊞ NLM
Some examples of the Cento 50 had Earles-type forks rather than telescopics.

1962 Capriolo 75 TV, 74.6cc face-cam unit-construction single, wet-sump lubrication, 4-speed gearbox.
£1,000–1,200
$1,400–1,700 ⊞ CYA
Capriolo manufactured a wide range of face-cam singles in 75, 100 and 125cc sizes. The face cam was carried at the top of the vertical shaft on the nearside of the cylinder. Off-road versions gained gold medals during the 1958 and 1959 ISDTs. A One-Day Trials model was also built.

Chater-Lea *(British 1900–37)*

◄ **1928 Chater-Lea Single,** 348cc overhead-valve Blackburne engine, front-mounted magneto.
£6,200–7,000
$8,900–10,000 ⊞ AtMc
Chater-Lea began by manufacturing bicycle components for other companies during the Victorian era, but progressed from this work to making motorcycles. During the 1920s, they were raced at Brooklands by Dougal Marchant, who broke several world records, including setting the absolute 350cc record at over 100mph. Chapter-Lea was one of the first manufacturers to use saddle tanks, introducing them in 1924.

Cimatti *(Italian 1937–84)*

Founded by Marco Cimatti – who had won a gold medal as a cycle racer in the 1932 Olympic Games – the Cimatti marque entered production in 1937, at the small provincial town of Porta Lame. Although the company prospered as a bicycle manufacturer, the factory was destroyed during the war years. Undaunted, however, Marco Cimatti started production again and, in 1949, branched out into powered two-wheelers. This was during an era when the supplier was king – virtually any type of motorcycle found willing buyers.

Even so, Cimatti concentrated its efforts on small, cheap designs, including mopeds. This policy paid dividends later in the 1950s, when many rival marques, offering larger, more expensive machinery, began to suffer serious financial problems. By contrast, Marco Cimatti saw his company expand and prosper.

In 1960, the factory was relocated to Pioppe di Salvaro, in the Appenines, and the 1960s saw the Cimatti works not only constructing a vast array of humble ride-to-work mopeds, but also winning the Italian national 50cc trials championship three years running – 1966, 1967 and 1968.

Cimatti introduced some larger-engined models, too, offering the 100cc and 175cc Sport Lusso for street use, and the Kaiman Cross *Competizione* for motocross racing.

At the beginning of the 1970s, a new 125cc motocrosser made its début, sporting a five-speed gearbox; a roadster version was also sold. All Cimatti's machines used proprietary two-stroke engines, bought in from the likes of Minerelli and Franco Morini.

An export drive was established under the direction of the founder's son, Enrico Cimatti. The principal markets were the USA, France, Norway and Tunisia. By 1977, production was up to around 50,000 units per year.

Cimatti was also keen to reduce its workforce through the wide use of automation. This, combined with a policy of cutting its range to concentrate purely on the 50cc sector, seemed to have paid off. But then came the recession of the early 1980s, and demand fell alarmingly, resulting in Cimatti being wound up in 1984.

► **1960 Cimatti Sport,** 49cc, Franco Morini 2-stroke single-cylinder engine, 4-speed gearbox, duplex swinging-arm frame, telescopic forks, front brake with air scoop, 50mph top speed.
£500–600
$700–850 ⊞ PMo

Comet *(Italian 1952–57)*

Although the Comet marque lasted less than five years, this Bologna based company was one of the most innovative of its era. 'One of the most interesting models on view', was how *Motor Cycling* described the 175cc Moto Comet in its review of the Milan show in December 1952.

Designed by the legendary FB Mondial engineer Ing. Alfonso Drusiani, this new motorcycle was of considerable technical interest. The engine was a vertical twin, with light-alloy cylinders and heads, the overhead camshaft being driven by a chain located between the cylinders. A particularly noteworthy feature was the use of overhung cranks – with gear primary and chain camshaft drives. In unit with the engine, a four-speed gearbox drove an in-built distributor located in the fuel-tank cut-away. Telescopic forks and hydraulically damped rear shock absorbers for the swinging-arm completed what was an exceptionally neat engineering and styling package.

A sports version was presented at the Milan show in November 1953. And the same venue was chosen in 1954 to display an experimental larger-capacity Comet model. Alfonso Drusiani had dreamed up a 250 four-stroke that employed the slide-valve principle. The barrel had no fewer than three bores in line, the main cylinder being sandwiched between two smaller ones. Three crankshaft assemblies were geared together, the 'valve-cylinder' pistons operating at half engine speed.

More conventional was a new 250cc Comet vertical twin, based on the existing 175. Also introduced at the same time was a racing 175 single, with overhead cam, outside flywheel and dual-spark ignition.

▶ **1955 Comet Twin,** 246cc chain-driven overhead-camshaft parallel twin, distributor ignition, overhung cranks with gear primary drive, 4-speed gearbox, telescopic forks, swinging-arm rear suspension.
£2,600–2,900
$3,700–4,100 ⊞ AtMC
The 250 Comet Twin was designed by Alfonso Drusiani; the company was based in Bologna.

Coventry Eagle *(British 1901–40)*

◀ **1931 Coventry Eagle F25,** 196cc Villiers 2-stroke single-cylinder engine, 61 x 67mm bore and stroke, 3-speed hand-change gearbox, rigid frame, girder forks.
£1,300–1,500
$1,800–2,000 ⊞ BB

DKW *(German 1919–81)*

► **1958 DKW RT200VS,** 191cc piston-port 2-stroke unit single, 62 x 64mm bore and stroke, 8.5bhp at 4,500rpm, 4-speed gearbox, 57mph top speed.
£700–800
$1,000–1,100 ⊞ PMo

Douglas *(British 1906–57)*

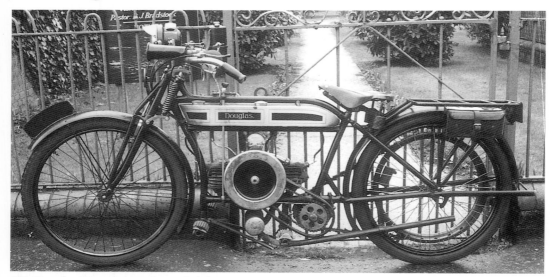

1914 Douglas 2-Speed, 346cc fore-and-aft flat-twin engine, outside flywheel, hand-change gearbox, belt final drive, flat tank.
£6,000–7,000
$9,700–11,300 ⊞ VER
Douglas, based in Bristol, was well established prior to the outbreak of WW1 in 1914, and even by then was famous for its flat-twin four-stroke engine.

1914 Douglas 2¾hp, 346cc fore-and-aft flat-twin engine, first registered 1920.
£3,600–4,400
$5,300–6,200 ⅃ BKS
The outbreak of war in 1914 heralded an unprecedented demand for Douglas machines, and the 2¾hp model was adopted by the British Army for despatch use. Subsequent experience with the machine at The Front resulted in a revision of the stand mounting, but otherwise it withstood the rigours of combat extremely well.

1957 Douglas Dragonfly, 348cc overhead-valve flat-twin, 60.8 x 60mm bore and stroke, coil ignition, Earles front forks, swinging-arm rear suspension, original specification.
£2,500–3,000
$3,600–4,300 ⊞ VER
The Dragonfly was offered between 1955 and 1957. It was known as the Dart during its development phase, the engine being a cross between the Mk V, the 90 Plus and a 500cc prototype exhibited in 1951, but never produced.

◀ **1924 Douglas Model OB,** 596cc overhead-valve fore-and-aft twin, hand-change gearbox, chain final drive.
£6,600–6,800
$9,600–8,400 ⊞ YEST

1930 Douglas Model T6, 596cc side-valve flat-twin, 68 x 82mm bore and stroke.
£4,000–4,800
$5,800–6,900 ⋌ BKS
The touring Douglas T6 was introduced at the 1929 Olympia show alongside the sporting S6, of the same displacement, and the S5 500cc model. Designed by Freddie Dixon, all retained the traditional Douglas 'fore-and-aft' layout, but incorporated a number of advanced features, including enclosed valve gear and an induction system that was cast into the timing cover to ensure adequate heating. The machines were among the most refined of their day, earning a reputation for silence and flexibility. The T6 incorporated a carrier and was offered with a choice of footboards or rests, all for £49 10s.

Ducati *(Italian 1946–)*

1958 Ducati 175 Sport, 174cc bevel-driven overhead-camshaft single, 62 x 57.8mm bore and stroke, 4-speed gearbox, 31.5mm front forks, full-width hubs, 'jelly-mould' fuel tank, rebuilt, excellent condition.
£3,500–4,000
$5,000–5,800 ⊞ MW
Founded by the Ducati brothers in 1926, the company that today is synonymous with high-performance world championship winning superbikes and Carl Fogarty, had its origins in a small suburb of Bologna, producing electrical equipment. The transition to motorcycles came in 1946, with the production of the *Cucciolo* (Little Puppy Dog). Then, in 1954, the famed engineer Fabio Taglioni joined the company and would go on to shape the evolution of future Ducati motorcycles.

Miller's is a price GUIDE not a price LIST

1959 Ducati 125 Turismo, 124cc overhead-valve unit single, 55.2 x 52mm bore and stroke, 4-speed gearbox, oil-in-frame model, complete in all major respects, in need of restoration.
£400–500
$580–720 ⊞ MAY

Miller's
Motorcycle Milestones

Ducati 175cc Turismo (Italian 1957)
Price range: £1,000–2,500 / $1,500–3,600

In the immediate post-war period, Ducati Meccanica rose from the ashes of Societa Scientifica Radiobrevetti Ducati, which had been founded on 4 July, 1926, by Antonio Cavalieri Ducati and his three young sons, Adriano, Bruno and Marcello. Specialising in the production of radio equipment, the company prospered, thanks in no small way to the part played by radio in the Fascist party's propaganda machine; by 1939, the company had 7,000 employees.

The war saw the virtual destruction of Ducati's Bologna plant. Post-war, a Turin based engineer, Aldo Farinelli, created a 48cc four-stroke engine, which could be clipped to a conventional pedal cycle. This not only saved Ducati from extinction, but in the process also sold in many thousands. This was the Cucciolo (puppy dog).

A larger 60cc version of Farinelli's engine powered Ducati's first complete motorcycle in 1950. From this came a whole series of pushrod lightweights, before Ing. Fabio Taglioni joined Ducati in May 1954, to herald a new era that saw the marque gain great success, both in the showroom and on the race circuit.

The first of Taglioni's new breed of single – with its camshaft driven by bevel gears and shafts – the 98cc Gran Sport racer, debuted in 1955. It was a class winner in both the Milano-Taranto and Giro D'Italia (Tour of Italy) long-distance road races.

The following year saw the twin-cam 124cc Grand Prix and three-camshaft Desmo racers, together with one of Ducati's most important street bikes of all time, the 175 Monoalbero (single-camshaft).

First displayed in public at the Milan show in November 1956, the 174.5cc (62 x 57.8mm) engine closely mirrored the 98GS. Its alloy cylinder, with cast-iron liner, was inclined slightly forward. Driven by a pair of bevel shafts and gears on the offside of the engine, its single-overhead-cam valve gear had enclosed (exposed on 98GS) rockers and hairpin valve springs. The geared primary drive and multi-plate clutch were on the nearside, transmitting power to a four-speed gearbox. The full-circle crankshaft featured a roller big-end bearing, while the small-end bush was phosphor-bronze. Lubrication was by wet sump, with a gear-type oil pump. Ignition was by battery/coil; the engine acted as a stressed member for the tubular-steel frame.

The first version, the 175T (Turismo) went on sale in 1957, soon followed by Sport and Formula 3 variants. 1958 saw the arrival of the 203.7cc (67 x 47.8mm) Elite. Thereafter came a vast array of other overhead-camshaft bevel singles, culminating in the 436cc in 1969. Production ceased in late 1974.

1960 Ducati 200 TS, 203cc bevel-driven overhead-camshaft single, 67 x 57.8mm bore and stroke, 4-speed gearbox, valanced mudguards, US specification, fully restored.
£2,000–2,200
$2,900–3,100 ⊞ MW
This model is now extremely rare.

1960s Ducati Mach 1 Replica, 248cc bevel-driven overhead-camshaft unit single, 5-speed gearbox, engine used as stressed frame member.
£2,800–3,300
$4,000–4,800 ⚲ COYS
This particular machine began life as a 1966 Monza 'narrow-case' 250, but with much work and the correct parts has been transformed into a Mach 1 replica of 1964 vintage. A genuine Mach 1 in this condition would be worth considerably more.

1966 Ducati Monza, 248cc bevel-driven, overhead-camshaft single, 5-speed gearbox, rebuilt in café-racer style with clip-ons, alloy rims, Vic Camp racing seat, megaphone silencer and small headlamp.
£1,600–1,800
$2,300–2,600 ⊞ MW

1967 Ducati Monza, 248cc belt-driven overhead-camshaft single, 74 x 57.8mm bore and stroke, 24mm Dell'Orto UBF carburettors, 5-speed gearbox, US model, fully restored to original specification, concours condition.
£2,200–2,300
$3,100–3,300 ⊞ MW

1969/70 Ducati 350 Mk 3D, 340cc overhead-camshaft single, 74 x 57.8mm bore and stroke, desmodromic valve gear, 29mm Dell'Orto carburettor, rev-counter, Silentium silencer, original specification, concours condition.
£3,500–3,600
$5,000–5,200 ⊞ MW
The 'D' suffix stood for 'Desmo'. This early 'wide-case'-framed single features the older 31.5mm enclosed front fork and single-leading-shoe, single-sided drum brake from the earlier 'narrow-case' range.

▶ **1970 Ducati 250 Mk 3D,** 248cc overhead-camshaft single, desmodromic valve gear, Dell'Orto VHB carburettor, fitted with optional rev-counter, steel rims, chrome tank, chrome tank panels.
£2,700–3,000
$3,900–4,300 ⊞ MW

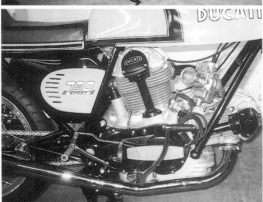

1972 Ducati 750 Sport, 748cc overhead-camshaft 90° V-twin, high-compression pistons, 32mm carburettors, 5-speed gearbox, Conti silencers, rebuilt to original specification apart from twin-disc front brake conversion, concours condition, one of first 750 Sport models built.
£8,000–9,000
$11,600–13,000 ⊞ MW
The paintwork on these early Sport models was different to later bikes. Today, they are extremely rare.

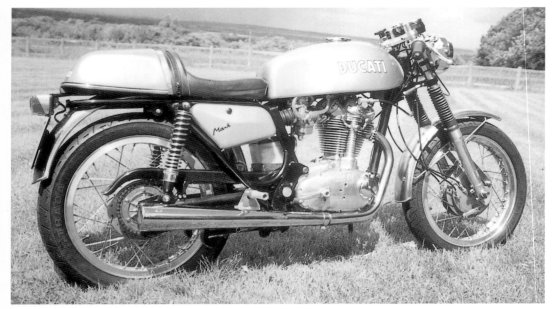

1972 Ducati 450 Mk 3, 436cc overhead-camshaft single, 86 x 75mm bore and stroke, 'wide-case' engine, electronic ignition, converted to café-racer specification with clip-ons, rearsets, 900SS single seat, Conti replica silencer, aluminium wheel rims, double-sided front brake, fork gaiters and stainless-steel mudguards.
£1,800–2,200
$2,600–3,200 ⊞ MW

1972 Ducati 350 Desmo Silver Shotgun, 340cc bevel-driven overhead-camshaft single, desmodromic valve gear, 5-speed gearbox, double-sided front brake, 35mm Marzocchi front forks, decals missing, otherwise standard specification.
£2,700–3,000
$3,900–4,300 ⊞ MW
The Silver Shotgun version of Desmo line was only made from late 1971 until early 1973.

▶ **1974 Ducati 250 Desmo Disc,** 248cc, 74 x 57.8mm bore and stroke, desmodromic valve gear, 35mm Ceriani forks, Brembo disc front brake with 2-piston caliper, original specification apart from rear shock absorbers.
£2,500–3,000
$3,600–4,300 ⋌ DOC

1973 Ducati 750GT, 748cc bevel-driven overhead-camshaft V-twin, 80 x 74.4mm bore and stroke, wet-sump lubrication, 5-speed gearbox, engine rebuilt to 750S specification with high-compression pistons and 32mm carburettors, one owner from new, concours condition.
£3,500–4,000
$5,000–5,800 ⊞ MW

◀ **1974 Ducati 750GT,** 748cc overhead-camshaft V-twin, spring valve gear, points ignition, 5-speed gearbox, central-axle forks, steel rims, square rear light, standard specification apart from dual disc conversion, K&N-type air filters and black silencers, one of last 750GTs made.
£2,600–3,200
$3,700–4,600 ⊞ MW
This is a US model with sealed-beam (Aprilia) headlamp, but flat European handlebars.

1974 Ducati 750 Sport, 748cc bevel-driven overhead-camshaft unit 90° V-twin, spring valve gear, 5-speed gearbox, wet clutch, double-disc front brake conversion, central-axle forks, alloy rims, Conti silencers, one of last built.
£4,000–5,000
$5,800–7,200 ⊞ MW

1975 Ducati 860 GT ES, 864cc overhead-camshaft V-twin, 86 x 74.4mm bore and stroke, spring valve gear, electric start, double-disc front brake conversion, 1980 Darmah Silentium silencers, 750 Sport-type instrument holders.
£1,000–1,400
$1,500–2,000 ⊞ MW

◄ **1977 Ducati 500 Sport Desmo,** 497cc chain-driven overhead-camshaft twin, desmodromic valve gear, wet-sump lubrication, 5-speed gearbox, electric start, triple Brembo disc brakes, original specification, concours condition.
£2,000–2,300
$2,900–3,000 ⊞ MW
The 500 Sport Desmo benefited from input by Leo Tartarini (styling) and Fabio Taglioni (desmo valve gear). Together with its smaller brother, the 350 Sport Desmo, it was certainly the best of Ducati's chain-driven overhead-camshaft parallel twins.

1977 Ducati 500 GTL, 497cc chain-driven overhead-camshaft unit V-twin, 5-speed gearbox, electric and kick start, side reflectors, sealed-beam headlamps, Lafranconi seamed silencers, Brembo dual disc front brakes, rear drum brake, 105mph top speed, US model, original, excellent condition.
£1,800–2,200
$2,600–3,100 ⊞ BLM

◄ **1978 Ducati 900 GTS,** 864cc, modified with fork gaiters, Japanese instruments, switchgear and direction indicators, Conti replica silencers and 860 GT saddle.
£2,600–3,100
$3,700–4,500 ➢ BKS
The 900GTS was introduced in 1978 and represented the culmination in the development of the valve-spring series of V-twins, which had begun with the 'round-case' 750 GT of 1971. The new model utilised the Darmah engine with valve-spring cylinder heads, Bosch ignition and an improved electric starter. Finished in red, green, blue or black, it earned a reputation as being one of the most reliable models to emerge from the factory, and certainly the best of the GT family after the unpopular Giorgetto Giugiaro-styled 860 of 1975.

1978/80 Ducati 900 SS, 864cc, 1978 engine, 1980 chassis, non-standard paintwork, fully restored by American Ducati specialist Syd Tunstall in 2000.
£4,000–4,400
$5,800–6,200 ⊞ MW

1979 Ducati 350 GTV, 349.82cc chain-driven overhead-camshaft parallel twin, 71.8 x 43.3mm bore and stroke, spring valve gear, wet-sump lubrication, 5-speed gearbox, cast alloy wheels, triple disc brakes, stainless-steel mudguards.
£1,700–1,800
$2,400–2,600 ⊞ MW
With the styling from the Tartarini-inspired Desmo Sport models, the GTV was the final expression of the parallel-twin theme, which had begun with the GTL in 1975. All three were offered in both 350 and 500cc engine sizes.

◄ **1980 Ducati 900 SS,** V-twin engine, 86 x 74.4mm bore and stroke, desmodromic valve gear, 40mm Dell'Orto carburettors, Conti silencers, Campagnolo wheels, drilled discs, 38mm Marzocchi forks, finished in black and gold, fitted optional dualseat and direction indicators, excellent condition.
£5,000–5,500
$7,200–7,900 ⊞ MW

1979 Ducati Mike Hailwood Replica, 864cc bevel-driven overhead-camshaft 90° V-twin, desmodromic valve gear, 40mm Dell'Orto carburettors, fairing, rearsets, footrests, clip-ons, Conti silencers, finished in red, green and white, one of the original 1979 hand-built limited-edition machines.
£6,000–7,000
$8,700–10,000 ⊞ MW

► **1982 Ducati 600 SL Pantah,** 583cc overhead-camshaft V-twin, 80 x 58mm bore and stroke, desmodromic valve gear, 5-speed gearbox, Silentium silencers, standard specification.
£2,200–2,400
$3,100–3,400 ⊞ MW

1983 Ducati 350 XL Pantah, 349cc overhead-camshaft V-twin, 66 x 51mm bore and stroke, 35mm Marzocchi front forks, small headlamp fairing.
£1,800–2,000
$2,600–2,900 ⊞ MW

1983 Ducati Pantah Special, 640cc belt-driven overhead-camshaft V-twin, desmodromic valve gear, 65bhp, 118mph top speed, D & R Raynor engine conversion, 2-into-1 exhaust, finished in red and black.
£2,000–2,300
$2,900–3,300 ⊞ MW

1985 Ducati MHR Mille, 973cc overhead-camshaft 90° V-twin, desmodromic valve gear, electric start, hydraulic clutch, 900SS-type fairing, concours condition.
£6,000+
$8,700+ ⊞ MW
Last of the famous bevel V-twins from Ducati, the Mille was built in two versions: the MHR (shown) and the S2. It was also the only bevel V-twin Ducati to feature plain-bearing big-ends.

1985 Ducati 750 F1, 748cc belt-driven overhead-camshaft V-twin, 88 x 61.5mm bore and stroke, desmodromic valve gear, 2-into-1 exhaust, monoshock rear suspension.
£3,000–3,500
$4,400–5,000 ⊞ MW
Fabio Taglioni's final design entered production in spring 1985 and a few weeks later (on 1 May) became the first Ducati to be sold under the new ownership of Cagiva. The 750 F1 and its limited-edition brothers, such as the Montjuich and Laguna Seca, are seen as the last of the raw-boned Ducati sports bikes.

1989 Ducati 851 Monoposto, 851cc double-overhead-camshaft liquid-cooled V-twin, Weber/Marelli fuel injection, 6-speed gearbox.
£4,000–4,500
$5,800–6,500 ⊞ MW
The 1989 Monoposto (single-seat) was the first mass-produced version of Ducati's new four-valves-per-cylinder, liquid-cooled, twin-cam, fuel-injected V-twin. The specification included 17in wheels, Marzocchi MIR forks and monoshock (rising-rate) rear suspension, while performance was 150+mph.

Dunelt *(British 1919–56)*

◄ **1931 Dunelt SD,** 495cc Sturmey Archer overhead-valve single-cylinder engine, 79 x 101mm bore and stroke, dry-sump lubrication, some components missing including the exhaust system.
£1,000–1,250
$1,450–2,000 ⚘ BKS
Dunelt (Dunford & Elliott) was based in Birmingham. One of the very rare four-stroke Dunelts made, the SD was an excellent motorcycle. In 1930, Dunelt won its second successive Mandes Trophy with an SD, covering 13,200 miles (around 300 laps of the Isle of Man TT course) in 16 days, climbing, as the company said, over 20 times the height of Mount Everest.

Excelsior *(British 1896–1964)*

Auction prices

Miller's only includes motorcycles declared sold. Our guide prices take into account the buyer's premium, VAT on the premium, and the extent of any published catalogue information relating to condition and provenance. Motorcycles sold at auction are identified by the ⚘ icon; full details of the auction house can be found on page 330.

► **1960 Excelsior F10 Consort,** 98cc Villiers 6F 2-stroke single-cylinder engine, telescopic forks, rigid frame.
£450–540
$650–750 ⚘ Bri

FN *(Belgian 1901–57)*

◄ **1911 FN Four,** 499cc 4-cylinder inline engine, front-mounted magneto, shaft final drive, pedalling gear.
£14,000–16,800
$20,300–24,000 ⊞ VER
The Belgian FN marque was one of the pioneers of the four-cylinder motorcycle.

► **1912 FN,** 285cc 4-stroke single, Bosch magneto, shaft final drive, fully restored.
£4,300–4,800
$6,200–7,000 ⚘ BKS
The famous Belgian arms manufacturer, FN, produced its first motorcycle during 1901. In 1903, it addressed one of the major impediments to motorcycle development when it adopted shaft final drive for its machines. The system enabled the use of a clutch and gears, did not slip in adverse weather conditions and was not prone to breaking, unlike the single-speed belt drive employed by the majority of its rivals. The system was employed until 1923 on the four- and single-cylinder models.

Francis-Barnett
(British 1919–64)

◄ **1939 Francis-Barnett J43 Seagull,** 249cc Villiers 2-stroke single-cylinder engine, 63 x 80mm bore and stroke, 3-speed gearbox.
£900–1,000
$1,300–1,450 ✦ H&H
Debuting at the 1938 Earls Court show, the Seagull went on sale shortly after for £36. This machine is pictured with Len Vale-Onslow, who carried out work on it at his Birmingham dealership.

Gilera *(Italian 1909–)*

1949 Gilera 125 Turismo, 124cc overhead-valve unit single, parallel valves, 3-speed gearbox, blade girder forks, swinging-arm rear suspension, original specification, in need of restoration.
£1,100–1,300
$1,600–1,800 ⊞ VICO
This was the first year of production for the 125 Turismo.

1953 Gilera 150 Turismo, 152.68cc overhead-valve unit single, 60 x 54mm bore and stroke, 6.5bhp at 5,600rpm, 4-speed gearbox, telescopic forks, swinging-arm rear suspension, unrestored.
£800–900
$1,100–1,300 ⊞ NLM

1960 Gilera 300B, 305cc overhead-valve unit twin, parallel valves, 15bhp at 6,800rpm, 4-speed gearbox, 78mph top speed.
£2,400–2,700
$3,400–3,900 ⊞ BB
The Gilera 300 twin was sold from 1953 until 1969. This later model has a larger front brake, Silentium silencers, a larger fuel tank and a dualseat.

1970 Gilera 98 Turismo, 98cc overhead-valve unit single, in need of cosmetic restoration.
£350–400
$500–600 ⊞ MAY
This was the final year of production for the 98 Turismo. The model was also known as the Giubileo (Jubilee), to celebrate the company's 50th anniversary in 1959.

► **1991 Gilera CX125,** 124cc liquid-cooled 2-stroke engine, reed-valve induction, 30bhp, 6-speed gearbox, aluminium frame, 100mph top speed, 48km from new, 'as-new' condition.
£2,200–2,700
$3,100–3,900 ⊞ NLM
The CX was designed by Frederico Martini, formerly of Bimota and the man largely responsible for the Tesi project. It featured single-sided forks front and rear, allowing quick wheel changes. This suspension also provided exceptional stability and comfort.

Henderson
(American 1912–1931)

1925 Henderson Four, 1300cc side-valve air-cooled 4-cylinder inline engine, chain final drive, shock-absorber front fork.
£15,000–17,000
$21,000–24,500 ⊞ VER
Henderson was founded in 1912 in Detroit by Tom and William Henderson, but in 1917 sold out to Ignaz Sohwinn, who added the marque to his Excelsior company. The brothers remained with the new grouping until 1919, when they left to create the Ace firm.

Hesketh *(British 1981–)*

◀ **1984 Hesketh V1000,** 992cc air-cooled double-overhead-camshaft V-twin, 1,100 miles from new.
£4,300–5,200
$6,200–7,500 ⚒ BKS
Lord Hesketh's brave attempt at producing a high-quality mount for discerning riders succumbed at an early stage to financial pressures. These were brought about by a number of factors – high development costs; high interest rates; and delays in delivery and production, resulting from the need to amend certain aspects of the machine at the last minute in response to criticism by the press. This example was built after the financial collapse of 1992 by Mick Broom.

1982 Hesketh V1000, 992cc V-twin, riveted wheels, Brembo brakes, nickel-plated frame, original factory-built bike, concours condition.
$5,600–7,000
$8,000–10,000 ⊞ BLM

Honda *(Japanese 1946–)*

1964 Honda C92, 124cc overhead-camshaft unit twin, 4-speed gearbox, fully enclosed final drive chain, electric start.
£600–700
$880–1,000 ⊞ MAY

1971 Honda CB500 Four, 498cc overhead-camshaft unit 4-cylinder across-the-frame engine, 5-speed gearbox, disc front brake, drum rear brake, US model with non-standard exhaust and front mudguard.
£700–800
$1,000–1,100 ⚒ H&H

c1965 Honda CB450, 444cc double-overhead-camshaft twin, 70 x 57.8mm bore and stroke, 43bhp at 8,500rpm, 4-speed foot-change gearbox, 18in wheels, concours condition.
£2,800–3,500
$4,000–5,000 ⊞ AtMC

▶ **1966 Honda CB450,** 445cc double-overhead-camshaft twin, 70 x 57.8mm bore and stroke, 43bhp at 8,500rpm, 4-speed gearbox.
£1,400–1,600
$2,000–2,300 ⚒ BKS
Nicknamed the 'Black Bomber' by the British motorcycle press, the CB450 marked an important step in Honda's progression to its position as the world's largest motorcycle marque. It exploded the myth than Honda was only interested in building small-capacity bikes.

1975 Honda CB750K5, 736cc, US model with non-standard gold wheel rims, otherwise original specification.
£2,600–2,700
$3,700–3,900 ⊞ MW
This US-market model is very rare in the UK.

1977 Honda CB400F, 408cc overhead-camshaft 4-cylinder engine, 51 x 48.8mm bore and stroke, 4-into-1 exhaust, 5-speed gearbox, original specification.
£1,800–2,000
$2,600–2,900 ⊞ PMo
The CB400F was largely designed for the European rider. A smaller CB350 four was sold elsewhere.

1981 Honda CD200TB, 194cc overhead-camshaft twin, electric start, full-width drum brakes front and rear, dualseat, direction indicators.
£170–200
$240–290 ⋔ PS
The CD200 superseded the CD185 in 1980, the first model being the T, followed by the TB in 1981. The first of the CD range had arrived in the early 1970s in the shape of the CD175. All were aimed at the 'ride-to-work' customer.

1976 Honda CL360, 357cc overhead-camshaft vertical twin, 67 x 50.6mm bore and stroke, electric start, 5-speed gearbox, high-level exhaust.
£1,300–1,500
$1,800–2,100 ⊞ PMo
The CL360 replaced the 325cc CL350; both models were very popular in the USA.

1980 Honda Super Dream Automatic, 400cc overhead-camshaft twin, 3-valve heads, Comstar wheels, chrome mudguards, 12 volt electrics, rare automatic model in original condition, unrestored.
£600–700
$850–950 ⊞ MAY

1981 Honda CX500, 500cc liquid-cooled V-twin, 78 x 52mm bore and stroke, 4 valves per cylinder, 50bhp, 5-speed gearbox, shaft final drive, Comstar wheels, double disc front brake, drum rear brake.
£1,300–1,500
$1,800–2,100 ⊞ RWHS
After a succession of prototypes, Honda finally got around to producing its first V-twin, the CX500, in 1977. It was very much a comfortable tourer with an advanced specification.

◄ **1982 Honda Ascot FT500,** 499cc overhead-camshaft single, 4-valves, twin exhaust ports, 2-into-1 exhaust, 5-speed gearbox, chain final drive, front and rear disc brakes, original specification, excellent condition.
£1,000–1,200
$1,400–1,800 ⊞ RWHS

Colour Review

1955 Ariel VH, 499cc overhead-valve single, 81.8 x 95mm bore and stroke, 24.6bhp at 6,000rpm, restored, concours condition.
£3,000–3,500
$4,350–5,000 ⊞ PM
This swinging-arm version of the VH was built from 1954 to 1959.

1964 Ariel Leader, 247cc air-cooled 2-stroke twin, 54 x 54mm bore and stroke.
£1,200–1,400
$1,750–2,250 🚲 DSCM
This Leader is fitted with many factory optional extras, including panniers, indicators and mirrors.

1981 BMW R80 G/S, 797cc overhead-valve twin, 84.6 x 70.6mm bore and stroke, alloy heads and barrels, 5-speed gearbox, shaft final drive, BMW carrier, US aftermarket side stand, good original condition.
£2,800–2,900
$4,000–4,300 ⊞ MW

> A known continuous history can add value to and enhance the enjoyment of a motorcycle.

1946 BSA B31, 348cc overhead-valve pre-unit single, iron head and barrel, 4-speed foot-change gearbox, restored, 1st-series B31 with rigid frame and telescopic front forks.
£1,800–2,000
$2,600–2,900 ⊞ MAY

1954 BSA A7 Shooting Star, swinging-arm frame, single-sided brakes, headlamp nacelle, fully restored, concours condition.
£3,000–3,500
$4,300–5,000 ⊞ CStC

1955 BSA M20, 496cc side-valve single, 82 x 94mm bore and stroke, telescopic forks, plunger frame.
£1,500–2,000
$2,200–2,900 ⊞ BLM
The M20 was not only popular for civilian use, but was also employed – with sidecar attached – by military and AA patrols.

1956 BSA DB34 Gold Star, 499cc overhead-valve pre-unit single, 85 x 88mm bore and stroke, 190mm front brake, alloy rims, full Clubmans specification, fitted with Amal Mk I Concentric carburettor for easier starting.
£7,000–8,000
$10,200–11,600 ⊞ VER

1962 BSA C15 Star, 247cc overhead-valve unit single, 67 x 70mm bore and stroke, 15bhp at 7,000rpm, restored.
£800–1,100
$1,100–1,600 ⊞ BLM

1961 BSA A10 Golden Flash, 646cc overhead-valve pre-unit twin, 70 x 84mm bore and stroke, iron head and barrel, 4-speed foot-change gearbox, full-width hubs, original specification.
£2,500–2,800
$3,600–4,000 ⊞ BLM

▶ **1966 BSA A65 Lightning,** overhead-valve unit twin, American specification with high bars and rear grab rail, updated with later twin-leading-shoe front brake, petrol tank with larger badges and rear light assembly.
£2,750–2,950
$4,000–4,400 ⊞ BLM

1969 BSA Bantam D175, 172cc piston-port 2-stroke single, alloy head, Amal Concentric carburettor, 4-speed gearbox, chrome headlamp.
£600–800
$870–1,150 ⊞ MAY
The final Bantam, the D175 of 1969, featured new crankcases, a central plug and needle-race clutch. Production ended in 1971.

1957 Douglas Dragonfly, 348cc overhead-valve flat-twin, 60.8 x 60mm bore and stroke, 4-speed foot-change gearbox, restored to original specification.
£2,400–2,600
$3,500–3,800 ⊞ MAY

▶ **1965 Ducati Mach 1,** 248cc overhead-camshaft single, 74 x 57.8mm bore and stroke, forged piston, shim-set rockers, 29mm Dell'Orto SSID carburettor, 30bhp, 100mph top speed, original specification, concours condition.
£4,000–5,000
$5,800–7,250 ⊞ MW

1974 Ducati 350 Desmo, bevel-driven overhead-camshaft single, desmodromic valve gear, double-sided Grimeca front brake, original specification, concours condition.
£4,500–4,800
$6,500–7,000 ⊞ MW

1971 Ducati 350 Scrambler, 340cc bevel-driven overhead-camshaft single, wide-case model, 76 x 75mm bore and stroke, camshaft-driven rev-counter, fork gaiters, alloy rims, full-width hubs, restored.
£2,000–2,100
$2,900–3,100 ⊞ MW

1972 Honda CB750 K2, 736cc overhead-camshaft 4-cylinder engine, 4-pipe exhaust, 5-speed gearbox, electric start, single disc front brake, rear drum brake, original specification, concours condition.
£3,500–3,900
$5,000–5,700 ⊞ RWHS

1981 Honda CX500, 500cc liquid-cooled V-twin, 4-valves-per-cylinder, 78 x 52mm bore and stroke, 5-speed gearbox, shaft final drive, Comstar wheels, tubeless tyres.
£1,250–1,400
$1,750–2,000 ⊞ RWHS

▶ **1970 Indian Velo,** 499cc overhead-camshaft single, alloy head and barrel.
£9,000–10,000
$13,000–14,500 ⊞ AtMC
Built while the Indian marque was owned by the publisher Floyd Clymer, the Indian Velo featured a duplex frame, Italian brakes and suspension, and a British 499cc Velocette Thruxton engine.

1974 Laverda 750 SFC, 744cc double-overhead-camshaft 4-stroke parallel twin, 4-bearing 360° crankshaft, twin carburettors, fitted with optional 2-into-1 exhaust, 5-speed gearbox.
£5,000–6,500
$7,250–9,400 ⊞ MW
The first disc-braked SFC arrived for the 1974 season, being known as the 16000 or 17000 series. All featured stronger 38mm Ceriani forks.

1958 Maserati Competizione, 49cc piston-port 2-stroke single, concours condition.
£5,000–5,200
$7,250–7,550 MW
Suitable for both fast road and racing use, the little Maserati was one of the fastest 50cc-class machines of its day. It could top 50mph with a silencer, but much more was possible with special tuning and an open exhaust.

1958 Matchless G3LS, 348cc overhead-valve pre-unit single, 69 x 93mm bore and stroke, 19bhp at 5,750rpm.
£2,000–2,500
$2,900–3,600 ⚙ AMOC
The G3LS was a long-stroke heavyweight single; 1958 was the first year it was offered with coil ignition.

▶ **1957 Matchless G11,** overhead-valve parallel twin, 72 x 72.8mm bore and stroke, 1st year of AMC gearbox, Norton-type clutch and Girling rear dampers, original specification.
£2,500–2,800
$2,900–4,000 ⊞ BLM
The softer G11 in 600 guise is considered the ideal engine size for AMC's twin.

1928 Moto Guzzi GT 2VT Special, 498.4cc overhead-valve single, exposed valve gear, 88 x 82mm bore and stroke, 17bhp at 4,200rpm, 3-speed gearbox with hand change.
£18,000–20,000
$26,000–29,000 ⊞ AtMc
The GT 2VT was introduced for the 1928 season.

1951 Moto Guzzi Falcone Sport, 498cc overhead-valve horizontal single, 88 x 82mm bore and stroke, 23bhp at 4,500rpm, concours condition.
£4,000–5,000
$5,800–6,500 ⊞ MW

1961 Moto Guzzi Lodola, 235cc overhead-valve unit-construction single, 68 x 64mm bore and stroke, 11bhp at 6,000rpm, 4-speed gearbox, unrestored.
£2,000–2,400
$2,900–3,500 ⊞ OBMS
The pushrod-engined version of the Lodola remained in production from 1960 to 1966.

1978 Moto Morini 500W Touring, 478.6cc overhead-valve 72° V-twin, 69 x 64 bore and stroke, 5-speed gearbox, electronic rev-counter, Marzocchi front forks, Grimeca double-disc front brake, grey cast alloy wheels, dualseat, Fiamm horns, largely standard specification.
£2,000–2,700
$2,900–3,900 ⊞ BLM

1979 Moto Morini 125 Series II, 122.7cc overhead-valve single, front disc brake, cast alloy wheels, matching instrumentation, original specification.
£400–800
$580–1,150 ⊞ MAY
The Series II 125 differed from the previous model in having a larger engine displacement and cast alloy wheels.

1981 Moto Morini 500 Six Speed, 478.6cc overhead-valve 72° V-twin, electric start, 12 volt electrics, Sport model with rearsets, low bars, steering damper and black exhaust.
£2,500–2,700
$3,600–4,000 ⊞ NLM

► **1984 Moto Morini Camel Series 2,** 478.6cc overhead-valve 72° V-twin, high-level exhaust, drum brakes, 6 volt electrics, standard specification.
£2,000–2,200
$2,900–3,200 ⊞ NLM
The Camel was Morini's first six-speed 500. This is an early model with twin-shock rear suspension.

1983 Moto Morini Kanguro X, 344cc overhead-valve 72°
V-twin, high-level exhaust, 6-speed gearbox, 6 volt electrics,
drum brakes, square-section swinging-arm.
£1,300–1,500
$1,900–2,200 ⊞ NLM
**During the early/mid-1980s, the 350 Kanguro was
Morini's bestselling bike on the Italian home market.**

1970 MV Agusta 125 Sport, 124cc overhead-valve single,
53 x 56mm bore and stroke, wet-sump lubrication,
15bhp at 8,500rpm, 5-speed gearbox, alloy rims,
concours condition.
£2,000–2,200
$2,900–3,200 ⊞ MW

► 1972 MV Agusta 600 Four,
double-overhead-camshaft 4-cylinder
engine, 58 x 56mm bore and stroke,
4 Dell'Orto MB24 carburettors, 52bhp
at 8,200rpm, 5-speed gearbox.
£12,000–13,000
$17,400–18,800 ⊞ MW
**Only 135 examples of the MV600
Four were sold in some six years
of production. The final batches,
built in 1971–72, featured a
double-sided twin-leading-shoe
Grimeca-made front brake.**

1973 MV Agusta 750GT, 743cc double-overhead-camshaft 4-cylinder engine, 65 x 56mm bore and stroke, 5-speed
gearbox, shaft final drive, concours condition.
£12,000–14,000
$17,400–20,300 ⊞ MW
The GT was made in much smaller numbers than the 750S. Today, it is very rare.

Indian *(American 1901–53)*

1933 Indian Four, 1265cc 4-cylinder inline engine, chain final drive, footboards, rigid frame, leaf-spring front forks, tank-mounted instruments, Indian-motif horn.
£20,000–22,000
$29,000–32,000 ⊞ VER

1941 Indian Scout Model 741, 600cc side-valve V-twin, hand-change gearbox, chain final drive, footboards, girder front forks, rigid frame.
£5,000–6,000
$7,200–8,700 ⊞ VER

Iso *(Italian 1948–64)*

◀ **1952 Iso 200,** 199cc 2-stroke split single, 44 x 2 x 64mm bore and stroke, foot-change gearbox, shaft final drive, leading-link front forks, plunger rear suspension, complete, in need of full restoration.
£2,000–2,400
$2,900–3,500 ⊞ NLM
Founded by Renzo Rivolta at Bresso in 1939, Iso did not begin making two-wheelers until 1948. From the early 1960s, it turned its attention to building supercars, such as the Rivolta and Grifo.

Itom *(Italian 1948–67)*

The very first Itom was a cyclemotor, which was designed in 1944. Based in Turin, the company soon built up an excellent reputation for its 50cc and later 65cc models, all of which were powered by a series of single-cylinder, two-stroke engines with piston-port induction.

During the late 1950s, the marque became involved in the 50cc racing boom, which ultimately led to the class being accepted for World Championship status in 1962. The early 'racing' models had a three-speed gearbox, geared primary drive and a hand-operated twistgrip gear-change. The Mk VII had four gears, as did the Mk VIII, which also benefited from foot-change.

Although the factory itself never entered works machines, privateer Itom riders made up the majority of any 50cc race programme for several years (from the late 1950s until around 1963), before being totally outclassed by 'official' production racers such as the double-overhead-camshaft Honda CR110 and the various Kreidlers, let alone the pukka works bikes from Derbi, Suzuki, Honda and Tomos, among others.

In December 1965, *The Motor Cycle* put one of the 49cc (40 x 39.5mm) competition models through its paces and was impressed enough to comment: 'It has disadvantages, true enough; but a remarkable, exceptionally smooth engine, allied with exemplary roadholding is compensation enough for any discomfort!' Costing the princely sum of £118, this fully road-legal Sports 50 was imported by A. H. Tooley of south-east London.

A few short months later, the factory was forced to close through falling orders – no doubt affected by the machine's racing decline.

▶ **1957 Itom 50 Competizione,** 49cc piston-port 2-stroke single, 3-speed hand-change gearbox, leading-link front forks, swinging-arm rear suspension, concours condition.
£1,800–2,600
$2,600–3,800 ⊞ MW
The first Itom was a cyclemotor, which was designed during the later stages of WWII. Based in Turin, Itom soon built up an excellent reputation for its 49 and 65cc models, all powered by single-cylinder piston-ported two-stroke engines of its own design and manufacture.

◀ **1961 Itom Astor Sport,** 49cc 2-stroke single, alloy head and iron barrel, backbone open frame, twist-grip 3-speed gear-change, full-width brake hubs, telescopic forks, swinging-arm rear suspension, original specification.
£650–750
$900–1,100 ⊞ VICO

James *(British 1902–64)*

1928 James Model B, 499cc side-valve V-twin, iron heads and cylinders, 64 x 77.5mm bore and stroke, forward-mounted magneto, hand-change gearbox, girder front forks, rigid frame, complete with rear carrier and leather side bags.
£6,000–6,500
$8,700–9,500 ⊞ VER

1950 James Comet 1, 98cc Villiers 1F 2-stroke engine, 47 x 57mm bore and stroke, 2.8bhp at 4,000rpm, 2-speed gearbox, rigid frame.
£500–600
$700–880 ⊕ NAC
The Comet 1 was in production from 1949 until 1955, but from 1953 it used the improved Villiers 4F engine.

Kawasaki *(Japanese 1962–)*

1974 Kawasaki Z1A, 903cc double-overhead-camshaft across-the-frame 4-cylinder engine, 66 x 66mm bore and stroke, wet-sump lubrication, coil ignition, 81bhp at 7,500rpm, original 4-pipe exhaust, 5-speed gearbox, single disc front/drum rear brakes, concours condition.
£3,600–4,000
$5,150–5,800 ⊞ RWHS

1974 Kawasaki Z750, 749cc double-overhead-camshaft parallel twin, 5-speed gearbox, single disc front brake, fitted with non-standard fairing, carrier, Marzocchi rear shocks and front mudguard, unrestored, now very rare.
£600–700
$870–1,000 ⊞ MAY

1976 Kawasaki 250KH, 249cc piston-port 2-stroke 3-cylinder engine, 3-pipe exhaust, disc front brake, drum rear brake, chrome mudguards, unrestored.
£1,300–1,500
$1,900–2,200 ⊞ PMo

Miller's
Motorcycle Milestones

Kawasaki Z1 903cc (Japanese 1973)
Price range: £3,000–5,000 / $4,400–7,250

During the early 1970s, Kawasaki's mighty Z1 was a dream bike for many teenagers. And when it was officially launched in Europe, at the Cologne show in Germany in September 1972, it was certainly the fastest and most powerful production roadster there had ever been.

Its twin-overhead-cam, across-the-frame four-cylinder engine put out a very impressive 82bhp at 8,500rpm. And it could zoom along a quarter of a mile from a standing start in only 12.3 seconds, while its maximum speed was a jaw-dropping 135mph.

In giving the Z1 this level of performance, Kawasaki engineers had not overtuned the 903cc (66 x 66mm) engine. In fact, it was able to run on lead-free petrol right from the start. It was also exceedingly flexible, being able to pull top gear from as low as 25mph.

Only 61 Z1s were sold in Britain during 1973, when the importers were Agrati Sales of Nottingham. However, this did not stop it from ending the Norton Commando's five-year run as the Motor Cycle News Machine of the Year. The Z1 went on to win again in 1974 and 1975.

The Z1's standard specification included 12 volt electrics, electric start, direction indicators, four-pipe exhaust, duplex full-cradle frame and four 28mm Mikuni carburettors.

But no bike is perfect, and the original 1973 Z1 had two major faults: handling and a high purchase price. It was 25 per cent more expensive than, for example, the Norton Commando and Suzuki GT750, and 20 per cent more than a Honda CB750.

1978 Kawasaki Z1-R, 1015cc double-overhead-camshaft across-the-frame 4-cylinder engine, electric start, 5-speed gearbox, triple drilled disc brakes, full cradle frame, standard specification.
£2,000–2,300
$2,900–3,350 ⊞ RWHS
The Z1-R was the performance model in the 1978 Kawasaki 1000 series line-up; its maximum power was an impressive 90bhp at 8,000rpm, giving 140+mph.

1981 Kawasaki Z1100ST, 1089cc double-overhead-camshaft 4-cylinder engine, 72.5 x 66mm bore and stroke, 5-speed gearbox, twin-shock rear suspension, fitted with touring half-fairing, carrier and pannier frames.
£2,000–2,300
$2,900–3,350 ⊞ RWHS
The Z1100 was intended primarily for touring, and was equipped with shaft final drive and a 16in rear wheel.

1984 Kawasaki Z750 Turbo, 738cc turbocharged double-overhead-camshaft 4-stroke 4-cylinder engine, 66 x 54mm bore and stroke, 112bhp at 9,000rpm, 150mph top speed, completely rebuilt 1999, 500 miles since, concours condition.
£2,300–2,750
$3,350–4,000 ⚡ BKS
Spurred on by the publicity generated by Honda's CX500 Turbo, the rest of Japan's 'Big Four' lost no time in jumping on the forced-induction bandwagon. By far the most successful offering came from Kawasaki, which bolted a turbocharger to its existing GPz750 and created one of the 1980s' most exciting sports motorcycles. By placing the turbo close to the exhaust ports, Kawasaki minimised throttle lag, while substituting electronic fuel injection for the original carburettors enabled combustion to be finely controlled. The result was 100+bhp at the rear wheel and a top speed of around 140mph. A subtly strengthened frame and swinging-arm helped enthusiastic owners keep the Turbo shiny side up.

Laverda *(Italian 1949–)*

◄ **1978 Laverda Alpine S,** 496.7cc double-overhead-camshaft twin, 4 valves per cylinder, 180° crankshaft, electronic ignition, 6-speed gearbox, 105mph top speed, standard specification, concours condition.
£2,200–2,800
$3,200–4,000 ⊞ MW

1972 Laverda SF1, 744cc double-overhead-camshaft vertical twin, 360° crankshaft, 5-speed gearbox, Nippon Denso instruments, dualseat, non-standard 2-into-1 exhaust.
£1,500–1,650
$2,750–2,375 ⊞ PMo

1982 Laverda Montjuic Series 2, 498cc double-overhead-camshaft twin, 2-into-1 exhaust, 6-speed gearbox, triple disc brakes, cast alloy wheels.
£2,500–3,000
$3,600–4,400 ⊞ MW

Miller's
Motorcycle Milestones

Laverda SFC 744cc (Italian 1975)
Price range: £5,000–8,000 / $7,250–11,600

Laverda's first motorcycles were humble 75cc pushrod singles, which debuted at the end of the 1940s. Success in the Italian long-distance road races of the 1950s helped establish the marque's sporting credentials. But it was really the appearance of a prototype 654cc (75 x 74mm) parallel twin, which had a four-bearing 180-degree crankshaft, duplex chain-driven single overhead camshaft, triplex chain primary drive, a multi-plate clutch and five-speed gearbox, that really started the ball rolling on an international scale.

By the Milan show at the end of 1967, it was clear that the production Laverda big twin would be a 750. This was achieved by increasing the capacity to 743.9cc.

Just as it had done years earlier with its tiny singles, Laverda decided to enter the racing arena to publicise its new twin. At first, this was done unofficially, but by 1970 Laverda had won the first 500 kilometre race for production motorcycles at the Monza circuit.

Then came a purpose-built competition machine, the 750 SFC. This was launched in 1971 as an endurance-racing version of Laverda's SF series, the C standing for Competizione. It duly won its first event, the gruelling Barcelona 24 Hours at Montjuic Park.

Although derived from the touring SF model, the SFC incorporated a number of important differences. Its engine was not only more highly tuned, but also more robust, with larger bearings and an increased-capacity oil pump. Its chassis featured a revised frame as well as the racing-style half-fairing, seat unit and controls.

However, these features did not deter enthusiastic road riders from using a large number of SFCs on the street. Initially equipped with Laverda's own drum front brake, the SFC was one of the fastest machines on the road in the early 1970s. And although expensive, there were always more potential buyers than could be satisfied by the 100 or so units built during each of the first three years of production.

In 1974, the SFC was updated with triple disc brakes, thicker fork tubes and other more minor changes. Later SFCs came with electronic ignition, and some even had cast alloy wheels. The final batch were the quickest; with special cam, and a top speed of 135mph.

During the SFC's six-year production life, only 549 examples were built, helping to make it even more valuable today.

Levis *(British 1911–40)*

1913 Levis, 211cc 2-stroke single, belt final drive, flat tank, carrier basket, tyre pump.
£4,400–4,800
$6,400–7,000 ⊞ VER
Levis built its reputation on the production of well-engineered two-stroke single-cylinder models, displacing 211 and 246cc.

1935 Levis Model A Special, 346cc overhead-valve 4-stroke single, 70 x 90mm bore and stroke, twin exhaust ports, iron head and barrel, high-level exhaust, excellent condition.
£4,200–4,400
$6,100–6,400 ⋏ BKS
The Model A made its debut in 1927 and remained in production until 1940, being updated continually. The Special version did not go on sale until 1935.

Lincoln *(British 1902–24)*

Auction prices

Miller's only includes motorcycles declared sold. Our guide prices take into account the buyer's premium, VAT on the premium, and the extent of any published catalogue information relating to condition and provenance. Motorcycles sold at auction are identified by the ⋏ icon; full details of the auction house can be found on page 330.

▶ **1912 Lincoln Elk,** side-valve single, forward-mounted magneto, pedalling gear, belt final drive, triangular frame, acetylene lighting, excellent condition.
£9,000–10,000
$13,000–14,500 ⊞ AtMC

Malanca *(Italian 1956–86)*

◀ **1972 Malanca 50 Sport,** 49cc piston-port 2-stroke single, flywheel magneto ignition, full-width aluminium brake hubs, telescopic forks, swinging-arm frame.
£300–400
$440–580 ⊞ VICO
Unlike the makers of many Italian ultra-lightweights, which used bought-in engines, Malanca developed its own power unit. The company built both street and racing models, always two-strokes. It was formed in 1956 by Mario Malanca in Pontecchio Marconi, a suburb of Bologna.

Maserati *(Italian 1953–61)*

1959 Maserati Sport, 49cc 2-stroke unit-construction single, full-width brake hubs, duplex frame, dualseat.
£2,150–2,600
$3,000–3,800 ⊞ NLM

Matchless *(British 1901–69, 1987–)*

1930 Matchless Silver Arrow Model A, 394cc side-valve narrow-angle V-twin, dry-sump lubrication, 3-speed hand-change gearbox, girder forks, original condition.
£5,000–5,500
$7,250–8,000 ⊞ VER
The cylinders of the Silver Arrow's engine were set at 26 degrees within a single casting under a single head. The engine and gearbox were carried in a tubular frame with pivoted rear suspension, controlled by coil springs and friction dampers mounted under the seat.

▶ **1934 Matchless Model X4,** 982cc side-valve V-twin, 85.5 x 85.5mm bore and stroke, dry-sump lubrication.
£5,750–6,900
$8,300–10,000 ⚒ BKS
During the early 1930s, the Model X catered for riders seeking a refined high-performance mount for either solo or sidecar use. A wheelbase approaching 60in ensured stable handling, while the engine – which was unusual in having the same bore and stroke dimensions, making it square rather than long-stroke – could deliver a top speed in the mid-90s. The Model X was produced in various guises throughout the 1930s.

c1948 Matchless Silver Hawk, 600cc overhead-camshaft narrow-angle V4.
£18,000–20,000
$26,000–29,000 ⊞ AtMC
The Silver Hawk retained the frame of the 400cc Silver Arrow, but offered improved performance from the larger engine.

1955 Matchless G80S, 497cc overhead-valve pre-unit single, 82.5 x 93mm bore and stroke, Burman 4-speed foot-change gearbox, full-width alloy hubs, AMC 'jampot' rear suspension units, standard specification.
£1,800–2,500
$2,600–3,600 ⊞ BLM

1959 Matchless G80S, 497cc, alloy head, iron barrel, Amal Monobloc carburettor, AMC gearbox, full-width hubs, Girling shock absorbers, original specification, good condition.
£1,700–2,700
$2,450–3,900 ⊞ BLM
The G80S (also sold as the AJS 18S) was a much stronger performer than the smaller-engined G3LS/16MS 350, which shared the same cycle parts.

1960 Matchless G12 CSR, 646cc overhead-valve pre-unit twin, 72 x 79.3mm bore and stroke, 8.5:1 compression ratio.
£2,100–2,600
$3,000–3,800 ↗ PS
The CSR was the sports model of the Matchless G12 650 series. It featured a more highly-tuned engine, siamesed exhaust, alloy mudguards and a shorter dualseat.

▶ **1960 Matchless De Luxe,** 646cc overhead-valve parallel twin, 72 x 79.3mm bore and stroke, 7.5:1 compression ratio, megaphone silencers, AMC gearbox, full-width hubs, Girling shocks, chrome tank, standard specification.
£2,200–2,800
$3,200–4,000 ⊞ PMo

1952 Matchless G9 Spring Twin, 498cc overhead-valve parallel twin, 66 x 72.8mm bore and stroke, 29bhp at 6,800rpm, 4-speed foot-change gearbox, telescopic forks, swinging-arm rear suspension, single-sided brakes.
£1,800–2,200
$2,600–3,200 ⊞ BLM
The G9 (also sold under the AJS label as the Model 20) was made from 1949 until 1961. A racing version, known as the G45 and using AJS 7R cycle parts, was built between late 1953 and mid-1957.

1959 Matchless G2, 248.5cc overhead-valve single, 69.85 x 64.85mm bore and stroke.
£1,000–1,150
$1,500–1,700 ⊞ BB
The Matchless (and AJS) lightweight 250 semi-unit-construction single was introduced in 1958. Features included 17in wheels, telescopic forks, full-width iron hubs and swinging-arm rear suspension. A more sporting and better equipped CSR version was also offered from 1962.

1959 Matchless G12, 646cc overhead-valve twin, 72 x 79.3mm bore and stroke, 4-speed foot-change gearbox.
£2,500–3,000
$3,600–4,400 ⚙ AMOC
For 1959, the old 600 engine was replaced by a new 650, which featured a longer cylinder barrel with an extra fin. It provided more power and torque, but was not as smooth as the previous unit.

Mi-Val *(Italian 1950–67)*

◄ **1954 Mi-Val 125 Sport,** 124cc piston-port 2-stroke single, foot-change gearbox, telescopic front forks, swinging-arm rear suspension, original specification.
£1,200–1,450
$1,750–2,100 ⊞ NLM
Metalimeccanica Italia Valtrompia SpA of Brescia was essentially a machine-tool manufacturer that produced motorcycles for a number of years. At first it built two-strokes, but later concentrated on 250, 350 and 500cc four-strokes.

MM *(Italian 1924–57)*

► **1955 MM 250 Turismo,** 247cc overhead-valve unit-construction single, wet-sump lubrication, 4-speed foot-change gearbox, full-width drum brakes, telescopic forks, swinging-arm rear suspension, some non-original parts.
£1,600–2,200
$2,300–3,200 ⊞ NLM
The MM marque was founded in Bologna by Mario Mazzetti and Alfonso Morini, hence the use of the double 'M'. However, the latter left to set up his rival Moto Morini concern at the end of the 1930s.

Mondial *(Italian 1948–79)*

1955 FB Mondial 175TV, 174cc overhead-camshaft single, battery/coil ignition, alloy rims, telescopic front forks, swinging-arm rear suspension, cradle frame, dualseat, excellent condition.
£3,800–4,000
$5,500–5,800 ⊞ MW

1969 FB Mondial 50 Enduro, 49cc piston-port 2-stroke single, foot-change gearbox, high-level exhaust, duplex frame.
£400–500
$580–720 ⊞ NLM
This was one of the last FB Mondial machines to be built before the factory ceased trading at the end of 1979.

Motobi *(Italian 1949–76)*

1971 Motobi Sports Special, 245cc overhead-valve unit-construction horizontal single, wet-sump lubrication, full-width hubs, open frame.
£1,800–2,000
$2,600–2,900 ⊞ MW
One of the six Benelli brothers, Giuseppe, left the company in 1949 to begin work on an independent design. Known as the 'B', the original machine made its debut in Milan in April 1950. Powered by a 98cc horizontal single-cylinder two-stroke engine, it would launch Motobi on its way and herald a whole line of models with horizontal cylinders in both two- and four-stroke guises; there were even some twin-cylinder versions. After Giuseppe died, his company 'rejoined' the Benelli family, which resulted in a new era of co-operation between the two marques, culminating in the De Tomaso-owned Benelli company absorbing Motobi in the early 1970s. Thereafter, Benelli models were badged as Motobis throughout the remainder of that decade.

Moto Guzzi *(Italian 1921–)*

1924 Moto Guzzi 500 Normale, 498.4cc inlet-over-exhaust single, 8bhp at 3,000rpm, 3-speed hand-change gearbox, girder forks, rigid frame.
£18,000–21,500
$26,000–30,600 ⊞ NLM
Built from 1921 until 1924, the Normale was Guzzi's first production model.

1925 Moto Guzzi 4V, 498.4cc overhead-camshaft horizontal single, Bosch magneto, 3-speed close-ratio gearbox, caliper front brake.
£35,000–42,000
$50,750–60,900 ⊞ NLM
The 4V (four-valve) is now extremely rare.

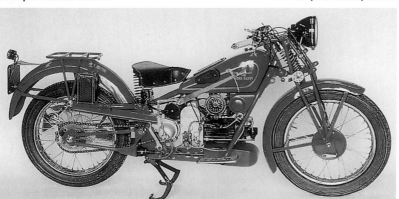

◀ **1931 Moto Guzzi Tipo GT,** 498.4cc inlet-over-exhaust horizontal single, chain final drive, girder front forks, sprung frame with springs contained in a box under engine, fully restored.
£4,000–4,800
$5,800–7,000 ⋗ TEN

Miller's
Motorcycle Milestones

Moto Guzzi C4V 498cc (Italian 1924)
Price range: £25,000–35,000 / $36,250–50,750

The unlikely setting of squadron life in the Italian Air Service during the latter stages of WWI in 1918 was instrumental in the creation of what is now generally regarded as Italy's most famous motorcycle marque, Moto Guzzi.

Two pilots, Giovanni Ravelli and Giorgio Parodi, together with Carlo Guzzi, their young mechanic/driver, talked of little else than an advanced design of motorcycle, which Guzzi had sketched out in his off-duty hours. Sadly, Ravelli would not see their dream come true, as he was killed in a flying accident shortly after the end of hostilities. But Parodi and Guzzi pressed on and, with backing from Parodi's father (a wealthy Genoese shipping magnate), began work in 1919.

The result of Guzzi's handiwork was the GP (Guzzi-Parodi), which debuted late in 1920, but the name was soon changed to the familiar Moto Guzzi. The fledgling company adopted as its trademark an eagle with wings spread in flight. This was in recognition of their fallen comrade, Ravelli.

For its time, the prototype machine was a revolutionary design. Its 498.4cc single-cylinder engine was laid horizontally and featured an overhead camshaft driven by shaft and bevel gears. Perhaps even more interesting were the four-valve

head layout and the engine's oversquare (short-stroke) dimensions of 88 x 82mm bore and stroke.

The first production model, the Normale, closely followed the original layout, but the overhead camshaft was ditched in favour of pushrod-operated valves, and two instead of four valves.

Guzzi's first racing model, the Corsa 2V (racing two-valve), appeared in 1923. It was replaced in 1924 by a much improved model, the C4V. This returned to many of the features of the original GP prototype, such as overhead camshaft and four valves.

Producing 22bhp at 5,500rpm and with a maximum speed of 94mph, the C4V made its debut in the famous Lario event (often named the Italian TT) where, ridden by Pietro Ghersi, it won at an average speed of 42.2mph. If this speed seems low, one should remember that the race was run over unsurfaced roads, and the course had numerous hairpin bends.

Later that year, a C4V won the European Championship, which was staged as a single event at the newly-completed Monza circuit; rider Guido Mentasi averaged 80.6mph.

The basic design of the Guzzi single, with its giant outside flywheel, semi-unit-construction gearbox and magneto ignition was to remain in production, albeit updated from time to time, until as late as 1976 – still retaining its original 88 x 82mm engine dimensions.

◀ **1935 Moto Guzzi Tipo Sport 15,** 498.4cc inlet-over-exhaust horizontal single, 4.5:1 compression ratio, 13.2bhp at 3,800rpm, 3-speed hand-change gearbox, 64mph top speed.
£5,650–6,800
$8,250–9,850 ⊞ NLM

1951 Moto Guzzi Airone Sport, 247cc overhead-valve horizontal single, 70 x 64mm bore and stroke, restored in Italy 1997.
£3,100–3,700
$4,550–5,300 ⚲ BKS

The first Airone appeared in 1939 and essentially was a development of the P.E. 232cc model with a redesigned 246cc engine and four-speed gearbox. In this form, it had a tubular frame of the type used by the P.E. However, this was soon replaced by one utilising steel pressings, which would continue in use until production ended in 1957 – with a break during the war years. The Airone became the most popular middleweight on the Italian market and remained so until production ceased.

1955 Moto Guzzi Falcone Sport, 498.4cc overhead-valve horizontal single, 88 x 82mm bore and stroke, Dell'Orto SS29A carburettor, 28bhp at 4,500rpm, 87mph top speed, fitted with period dualseat.
£6,900–8,300
$10,000–12,000 ⊞ **NLM**

1957 Moto Guzzi Lodola, 174.4cc overhead-camshaft single, cylinder inclined at 45°, 62 x 57mm bore and stroke, in need of restoration.
£800–950
$1,150–1,380 ⊞ **NLM**
Carlo Guzzi's final design, the Lodola (Lark) was shown for the first time at Milan in April 1956. For 1960, the 175 was replaced by a larger 235cc model with pushrods.

1958 Moto Guzzi Cardellino Lusso, 73cc disc-valve 2-stroke single, 45 x 46mm bore and stroke, 2.6bhp at 5,000rpm, in need of complete restoration.
£750–900
$1,100–1,300 ⊞ **NLM**

1958 Moto Guzzi Cardellino Lusso, 73cc disc-valve 2-stroke single, 2.6bhp at 5,200rpm, 3-speed gearbox, dualseat, in need of restoration.
£350–400
$500–580 ⊞ **MAY**

▶ **1957 Moto Guzzi Zigolo Series I,** 98cc disc-valve horizontal single, 50 x 50mm bore and stroke, 3-speed gearbox, concours condition.
£1,500–2,100
$2,150–3,000 ⊞ **MW**
The original Zigolo, with 98cc engine, made its debut in 1953, and 1957 was the final year of production. It was replaced for 1958 by the Series 2, then finally by a 110cc version, which was offered from 1960 until 1966.

◀ **1962 Moto Guzzi Lodola,** 235cc overhead-valve unit single, 68 x 64mm bore and stroke, restored.
£2,500–3,000
$3,600–4,400 ⊞ **OBMS**
The 235cc version of the Lodola was slower (72mph) than the 175 overhead-cam Sport model, but offered improved torque. Unlike the 175, which had an aluminium cylinder barrel with an iron liner, the 235 had a barrel made entirely of iron.

1960 Moto Guzzi Zigolo Series 2, 110cc rotary-valve 2-stroke horizontal single, 52 x 52mm bore and stroke, 4.8bhp at 5,200rpm, 3-speed gearbox, unrestored, good original condition.
£900–1,000
$1,300–1,500 ⊞ MAY

1961 Moto Guzzi Cardellino, 73cc disc-valve 2-stroke single, 45 x 46 bore and stroke, original, unrestored.
£400–500
$580–720 ⊞ MAY

1974 Moto Guzzi Nuovo Falcone, 498.4cc overhead-valve unit-construction single, aluminium head and barrel, wet-sump lubrication, 12 volt electrics, electric start, 4-speed gearbox, Grimeca full-width alloy brake hubs.
£2,600–3,100
$3,800–4,550 ⊞ NLM
The Nuovo Falcone was developed originally with police and military contracts in mind. It appeared in prototype form at the end of 1969, the civilian version entering production during 1971.

1977 Moto Guzzi Le Mans One, 844cc overhead-valve 90° V-twin, 83 x 78mm bore and stroke, 70bhp, 5-speed gearbox, shaft final drive, 125mph top speed.
£3,500–4,000
$5,000–5,800 ⊞ PMo
To many, the Le Mans One, introduced in 1976, was the best of the series, having more rounded lines than later versions.

1980 Moto Guzzi Convert Automatic, 948.8cc overhead-valve 90° V-twin, 30mm Dell'Orto carburettors, German Sachs torque convertor, 2-speed gearbox, shaft final drive.
£2,250–2,500
$3,300–3,600 ⊞ PMo
Like most automatic cars, the automatic Moto Guzzi V-twin was closely based on an existing manual-gearchange model – in this case the 850T3. However, the Convert had an increase in displacement from 844 to 948.8cc.

▶ **1982 Moto Guzzi Le Mans Series III,** 844cc overhead-valve 90° V-twin, 76bhp at 7,700rpm, 5-speed gearbox, 130mph top speed, fitted with non-standard fairing.
£2,500–2,700
$3,600–3,900 ⊞ BLM
The Le Mans Series III was a major redesign – with a new fairing, tank, seat, panels, exhaust system and modified engine top end, which featured square, instead of round, finning. It was built between 1981 and 1984.

1981 Moto Guzzi 350 Imola, 346.2cc overhead-valve 90° V-twin, 66 x 50mm bore and stroke, 28bhp at 8,000rpm, shaft drive, 99mph top speed, standard specification apart from carrier, fairing sides and belly pan.
£1,400–1,600
$2,000–2,300 ⊞ RWHS
With sporty looks, but hardly any improvement in performance, the V35 Imola was launched in 1979.

Motom
(Italian 1947–early 1960s)

◄ **1959 Motom Super Sport,** 49.8cc overhead-valve unit single, 40 x 39.8mm bore and stroke.
£1,400–1,700
$2,000–2,450 ⚖ BKS
Motom began production in 1947 in Milan. Initially, production concentrated on 50cc-class machines, utilising a four-stroke engine. Machines of this size would remain the focus of the firm's efforts, although models of up to 160cc would leave the factory in later years. The 50cc four-stroke single proved both durable and amenable to tuning, with top speeds in excess of 50mph being gained with comparative ease.

Moto Morini *(Italian 1937–)*

◄ **1956 Moto Morini Sbarazzino,** 98.1cc overhead-valve unit single, 50 x 50mm bore and stroke, foot-change gearbox, original specification, unrestored.
£800–950
$1,150–1,380 ⊞ NLM
'Sbarazzino' means rascal in respect of children in the Italian language. The machine made its debut at the Milan show in late 1956. It proved a popular bike and sold in many thousands over its long life.

1956 Moto Morini Briscola, 172.6cc overhead-valve unit-construction single, 60 x 61mm bore and stroke, wet-sump lubrication, 8.5bhp, 4-speed gearbox, 76mph top speed, original, unrestored.
£1,800–2,200
$2,600–3,200 ⊞ NLM
A trio of new 175 Morini singles arrived in 1955: the Briscola, Tressette and Settebello (all popular card games in Italy). The Briscola was the touring model.

1973 Moto Morini 3½ Strada, 344cc overhead-valve 72° V-twin, belt-driven camshaft, parallel valves, Heron combustion chambers, good condition.
£1,000–2,200
$1,500–3,200 ⊞ NLM
First shown at the Milan show in November 1971, Morini's new 350 V-twin did not enter production until early 1973. It was the company's first multi-cylinder model.

◄ **1974 Moto Morini 3½ Strada S1,** 344cc overhead-valve V-twin, 62 x 57mm bore and stroke, electronic ignition, 35bhp at 8,250rpm, fitted with carrier and top box, otherwise standard specification.
£2,200–2,650
$3,200–3,850 ⊞ NLM

1978 Moto Morini 250T, 239.3cc overhead-valve unit-construction single, 69 x 64mm bore and stroke, 9.5:1 compression ratio, 18.5bhp at 7,000rpm, 5-speed gearbox, 6 volt electrics.
£800–950
$1,150–1,380 ⊞ NLM
Making full use of its modular design principals, Morini built not only a range of V-twins, but also several singles. The first of these – a 250 – arrived in 1976. Essentially, it used half of the 500V's engine.

Restored values
The cost of a professional restoration will have an influence on, but no direct relation to, a motorcycle's market value. A restored motorcycle can have a market value lower than the cost of its restoration.

1979 Moto Morini 500 Touring, 478.6cc overhead-valve 72° V-twin, 5-speed gearbox, 12 volt electrics, kickstart only, cast alloy wheels, dual disc front brakes, non-standard 2-into-1 exhaust and rear sets.
£1,850–2,250
$2,700–3,300 ⊞ NLM

1979 Moto Morini 3½ Strada Disc, 344cc overhead-valve 72° V-twin, 6-speed gearbox, electric start, 12 volt electrics, Grimeca single front disc brake, drum rear brake, cast alloy wheels.
£1,800–2,200
$2,600–3,200 ⊞ NLM

1976 Moto Morini 3½ Strada Disc, 344cc overhead-valve 72° V-twin, wet-sump lubrication, 6-speed gearbox, front disc brake, wire wheels, 35mm forks, duplex tubular steel frame, non-standard seat and black-painted exhaust, otherwise original specification.
£1,800–2,000
$2,600–2,900 ⊞ NLM

1979 Moto Morini 125U Series 2, 122.7cc overhead-valve single, 59 x 45mm bore and stroke, 5-speed gearbox, 6 volt electrics, cast alloy wheels, indicators, standard specification apart from mirrors and fork gaiters.
£700–900
$1,000–1,300 ⊞ NLM

1981 Moto Morini 500 Sport, 478.6cc overhead-valve 72° V-twin, 69 x 64mm bore and stroke, 6-speed gearbox, fork gaiters, stainless-steel silencers, dog-leg control levers, 107mph top speed.
£2,500–3,000
$3,600–4,400 ⊞ NLM

1981 Moto Morini 3½ Strada, 344cc overhead-valve 72° V-twin, electronic ignition, 12 volt electrics, electric start, disc front brake, plastic chainguard.
£1,900–2,300
$2,750–3,350 ⊞ NLM

► **1985 Moto Morini Kanguro XI,** 344cc overhead-valve 72° V-twin, high-level exhaust, disc front brake, 21in front wheel, 84mph top speed, fitted with carrier and handlebar protectors.
£1,200–1,400
$1,750–2,000 ⊞ NLM

1983 Moto Morini 500 Camel, 478.6cc, original, good condition.
£2,000–2,300
$2,900–3,350 ⊞ NLM
The Camel was a development of factory bikes that had been entered in such events as the Paris-Dakar Rally and the ISDT. The 500 Camel had revised styling compared to the 350 Kanguro, but retained that bike's drum brakes.

1983 Moto Morini Kanguro X, 344cc overhead-valve 72° V-twin, high-level exhaust, 6-speed gearbox, disc front brake, duplex frame, leading-axle front forks, sump bash plate.
£1,300–1,600
$1,900–2,300 ⊞ NLM

◄ **1992 Moto Morini 501 Excalibur RLX,** 507cc overhead-valve 72° V-twin, 6-speed gearbox, electric start, 12 volt electrics, leading-axle front forks, twin-shock rear suspension.
£2,500–2,700
$3,600–3,900 ⊞ NLM
This custom cruiser employed a Camel-type 507cc engine with Nickasil cylinder bores, Japanese Kokusan electrics and other improvements.

Moto Reve *(Swiss 1902–25)*

1908 Moto Reve, 248cc inlet-over-exhaust narrow-angle V-twin, pedalling gear, belt final drive, sprung saddle, cycle-type caliper front brake.
£5,500–6,000
$7,900–8,700 ⊞ VER

MV Agusta
(Italian 1945–78, 1998–)

◄ **1957 MV Agusta Turismo Rapido,** 123.5cc overhead-valve unit-construction single, 54 x 54mm bore and stroke, 4-speed gearbox, telescopic front forks, swinging-arm rear suspension, full-width alloy drum brakes, 6 volt electrics, valanced mudguards, concours condition.
£2,200–2,500
$3,100–3,600 ⊞ BB
The Turismo Rapido (TR) was built from 1955 to 1957.

A known continuous history can add value to and enhance the enjoyment of a motorcycle.

► **1957 MV Agusta 175 Turismo,** 172cc overhead-camshaft single, 59.5 x 62mm bore and stroke, 8bhp at 5,600 rpm, 4-speed gearbox, in need of restoration.
£1,000–1,200
$1,400–1,600 ⊞ MAY

Miller's
Motorcycle Milestones

MV Agusta GP 497cc (Italian 1956)
Price range: £100,000–150,000
$145,000–217,500

Giovanni Agusta was one of Italy's aviation pioneers, flying his own prototype aeroplane at Capau, just north of Naples in 1907. Although he died in 1927, the company he founded went on to become a major fixed-wing aircraft constructor during the inter-war period and WWII, thereafter specialising in helicopter design. In addition, for some three decades, MV Agusta was a major motorcycle marque.

MV's first motorcycle, a 98cc two-stroke single, appeared in 1946 and was soon followed that year by a racing version. The first four-stroke was a 249cc overhead-valve single, while the first racing four-stroke appeared in 1950, in the shape of a twin-cam, 123.5cc single and a 494.4cc (54 x 54mm) four. The latter machine was unexpectedly presented at the 1950 Milan Trade Fair – a rare, if not unique, example of a racing machine being exhibited to the public before it appeared on the circuits. The bike, designed by former Gilera chief engineer Pietro Remor, possessed several features not normally found in racing designs, most notably shaft drive and torsion-bar suspension.

The four-cylinder MV's first race was no less than the Belgian GP in July 1950. Ridden by Areiso Artesiani, the newcomer managed a very creditable

fifth, behind works entries from Gilera and AJS.

Always a speedy machine, the MV's main problem centred around its road-holding, and the following year it was equipped with conventional telescopic front forks.

Next, in 1952, came a heavily modified version with new bore and stroke dimensions of 53 x 56.4mm to produce 497.5cc. With larger valves, hotter cams and other changes, allied to four instead of two carburettors, power rose to 45bhp. Moreover, the gearbox was uprated from four to five ratios, and the drive shaft was replaced by a chain. A new frame completed the picture. Subsequently, Earles-type front forks were tried, but after team leader Les Graham's fatal accident in the 1953 Senior TT, MV quickly returned to the telescopic type.

But the real breakthrough for MV came in 1956, when the company signed the rising British star John Surtees, and the combination won the marque's first 500cc world title. Surtees went on to win a further six titles (three 350cc and three 500cc) before retiring at the end of 1960. Other MV 500cc world champions were Gary Hocking, Mike Hailwood, Giacomo Agostini and Phil Read.

By the time it quit the sport at the end of 1976, MV had won over 3,000 international races, 38 individual world championships and 37 manufacturer's titles, and had become the most successful team ever.

1971 MV Agusta 350B Elettronica, 349cc overhead-valve unit twin, 63 x 56mm bore and stroke, 32 bhp at 7,650rpm, 5-speed gearbox, 99mph top speed.
£2,200–2,500
$3,100–3,600 ⊞ NLM

1973 MV Agusta 350S Elettronica, overhead-valve unit-construction twin, 5-speed gearbox, full-width alloy hubs.
£2,200–2,500
$3,100–3,600 ⚲ BKS
The MV Agusta 350 twin, first seen at the 1969 Milan motorcycle show, was a development of the existing 250 twin. The increase in displacement was achieved by enlarging the bore from 53 to 63mm and resulted in a free-revving unit. When first introduced, the bike relied on conventional coil ignition; in 1971, however, a revised line-up was announced featuring electronic ignition. The S version was equipped with clip-on handlebars, alloy rims, a sports seat and rearsets.

1972 MV Agusta 750S, 743cc double-overhead-camshaft 4-cylinder engine, 65 x 56mm bore and stroke, 5-speed gearbox, concours condition.
£15,000–16,000
$21,000–23,000 ⚲ BKS
MV Agusta had tantalised the public during the mid-1950s with a prototype four-cylinder machine that obviously was derived from the factory racing machines. However, it was not until 1965 that a four finally emerged for public consumption. The new model, a 600cc, twin-carburettor tourer with styling that could most politely be described as 'unusual' failed to interest the public, who wanted something more sporting. In 1969, enthusiasts' prayers were finally answered with the introduction of the 750S. Displacing 743cc, the new model featured clip-on handlebars, rearsets, a humped seat, stainless-steel mudguards and four individual silencers, two per side. Early versions utilised a twin-leading-shoe drum brake at the front, although later models adopted discs. Finished in red, white and blue, the 750S provided performance, handling and looks.

Auction prices

Miller's only includes motorcycles declared sold. Our guide prices take into account the buyer's premium, VAT on the premium, and the extent of any published catalogue information relating to condition and provenance. Motorcycles sold at auction are identified by the ⚲ icon; full details of the auction house can be found on page 167.

1976 Agusta Model 216 350 Sport, 349cc overhead-valve twin, 63 x 56mm bore and stroke, square-case engine, 5-speed gearbox, triple Scarab disc brakes, cast alloy wheels, aluminium side panels.
£2,000–2,500
$2,900–3,600 ⊞ MW

1978 MV Agusta 750 America, 790cc double-overhead-camshaft 4-cylinder engine, 67 x 56mm bore and stroke, 75bhp at 8,500rpm, 5-speed gearbox, 4-into-1 exhaust and Marzocchi rear shock absorber, otherwise largely standard.
£13,000–15,000
$18,800–21,750 ⊞ MW

1972 MV Agusta 750 Super Sport, 748cc double-overhead-camshaft across-the-frame 4-cylinder engine, 5-speed gearbox, shaft final drive.
£25,000–30,000
$36,000–43,500 ⊞ MW
The 750 Super Sport is a very rare version of the standard 750S. Giacomo Agostini rode a racing version in the 1972 Imola 200 race. The Super Sport came with a full fairing and a different colour scheme to the S model.

MZ *(German 1953–)*

1980 MZ Super 5, 247cc piston-port 2-stroke single, 5-speed gearbox, drum brakes, alloy rims, standard specification, exhaust in need of replating.
£400–500
$580–725 ⊞ BLM

Neracar
(American/British 1921–26)

◀ **1922 Neracar A2,** 285cc 2-stroke single.
£2,000–2,500
$2,900–3,600 ⚡ BKS
Designed by J. Neracher, the Neracar was built in both America and Britain. Initially, a 285cc two-stroke engine provided the motive power, relying on friction drive to the rear wheel. Later variants produced in Britain utilised more conventional transmission systems, with chain final drive and Blackburne 348cc engines in overhead-valve and side-valve configurations. The frame was manufactured from steel pressings and incorporated the mudguards, which combined with the foot-forward riding position to produce a machine of unique appearance that handled exceptionally well.

New Hudson *(British 1909–57)*

◀ **1921 New Hudson 2-Speed,** 229cc deflector-piston 2-stroke single, in need of complete restoration.
£1,600–1,900
$2,300–2,750 ⚡ PS
New Hudson motorcycles were manufactured until 1933, when the marque was acquired by BSA. Thereafter, the company concentrated on autocycles.

▶ **1926 New Hudson 2¾hp Semi Sports,** 348cc side-valve single, hand-change gearbox, chain final drive, drum brakes, fully restored, concours condition.
£4,500–5,000
$6,500–7,000 ⊞ VER

New Imperial
(British 1910–39)

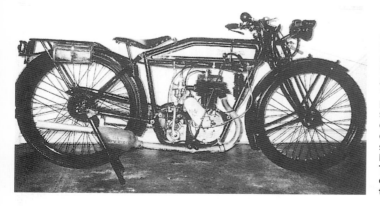

◀ **1927 New Imperial Semi Sports De Luxe,** 293cc JAP side-valve single.
£1,600–2,000
$2,000–2,900 ⚡ BKS
After an abortive experiment in 1901, New Imperial began production in 1910 with a 293cc side-valve JAP-engined model equipped with a two-speed countershaft gearbox, the latter something of a novelty in a lightweight machine of the period. The success of the Model 1 ensured the company's prosperity throughout the 1920s.

Norton *(British 1902–)*

1928 Norton CS1, 490cc overhead-camshaft single, 79 x 100mm bore and stroke.
£8,000–10,000
$11,500–14,500 ⊞ YEST

1931 Norton Model 18, 490cc overhead-valve single,
79 x 100mm bore and stroke, girder forks, rigid frame.
£6,300–6,700
$9,100–9,600 ⊞ PM

1933 Norton CJ, 348cc overhead-camshaft single,
71 x 88mm bore and stroke.
£5,700–6,900
$8,100–10,000 ⚲ BKS

The appearance of the overhead-cam Norton in 1927 marked the beginning of two decades that constitute one of the most glorious phases in the marque's long and illustrious history. During this period, single-cam Nortons attained an astonishing record in competition at both national and international level. The name chosen for the revised model that replaced the CS1 in 1931, International, demonstrated no immodesty on the part of the Bracebridge Street concern. It simply reflected the outstanding quality of Norton's product and its success. The new engine was the work of Arthur Carrol, who specified dry-sump lubrication and a change of position for the magneto to the rear of the cylinder.

The CS1 – Norton's First Camshaft Model

The honour of being the first 'cammy' Norton single goes to the CS1 (Cam Shaft One). Its design was the work of Walter Moore, who had joined the company in 1924 to take over from the ailing James ('Pa') Norton.

Conceived during 1926, the engine, which replaced the overhead-valve Model 18 at the top of Norton's range, was first used during the Isle of Man TT series in 1927. As the story goes, the engine had never been fully tested, and Walter Moore himself took the first two completed engine assemblies to the Island, hiring a small boat to take him there overnight. He personally persuaded the team riders, including Alec Bennett, to use them. This confidence proved to be fully justified, as Bennett rode the new CS1 to a win in the Senior TT, leading by over eight minutes. What an incredible debut, and one of the best ever in motorcycle racing history. Alec Bennett's winning speed (a new record) was 68.41mph.

The CS1 employed the traditional long-stroke Norton dimensions of 79 x 100mm. In fact, Moore utilised several existing overhead-valve engine components, including the crankcases, crankshaft flywheels, connecting rod and piston from the Model 18. But the big difference was the set of bevel gears and shafts that ran up the offside of the cylinder and crankshaft to drive the camshaft. Again, Moore borrowed the oil-pump design from a type first used in 1925, this being enclosed in the bottom bevel housing. The magneto, situated at the rear of the barrel, was driven by a chain.

Ultimately, though, the CS1 was relatively short-lived due to a combination of events. First, Moore tried, unsuccessfully, to extract extra performance for 1928, which affected reliability. Then, in 1929, he left to work for NSU in Germany, where his first design was virtually an unlicensed copy of the CS1! This was the final straw as far as the Norton management was concerned, the result being a new camshaft engine designed by Arthur Carroll, which was to lead into the International and Manx models.

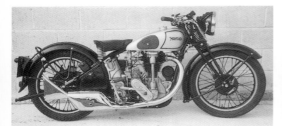

1938 Norton International, 490cc bevel-driven overhead-camshaft single, 79 x 100mm bore and stroke, foot-change gearbox, girder forks, rigid frame, 'Brooklands can' silencer.
£5,500–6,500
$8,000–9,500 ⊞ BLM
This International is in sports/touring guise.

1949 Norton ES2, 490cc overhead-valve single, telescopic forks, plunger frame, rider's seat and pillion pad, original specification, very good condition.
£3,500–3,800
$5,000–5,500 ⊞ VER

1950 Norton Model 30 International, 490cc bevel-driven overhead-camshaft single, 4-speed foot-change gearbox, telescopic forks, plunger rear suspension, largely original apart from Manx front brake and chrome fuel and oil tanks, concours condition.
£8,000–10,000
$11,600–14,500 ⚒ BKS

▶ **1951 Norton ES2,** 490cc overhead-valve single, laid-down gearbox, telescopic forks, plunger frame, non-period dualseat.
£2,800–3,200
$4,000–4,650 ⊞ BLM

◀ **1951 Norton Model 7 Dominator,** 497cc overhead-valve parallel twin, 66 x 72.6mm bore and stroke, iron head and barrel, telescopic forks, plunger frame, 7in front brake.
£3,500–3,900
$5,000–5,600 ⊞ PMo
Designed by Bert Hopwood, the Dominator twin was probably the most important Norton model of the immediate post-war era; the first model was coded 7 and arrived in 1948.

▶ **1953 Norton ES2,** 490cc overhead-valve single, 70 x 100mm bore and stroke, die-cast alloy front brake plate and 8in drum.
£2,500–3,000
$3,600–4,400 ⊞ BLM
For 1953, the ES2 gained a swinging-arm frame, Girling rear shock absorbers, a smaller exhaust pipe, a quickly-detachable rear wheel and a dualseat.

1956 Norton 19S, 597cc overhead-valve single, 82 x 113mm bore and stroke, 25bhp at 4,200rpm, full-width hubs, Roadholder forks, single-down-tube frame, Girling rear shock absorbers.
£2,800–3,400
$4,000–4,900 ⚞ PS
The 19S arrived for the 1955 model year and essentially was a larger-engined ES2.

1961 Norton Dominator 99, 597cc near-standard apart from aftermarket dualseat.
£3,500–3,800
$5,000–5,500 ⊞ BLM
This was the final year of the 600 Model 99.

▶ **1962 Norton ES2,** 490cc overhead-valve single, AMC gearbox, wideline Featherbed frame, near-original specification apart from valanced mudguards and later twin-leading-shoe front brake conversion, very good condition.
£3,800–4,000
$5,500–5,800 ⊞ VER

1957 Norton International Model 30, 490cc overhead-camshaft single.
£6,900–8,200
$10,000–11,900 ⚞ BKS
Perhaps the most significant development in the history of the long running Norton International was the announcement of the Featherbed frame and all-alloy engine in 1953. The new versions of the Model 30 and Model 40 would continue in production in essentially the same form until 1955. From then on, they no longer appeared in the catalogue, but were still available to special order until 1958. Minor modifications were introduced in the 1955–58 period, reflecting improvements introduced on other road-going Featherbed-framed models, although the International always retained the laid-down gearbox.

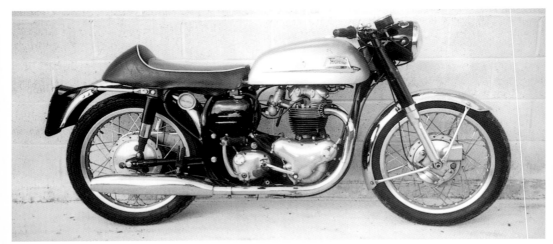

1962 Norton 650SS, 647cc overhead-valve twin, 68 x 89mm bore and stroke, 49bhp at 6,800rpm, camshaft-driven rev-counter, original 650SS model updated with sports seat, twin-leading-shoe front brake, flangeless aluminium wheel rims and Amal Concentric Mk 1 carburettors instead of Monoblocs.
£3,400–3,700
$5,000–5,400 ⊞ BLM
The 650SS remained in production for almost a decade, from 1961 until 1970.

▶ **1963 Norton 650SS,** 647cc overhead-valve twin, alloy head, iron barrel, AMC gearbox, slimline frame, Roadholder forks, full-width hubs, black painted mudguards instead of chrome, no rev-counter, non-standard dualseat.
£3,300–3,900
$4,800–5,600 ⊞ OBMS

1969 Norton Commando S-Type, 745cc overhead-valve twin, 73 x 89mm bore and stroke, 60bhp at 6,800rpm, chrome grab rail, perforated exhaust heat shields, fully restored, concours condition.
£3,800–4,200
$5,500–6,100 ⊞ BLM
The S-Type was made for the American market, with high-level exhaust, high bars and a chrome ring around the headlamp.

▶ **1969 Norton Mercury,** 646cc overhead-valve parallel twin, non-standard siamesed exhaust, chromed headlamp brackets.
£2,800–3,200
$4,000–4,600 ⊞ PMo
The Mercury was the last of the 650 Norton twins to be made. It was built between 1968 and 1970 only.

1969 Norton Mercury, 646cc, slimline frame, factory optional stainless-steel mudguards.
£2,700–3,200
$3,900–4,600 ⊞ BLM

1971 Norton Commando, 745cc overhead-valve pre-unit parallel twin, Fastback-type exhaust, Isolastic suspension, twin-leading-shoe front brake, larger-capacity fuel tank.
£2,200–2,700
$3,200–3,900 ⊞ MAY

1973 Norton JPS, restored.
£4,000–4,500
$5,800–6,500 ⊞ PMo

1973 Norton Commando Interstate, 745cc overhead-valve parallel twin, electronic ignition, disc front brakes, rear drum brakes, vernier Isolastic mountings, stainless-steel fasteners, known history.
£4,000–4,500
$5,800–6,500 ⊞ WbC

1971 Norton Commando Fastback, 745cc overhead-valve twin, 73 x 89mm bore and stroke, Isolastic suspension, twin-leading-shoe front brake, completely restored.
£4,000–5,000
$5,800–7,000 ⊞ BLM

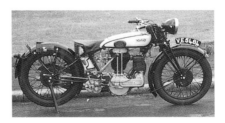

1975 Norton Commando Roadster, 745cc overhead-valve twin, 73 x 89mm bore and stroke, 60bhp at 6,800rpm, single front disc brake, rear drum brake, standard US model with enlarged oil tank and cartridge filter.
£3,000–3,500
$4,400–5,000 ⊞ BLM

1977 Norton Commando, 829cc overhead-valve twin, 4-speed gearbox, electric start, front and rear disc brakes, JPS (John Player Special) colour scheme, standard specification.
£3,500–4,000
$5,000–5,800 ⊞ PMo
This was the final year of Commando production.

1977 Norton 850 Commando Interstate Mk3, 829cc overhead-valve twin, electric start, fork gaiters, rev-counter, direction indicators, finished in silver and black, one of last Commandos built, 1,100 miles from new, concours condition.
£5,000–6,000
$7,250–8,700 ⊞ NLM

Miller's is a price GUIDE not a price LIST

OEC *(British 1901–54)*

◀ **1934 OEC Model 34/8,** 592cc water-cooled 4-cylinder engine, hand-change gearbox, chain final drive, drum brakes.
£22,500–25,000
$32,000–36,000 ⊞ AtMC
Based in Gosport, Hampshire, OEC (Osborn Engineering Company) was best known for its duplex steering system, designed by Fred Wood and introduced in 1927. The duplex system was far heavier, but much stiffer, than girder forks, giving much improved stability at speed.

Panther *(British 1900–66)*

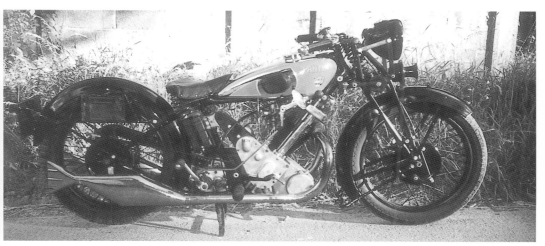

1930 Panther Redwing 90, 490cc overhead-valve twin-port single, sloping cylinder, twin 'Brooklands can' exhausts.
£3,000–3,200
$4,400–4,650 ⊞ CotC
Panther was originally known as P & M (Phelon & Moore) and was based in Cleckheaton, West Yorkshire.

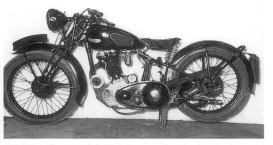

1938 Panther Model 20, 249cc overhead-valve single, wet-sump lubrication, girder forks, rigid frame, sprung saddle.
£900–1,100
$1,300–1,600 ⊞ MW
Pride & Clarke sold this Panther model for less than £30 when new.

1956 Panther Model 100, 594cc overhead-valve twin-port single, 87 x 100mm bore and stroke, sloping cylinder, large-diameter drum brakes, telescopic forks, swinging-arm rear suspension, dualseat, original and unrestored.
£1,500–1,800
$2,100–2,600 ⊞ BLM

Restored values

The cost of a professional restoration will have an influence on, but no direct relation to, a motorcycle's market value. A restored motorcycle can have a market value lower than the cost of its restoration.

1962 Panther Model 10/4, 197cc Villiers 9E 2-stroke single, 59 x 72mm bore and stroke, alloy head, iron barrel, 3-speed gearbox, Earles forks, swinging-arm rear suspension, dualseat, original specification.
£600–900
$870–1,300 ⊞ BLM
The Model 10/4 was built between 1955 and 1962.

Parilla *(Italian 1946–67)*

1957 Parilla MSDS 175, 174cc high-camshaft single, 59.8 x 62mm bore and stroke, 4-speed close-ratio gearbox, alloy rims, Dell'Orto SSI carburettor, restored to original specification, concours condition.
£4,000–4,500
$5,800–6,500 ⊞ MW
The MSDS 175 was a limited-edition Milano-Taranto type machine with brake-tested engine. It was capable of over 90mph.

Peugeot *(French 1899–)*

c1902 Peugeot 2hp Perfecta, single-cylinder engine, in need of restoration.
£3,500–4,200
$5,000–6,100 ⚲ BKS
Peugeot was a pioneer of the early car and motorcycle industries and soon became known for building both single-cylinder and V-twin engines; in 1904, it provided the engine for the first motorcycle manufactured by Norton. However, Peugeot's first production model was a motorised bicycle with a 1.5hp engine. Perfecta was another French factory which, at one time made tricycles and also clip-on, single-cylinder power units at the turn of the 20th century.

Premier
(British 1908–20)

1913 Premier, 490cc inlet-over-exhaust single, 3-speed hand-change gearbox, magneto ignition, pedalling gear, belt final drive.
£6,000–6,500
$8,700–9,400 ⊞ VER

▶ **1908 Premier Lightweight,** 200cc inlet-over-exhaust single, pedalling gear, belt final drive, in need of restoration.
£1,750–1,850
$2,450–2,600 ⊞ YEST

Quadrant *(British 1901–29)*

▶ **1906 Quadrant 4hp Tourer,** 498cc single, upright cylinder, pedalling gear, belt final drive, acetylene lighting.
£8,000–9,000
$11,600–13,000 ⊞ VER

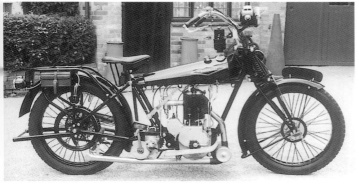

◀ **1925 Quadrant,** 654cc side-valve single, vertical cylinder, iron head and barrel, magneto ignition, hand-change gearbox, drum front/caliper rear brakes, girder forks, rigid frame.
£5,000–5,500
$7,250–8,000 ⊞ VER

Raleigh *(British 1899–1970s)*

◄ **1924 Raleigh Model 6 Sports,** 348cc side-valve single, forward-mounted magneto, Sturmey Archer hand-change gearbox, chain final drive, caliper front brake.
£3,000–3,500
$4,400–5,000 🚲 RSS
The Raleigh company, based in Nottingham, produced motorcycles from 1899 until 1906, then restarted production after WW1. It also sold engines and gearboxes to other firms under the Sturmey Archer name, and this business continued until 1934.

1929 Raleigh Model 12 De Luxe, 248cc side-valve single, chain final drive, drum brakes, fully restored.
£2,500–3,000
$3,600–4,400 🚲 RSS

1927 Raleigh 350, 348cc side-valve single, iron head and barrel, hand-change gearbox, chain final drive, drum brakes.
£3,500–3,800
$5,000–5,500 ▦ VER

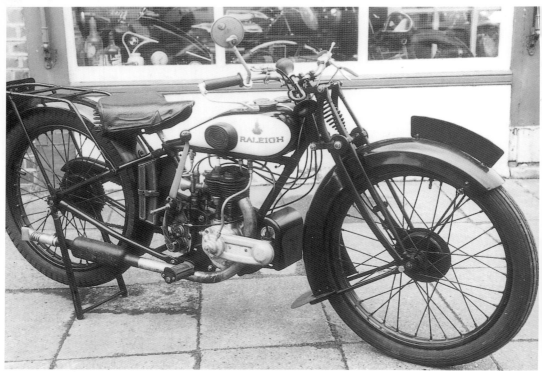

1925 Raleigh 250, 248cc side-valve single, magneto ignition, hand-change Sturmey Archer gearbox, girder forks, rigid frame, sprung saddle.
£2,700–3,200
$3,900–4,650 ▦ AtMc

Rickman *(British 1959–80s)*

◀ **1977 Rickman-Kawasaki,** 1000cc double-overhead-camshaft Kawasaki 4-cylinder engine, Rickman cycle parts including frame, forks and bodywork.
£1,200–2,000
$1,750–2,900 ⚒ COYS
The Rickman brothers, Don and Derek, were well-known motocross stars, who had achieved success riding machines that employed their own design of frame, called the Metisse. During the mid-1960s, they turned their expertise to the tarmac, first through road-racing, then with production roadsters. Their factory, at New Milton, Hampshire, produced bikes with British and Japanese engines.

Rover *(British 1902–25)*

1914 Rover 3½hp, side-valve single, 3-speed hand-change gearbox, Sturmey Archer hub gear, belt final drive, restored.
£5,600–6,200
$8,100–8,800 ⚒ BKS
With roots in J.K. Starley's cycle manufacturing business at Meteor Works, Coventry, Rover began making motorcycles in 1902, although production in earnest did not get under way until around 1910. The first 3½hp machine was marketed for the 1911 season and sold well. It found favour with the Post Office in Scotland, and attracted orders from the Russian government during WWI, by which time it had gained a three-speed countershaft gearbox with gear-change effected through the petrol tank.

▶ **1917 Rover V-Twin,** 676cc side-valve JAP narrow-angle V-twin, single carburettor, fully enclosed chain final drive, footboards, excellent condition.
£6,500–7,000
$9,400–10,200 ⊞ VER

Royal Enfield *(British 1901–70)*

1910 Royal Enfield 2¼hp, belt final drive, pedal starting.
£6,000–6,500
$8,700–9,400 ⊞ MW
'Made like a gun' was the slogan most widely used to describe the Royal Enfield marque. This was in response to its badge, which for many years incorporated an illustration of a small field gun.

1921 Royal Enfield Model 200, 2.25hp 2-stroke single, chain final drive, caliper brakes, legshields, footboards.
£1,100–1,300
$1,600–1,900 ⋏ H&H

1914 Royal Enfield V-Twin, 600cc inlet-over-exhaust V-twin, enclosed valve gear, hand-operated oil pump, 2-speed countershaft gearbox, chain final drive, caliper brakes.
£8,500–8,900
$11,600–12,800 ⊞ VER
Based in Redditch, Worcestershire, the Enfield concern made sewing needles and machine parts during the 19th century. Then, in the 1880s, 'Royal' was added to its name. The first motorcycle was built in 1901.

1925 Royal Enfield 2¾hp Sports, 350cc side-valve single, hand-change gearbox, chain final drive, girder forks, rigid frame.
£1,500–1,900
$2,175–2,750 ⊞ BLM

1958 Royal Enfield Crusader Airflow, 248cc overhead-valve unit single, 70 x 64.5mm bore and stroke, 4-speed gearbox, full-width aluminium brake hubs, Airflow fairing, dualseat.
£1,000–1,400
$1,500–2,000 ⊞ BLM
Royal Enfield was one of the first factories in the world to offer true weather protection. The original Airflow fairing was manufactured for Enfield by the Bristol Aviation Company.

1949 Royal Enfield J2, 499cc overhead-valve single, 84 x 90mm bore and stroke, iron head and barrel, 4-speed foot-change gearbox, telescopic forks, rigid frame, original specification, excellent condition.
£3,400–3,600
$4,800–5,200 ⊞ VER
The J2 model featured a twin-port cylinder head. It continued to be produced until 1955, mainly for sidecar enthusiasts who preferred a rigid frame.

1959 Royal Enfield Meteor Minor, 496cc overhead-valve parallel twin, 70 x 64.5mm bore and stroke, full-width alloy brake hubs, 17in wheels.
£2,000–2,700
$2,900–3,900 ⊞ BLM
The Meteor Minor was the last 500 Enfield twin built, and it was available from 1958 until 1968.

1959 Royal Enfield Bullet, 346cc overhead-valve single, alloy head, iron barrel, 4-speed foot-change gearbox, chrome mudguards, twin pilot lights.
£1,500–1,700
$2,175–2,450 ⊞ BLM
The Bullet was offered for the 1959 model year with revised engine internals, a larger tank, 17in wheels and 7in brakes.

1961 Royal Enfield 350 Bullet, 346cc overhead-valve semi-unit single, sweptback exhaust pipe, 4-speed foot-change gearbox, painted mudguards.
£1,400–1,800
$2,000–2,600 ⊞ BLM

1970s Royal Enfield Interceptor, 736cc overhead-valve parallel twin, 4-speed gearbox, assembled in touring trim from a variety of Interceptor and Constellation parts, Norton Commando fork legs, Norvil disc front brake, high bars, chrome Lucas headlamp, in need of cosmetic attention.
£1,000–1,400
$1,500–2,000 ⊞ BLM

◄ **1991 Royal Enfield India,** 499cc overhead-valve single, 84 x 90mm bore and stroke, alloy head, iron barrel, 12 volt electrics, direction indicators, chrome mudguards.
£900–1,100
$1,300–1,600 ⊞ BLM
Although production of the Bullet ceased at Redditch in the mid-1960s, the model has been built in Madras, India, since that time. Currently, it is available in both 350 and 500cc engine sizes.

Rudge *(British 1911–40)*

1919 Rudge Multi, 499cc inlet-over-exhaust single, 85 x 88mm bore and stroke, iron head and barrel, incomplete but including 2 new Dunlop tyres, in need of complete restoration.
£3,200–3,800
$4,650–5,500 ✈ TEN
This model was equipped with the famous variable 'multi' gear, which allowed up to 20 gear positions. A Rudge using this feature was victorious in the 1914 TT.

▶ **1925 Rudge Four,** 499cc overhead-valve single, 85 x 88mm bore and stroke, 25bhp, 4-speed hand-change gearbox, 85mph top speed.
£3,700–4,000
$4,200–5,800 ⊞ VER
Originally the Four (four-valve) was available in both 348 and 499cc engine sizes, but from 1925 only the larger model was available.

1921 Royal Rudge TT Multi, 499cc inlet-over-exhaust single, belt final drive, rigid frame, older restoration, running condition.
£6,500–7,000
$9,400–10,200 ⊞ BLM
This TT Multi spent most of its life on the Isle of Man and was discovered around 20 years ago in poor condition on a farm in Wales.

1930 Rudge 250 Sports, 245cc JAP overhead-valve twin-port single, 62 x 5.80mm bore and stroke, hand-change gearbox.
£3,000–3,200
$4,400–4,650 ⊞ VER
This was the final year of manufacture for the 250 Sports.

▶ **1931 Rudge Radial,** 348cc overhead-valve twin-port single, 70 x 90.5mm bore and stroke, iron head and barrel, girder forks, rigid frame.
£5,00–5,500
$7,250–8,000 ⊞ PM
The Radial was fitted with a four-valve cylinder head.

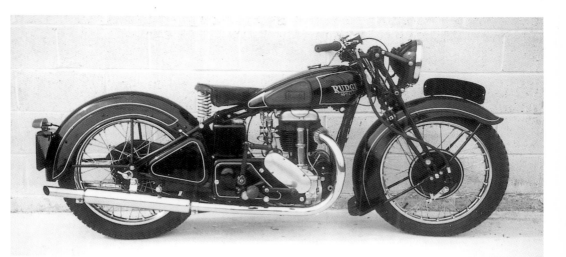

1937 Rudge Special, 493cc overhead-valve twin-port single, 84.5 x 88mm bore and stroke, 4-speed foot-change gearbox, concours condition.
£4,500–5,000
$6,500–7,250 ⊞ BLM
The Special was essentially the touring version of the famous Ulster sports model.

Rumi *(Italian 1949–late 1950s)*

1954 Rumi 125 Sport, 124cc horizontal twin, 42 x 45mm bore and stroke, telescopic forks, plunger frame, excellent condition.
£5,600–6,600
$8,200–9,500 ⊞ NLM
The Rumi twin-cylinder engine was extremely successful, not only as a power unit for road-going motorcycles and scooters, but also in racing. It was even fitted to machines that contested such endurance events as the 24-hour French famous Bol d'Or.

▶ **1954 Rumi 125 Lusso,** 124cc 2-stroke horizontal twin, alloy heads, iron barrels, telescopic forks, plunger rear suspension, fork gaiters, dualseat.
£4,600–5,600
$6,700–8,200 ⊞ NLM

Scott *(British 1909–late 1960s)*

◀ **1925 Scott Two-Speed,** 596cc liquid-cooled 2-stroke twin, not completely original, very good condition.
£6,500–7,000
$9,400–10,200 ⊞ VER

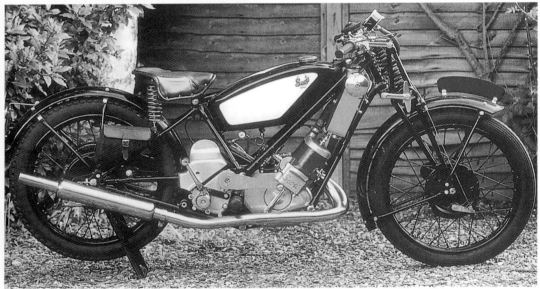

1928 Scott Squirrel, 499cc liquid-cooled 2-stroke twin, 68.25 x 68.25mm bore and stroke.
£3,200–3,800
$4,650–5,500 ⚲ BKS

Alfred Angas Scott's experiments with two-stroke motorcycle engines began in the closing years of the 19th century. The first complete Scott motorcycle followed in 1908, its twin-cylinder engine, two-speed foot-change gearbox and all-chain drive marking it out as an exceptionally advanced design for its day. Light weight, ample power and sure-footed handling, thanks to a low centre of gravity, were Scott virtues right from the outset. In 1909, the marque made its first appearance at the Isle of Man TT. Revisions to the existing design saw water-cooling adopted for cylinder head and barrel – previously the latter had been air-cooled. In 1912, Scott's works rider, Frank Appleby, won the Senior TT, having led from the start. It was the first time such a feat had been achieved, and the first senior victory for a two-stroke. Although recognisably derived from Scott's earliest designs, the Scott motorcycle of the 1920s gained steadily in complexity and weight. A three-speed countershaft gearbox had been introduced for 1923 and, as a result of the racing programme, there was a new duplex frame and bigger brakes for 1927. For the traditionalists, the old-style two-speed model soldiered on, remaining in production into the 1930s.

1930 Scott Flying Squirrel, 597cc liquid-cooled 2-stroke twin, 74.6 x 68.25mm bore and stroke, 3-speed hand-change gearbox, excellent condition.
£5,000–5,500
$7,250–8,000 ⊞ VER

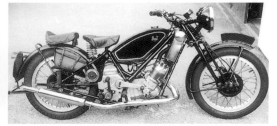

1938 Scott Flying Squirrel, 598cc liquid-cooled 2-stroke twin, inclined cylinders, siamesed exhaust, foot-change gearbox, front wheel speedometer drive, aluminium wheel rims.
£1,750–2,250
$2,575–3,275 ⊞ VER

The distinctive yowl from the Scott's exhaust set it apart from other machines, and also helped to endear the marque to many enthusiasts.

> A known continuous history can add value to and enhance the enjoyment of a motorcycle.

◀ **1947 Scott Flying Squirrel,** 598cc liquid-cooled 2-stroke twin, foot-change gearbox.
£3,200–3,800
$4,650–5,500 ⊞ NLM
The 1947 Flying Squirrel was much as the pre-war model, apart from telescopic front forks and a full-width front drum brake.

Sertum *(Italian 1922–51)*

This famous Milan factory originally manufactured precision instruments. But in 1922, its owner, Fausto Alberti, decided to enter the two-wheel world. The company's first design was a 174cc side-valve model, which was soon followed by a cheaper 119cc two-stroke.

Thereafter, throughout the mid- and late 1930s, Sertum manufactured a wide range of strong, dependable singles and twins, employing not only side-valve engines, but also overhead-camshaft units.

The Milanese concern was involved in motorcycle sport, too, most notably the ISDT and the long-distance road races, such as the Milano-Taranto.

After the war, Sertum was one of the first Italian manufacturers to resume production, and at the 1947 Milan Show it was able to boast of being the only Italian company to support that year's ISDT. At the exhibition, Sertum showed two basic models: a girder-fork, rear-sprung, 250cc overhead-valve single, and a similar 500. It also had a 500cc vertical twin, but was undecided about production. The neatest bike on the stand was a new Sports 250 with pressed-steel frame.

The following year, Gilera, Bianchi, Parilla, Moto Guzzi and Sertum were responsible for 97.74 per cent of all Italian motorcycle registrations – with the remaining 33 manufacturers having to divide a measly 2.26 per cent between them!

But from this high, sales declined rapidly, to a point where the Milan company was forced to close its doors – the first major post-war casualty of the Italian motorcycle industry.

▶ **1945 Sertum 250 Turismo,** 247cc side-valve single, foot-change gearbox, blade girder forks, full-width drum brakes, original, in need of cosmetic restoration.
£1,100–1,300
$1,500–1,800 ⊞ VICO

Sun *(British 1911–61)*

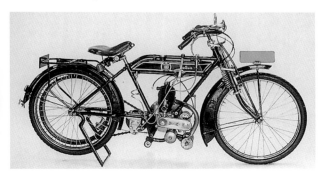

◀ **1914 Sun,** 269cc Villiers 2-stroke engine, Albion 2-speed gearbox, restored mid-1990s.
£2,100–2,600
$3,000–3,800 ↗ TEN
Like many of its ilk, the Sun marque could trace its origins to the cycle industry and hailed from Birmingham. Motorcycle production began prior to WW1 and continued after the war with JAP, Villiers and other engines, including a disc-valve two-stroke. This particular machine took part in the first London–Brighton Pioneer Run held in 1930.

Sunbeam *(British 1912–57)*

1915 Sunbeam, 499cc inlet-over-exhaust single, iron head and barrel, magneto ignition, fully enclosed chain final drive, footboards, lighting equipment.
£6,500–7,000
$9,400–10,200 ⊞ VER

1916 Sunbeam, 499cc side-valve single, hand-change gearbox, all-chain drive, primary and final drive in oil-bath cases.
£6,600–8,000
$9,500–11,600 ⚒ BKS
John Marston waited until 1912 before beginning motorcycle production, but his beautiful Sunbeam machines soon found an eager market. Although he was rather late to enter the field, the most remarkable fact was that when he did, it was at the grand age of 76. His family firm had many years of experience in metal finishing, and as it was one of the first in Britain to perfect the technique of applying a high-gloss baked finish, its machines benefited accordingly, exuding an air of high quality.

1925 Sunbeam Light Solo, 499cc side-valve single, hand-change gearbox, fully enclosed primary and final drive chains, sprung saddle and pillion pad.
£5,500–6,000
$8,000–8,700 ⊞ VER

1926 Sunbeam Model 2, 347cc side-valve single, fitted optional 26 x 3in tyres and sports (exposed) rear chain guard, unrestored.
£2,100–2,500
$3,000–3,600 ⚒ H&H

◄ **1927 Sunbeam Model 2,** 347cc side-valve single, 70 x 90mm bore and stroke, sprung forks and saddle.
£3,800–4,500
$5,500–6,500 ⊞ VER
Production of the Model 2 ceased at the end of 1930.

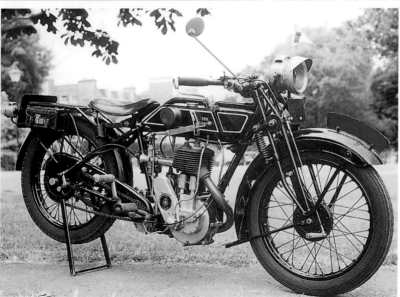

◄ **1928 Sunbeam Model 6,** 491cc side-valve single, 77 x 105.5mm bore and stroke, hand-change gearbox, hub brakes, full lighting equipment.
£3,500–4,000
$5,000–5,800 ⚒ BKS
The Model 6 was built until the end of 1930. Thereafter, Sunbeam concentrated its efforts upon overhead-valve rather than side-valve engines.

◄ **1929 Sunbeam Model 5,** 491cc side-valve single, iron head and barrel, hand-change gearbox.
£3,200–3,800
$4,650–5,500 ⚸ BKS
Both the Model 5 and Model 6 used Sunbeam's own 'Longstroke' engine, so-called because its 77 x 105.5mm bore and stroke dimensions were not only exceedingly long-stroke, but also because it was the company's longest running engine, remaining in production from 1922 until 1940 (from 1931 as the Lion, and later still as the 30 Series).

1930 Sunbeam Model 9, 493cc overhead-valve single, 80 x 98mm bore and stroke, hand-change gearbox, unrestored.
£3,200–3,800
$4,650–5,500 ⚸ BKS
The 'LL' prefix of the Model 9's engine number stood for 'Twin Port'. The machine was manufactured from 1929 until 1938.

1931 Sunbeam Model 6, side-valve single, 85 x 105.5mm bore and stroke, hand-change gearbox.
£2,000–2,750
$2,900–3,900 ⊞ BLM
This was the final year of production for the Model 6; thereafter it was sold as the Lion.

1934 Sunbeam Model 8, 348cc overhead-valve twin-port single, magneto ignition, hand-change gearbox, girder forks, rigid frame, drum brakes, concours condition.
£5,500–6,000
$8,000–8,700 ⊞ MAY
The Model 8 was reintroduced for the 1933 season (production having ceased at the end of 1930). It was finally axed at the end of 1937, being superseded by the A24.

1938 Sunbeam Model A29 Lion, 489cc side-valve single, 77 x 105.5mm bore and stroke, foot-change gearbox, girder forks, rigid frame, concours condition.
£3,500–3,800
$5,000–5,500 ⊞ VER

1949 Sunbeam S7, 489cc overhead-camshaft inline twin, 70 x 63.5mm bore and stroke, 4-speed foot-change gearbox, shaft final drive.
£3,500–4,000
$5,000–5,800 ⊞ PMo
After being taken over by AMC in 1937, then BSA in 1943, Sunbeam became one of the first British marques to offer a totally new design after WWII. That model was the S7.

1950 Sunbeam S8, 489cc overhead-camshaft inline twin, 4-speed foot-change gearbox, shaft final drive, 76mph top speed.
£2,200–2,500
$2,900–3,600 ⊞ CotC
First offered for the 1949 season as an alternative to the balloon-tyred S7, from which it was derived, the S8 was given a more conventional appearance thanks to its narrower-section tyres, slimmer BSA forks and 7in single-sided BSA front brake. It was supposed to be the 'sports' version of the S7, but at heart it was still very much a tourer rather than a roadburner.

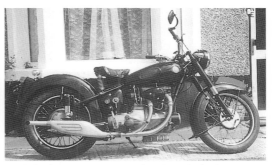

1949 Sunbeam S8, 489cc overhead-camshaft inline twin, shaft final drive, telescopic front forks, plunger rear suspension, fully rebuilt.
£2,200–2,500
$3,200–3,600 ⊞ MW

1952 Sunbeam S8, 489cc overhead-camshaft inline twin, original, unrestored.
£2,000–2,800
$2,900–4,000 ⋏ TEN

1956 Sunbeam S8, 489cc overhead-camshaft inline twin, 4-speed foot-change gearbox, shaft final drive, BSA-type forks, cast alloy silencer, original, unrestored.
£2,200–2,500
$3,200–3,600 ⊞ BLM
This was the last year of production for the S8.

Suzuki *(Japanese 1952–)*

1968 Suzuki T20 Super Six, 247cc piston-port 2-stroke parallel twin, 54 x 54mm bore and stroke, 29bhp at 7,500rpm, 6-speed gearbox, fitted with TC250-type raised exhaust.
£1,700–1,900
$2,450–2,750 ⊞ PMo
Together with the Ducati Mach 1, Suzuki's T20 Super Six met the need for performance 250s in the mid-/late 1960s, both being capable of 100mph.

1974 Suzuki GT750L, 736cc 2-stroke water-cooled 3-cylinder engine, 70 x 64mm bore and stroke, double disc front brake.
£2,300–2,500
$3,350–3,600 ⊶ SOC
This machine was used in the preparation of the Haynes Workshop Manual for the model.

1979 Suzuki GS850G, 850cc air-cooled double-overhead-camshaft across-the-frame 4-cylinder engine, 5-speed gearbox, shaft final drive, cast alloy wheels, triple disc brakes with 2-piston calipers, aftermarket fairing and carriers, otherwise standard specification.
£1,700–1,900
$2,450–2,750 ⊞ RWHS

▶ **1982 Suzuki XN 85 Turbo,** 650cc double-overhead-camshaft turbocharged 4-cylinder engine, triple disc brakes, anti-dive front forks, monoshock rear suspension, 16in front wheel, aftermarket 4-into-1 exhaust, otherwise standard.
£1,700–1,900
$2,450–2,750 ⊞ RWHS

1973 Suzuki T500, 493cc piston-port 2-stroke parallel twin, 70 x 64mm bore and stroke, 47bhp at 7,000rpm, 5-speed gearbox, 109mph top speed, drum-brake model to original specification apart from aftermarket Allspeed expansion-chamber exhausts, unrestored.
£500–800
$720–1,150 ⚒ PS

1975 Suzuki RE5 Rotary Mark 1, 497cc single-rotor Wankel engine, 62bhp at 6,500rpm, 5-speed gearbox, double 300mm disc front brake, 180mm drum rear brake, Vetter-type full fairing, otherwise original specification.
£3,500–4,000
$5,000–5,800 ⊞ PMo
The RE5 was built between 1974 and 1977.

1980 Suzuki GS1000E, 998cc air-cooled double-overhead-camshaft 4-cylinder engine, 5-speed gearbox, chain final drive, electric start, full instrumentation, chrome mudguards, original, unrestored, very good condition.
£1,800–2,000
$2,600–2,900 ⊞ RWHS

Triumph *(British 1902–)*

In the Turner era, as marque specialist Ivor Davies was once heard to remark, 'A love-hate relationship with motorcycle racing existed.' And this was one of the few mistakes in an otherwise glittering design career that made Triumph a household name.

Edward Turner joined Triumph in 1934 after designing the famous Square Four for the Ariel concern in 1930. At both companies he was under the charismatic Jack 'JY' Sangster, whose father had been responsible for creating the Ariel marque at the turn of the century.

Turner had been born in London on 24 January, 1901, his christian name arising from the fact that his birth came within hours of Queen Victoria's death, so he was the first true Edwardian in the family of seven children. His father owned a light engineering concern that manufactured a wide range of products for the tradesmen of the day.

While at Ariel, Turner also planned the famous Red Hunter overhead-valve single, before moving to Triumph where he became managing director and chief designer. But it was his Speed Twin of 1938 that really cemented his reputation. This overhead-valve 500 vertical twin set new standards for both weight and performance, being lighter and faster than virtually any existing single-cylinder model. A sports version, the Tiger 100, appeared in 1939, on the very eve of WWII.

Edward Turner was responsible for Triumph's high level of success in the immediate post-war period with designs such as the sprung-hub, Terrier, Cub, Thunderbird, Twenty One and, of course, the legendary Bonneville. In fact, under his management, this was the most successful period in the marque's history.

In 1960, Turner visited Japan and, upon his return, wrote a detailed report on the Japanese threat. Unfortunately, his views were not acted upon and thus no creditable challenge was mounted by the British industry to counter Japan's growing dominance during the 1960s. After designing the 350cc overhead-camshaft twin Bandit roadster, which appeared in the 1971 programme, Edward Turner retired. He died in 1973.

1911 Triumph 3½hp Model D, 499cc side-valve single, double-barrel carburettor, forward-mounted magneto.
£4,000–5,000
$5,800–7,250 ⊞ YEST

1930 Triumph Model NSD, 549cc side-valve single, 84 x 99mm bore and stroke, iron head and barrel, chain final drive.
£2,700–2,900
$3,900–4,200 ⊞ BLM

1923 Triumph Model H, 549cc side-valve single, hand-change gearbox, belt final drive, front wheel-driven speedometer.
£4,800–5,000
$7,000–7,250 ⊞ VER

1937 Triumph Tiger 80, 343cc overhead-valve single, 70 x 89mm bore and stroke, 4-speed foot-change gearbox, girder forks, rigid frame.
£2,400–3,000
$3,500–4,400 ⚞ COYS
Edward Turner's first main task at Triumph was to update the ageing range of singles, which were suffering from the onslaught of the opposition. The resulting line-up comprised the Tiger 70, Tiger 80 and Tiger 90, the model number being an indication of the top speed achievable by each machine. The redesigned singles were fast, stylish and enormously popular. Ace tuner Freddie Clarke was the first to demonstrate the potential of the Tiger 80, capturing the Brooklands lap record at 105.7mph. A road test of the Tiger 80 undertaken by *Motor Cycling* reported that the motorcycle, '...was gentlemanly in every respect but nevertheless, a veritable tiger, living up to its name, when it was a matter of sheer performance.'

1938 Triumph Tiger 80, 343cc overhead-valve single, dry-sump lubrication, low-level exhaust system, 4-speed foot-change gearbox, fully restored.
£2,400–3,200
$3,500–4,600 ⚞ H&H

1949 Triumph Tiger 100, 498.8cc overhead-valve pre-unit parallel twin, 30bhp, foot-change gearbox, telescopic front forks, sprung rear hub, dualseat, 99mph top speed.
£4,500–5,000
$6,500–7,250 ⊞ PMo
In October 1948, the Tiger 100 and Speed Twin were updated with the deletion of the tank-top instrument panel and the introduction of a headlamp nacelle.

◄ **1947 Triumph Tiger 100,** 498.8cc overhead-valve pre-unit twin, 63 x 80mm bore and stroke, iron head and barrel, single carburettor, telescopic forks, rigid frame, tank-top instrument panel, chrome-plated headlamp shell.
£5,000–5,500
$7,250–8,000 ⊞ PMo

1951 Triumph 3T, 349cc overhead-valve pre-unit twin, iron head and barrel, magneto/dynamo ignition, 4-speed gearbox, telescopic forks, rigid frame, sprung seat, pillion pad, original condition, unrestored.
£1,300–1,500
$1,900–2,175 ⚞ PS
The 3T ran from 1946 until 1951, but compared to the other pre-unit twins, it was underpowered for its weight and was a poor performer.

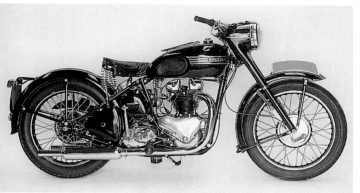

◄ **1952 Triumph 6T Thunderbird,** 649cc overhead-valve pre-unit twin, 71 x 82mm bore and stroke, 34bhp at 6,300rpm, telescopic forks, rigid frame, 105mph top speed, fully restored to original specification.
£2,800–3,000
$4,000–4,400 ⚒ TEN
The Thunderbird came about after pressure for a larger twin from North America. In the end, Edward Turner agreed, and in September 1949, the Thunderbird was launched with a highly publicised, high-speed demonstration by three machines at the Montlhéry circuit near Paris.

1951 Triumph 5T Speed Twin, 498.8cc overhead-valve twin, 27bhp at 6,300rpm, 94mph top speed, sprung rear hub, parcel grid, headlamp nacelle, dualseat, original specification.
£3,800–4,200
$5,500–6,100 ⊞ PMo

1953 Triumph Tiger 100, 498.8cc overhead-valve pre-unit parallel twin, all-alloy engine, sprung rear hub, tank-top parcel grid, headlamp nacelle, dualseat.
£4,000–4,500
$5,800–6,500 ⊞ BLM
This was the last year of the sprung-hub model. It was replaced at the end of the year by a revised machine with a new swinging-arm frame.

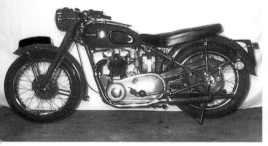

1953 Triumph 5T Speed Twin, 498.8cc overhead-valve pre-unit twin, telescopic forks, sprung rear hub, alternator, key-operated ignition switch in headlamp nacelle.
£2,000–2,400
$2,900–3,500 ⚒ PS

1953 Triumph 6T Thunderbird, 649cc overhead-valve pre-unit twin, iron head and barrel, 4-speed foot-change gearbox, magneto/dynamo, Mk 2 sprung rear hub, telescopic forks, dualseat, headlamp nacelle.
£5,000–5,500
$7,250–8,000 ⊞ PM

◄ **1954 Triumph T15 Terrier,** 149cc overhead-valve unit single, 57 x 58.5mm bore and stroke, 8.3bhp at 6,500rpm, 4-speed gearbox, plunger rear suspension, telescopic forks.
£800–1,200
$1,150–1,750 ⚒ PS
Launched at the tail end of 1952, the Terrier was designed by Edward Turner and went on sale early the following year. Later it was enlarged to 199cc and sold as the Tiger Cub.

◀ **1954 Triumph 6T Thunderbird,**
649cc overhead-valve pre-unit
parallel twin, iron head and barrel,
SU carburettor, alternator, sprung
rear hub, single sided front brake,
dualseat, headlamp nacelle,
parcel grid.
£4,500–5,000
$6,500–7,250 ⊞ PM
The 1954 model was the last of the
sprung-hub Thunderbirds.

1955 Triumph 5T Speed Twin, 499cc overhead-valve pre-
unit twin, 63 x 80mm bore and stroke, 27bhp at 6,300rpm.
£2,800–3,200
$4,000–4,650 ⊞ BLM
For 1955, the Speed Twin (and other models)
gained improved main bearings and shell-type
big-end bearings.

1956 Triumph T110, 649cc overhead-valve pre-unit twin,
4-speed foot-change gearbox, magneto/dynamo, swinging-
arm frame, ventilated front brake, headlamp nacelle,
aftermarket rear carrier, otherwise standard specification.
£3,000–3,500
$4,400–5,000 ⊞ MAY
This was the first year of the alloy head and
ventilated front brake for the T110.

> **Cross Reference**
> See Colour Review (page 123)

◀ **1956 Triumph 6T Thunderbird,** 649cc overhead-valve
pre-unit twin, iron head and barrel, single Amal
Monobloc carburettor, 4-speed gearbox, alternator,
swinging-arm frame.
£4,500–4,800
$6,500–7,000 ⊞ VER

1956 Triumph T110, 649cc overhead-valve pre-unit parallel twin, 4-speed foot-change gearbox, restored,
excellent condition.
£4,500–4,800
$6,500–7,000 ⊞ BLM
The T110 was the sports model of the 650 Triumph range, with alloy head, magneto/dynamo, and ventilated
8in front brake with aluminium brake plate.

1956 Triumph Tiger 100, 499cc, siamesed exhaust, fork gaiters, otherwise standard specification.
£4,000–4,800
$5,800–7,000 ✗ BKS
When tested by *Motor Cycling*, a sprung-hub T100 achieved a maximum speed of 93mph, prompting the magazine to describe the model as 'a sound example of British engineering at its best.' For the 1951 season, the model gained an all-alloy engine and an increase in performance. The next major revision came in 1954, when the cycle parts were updated by the adoption of a swinging-arm frame and an 8in front brake, followed in 1955 by an increase in compression ratio to 8:1 and improvements to the front fork damping.

1957 Triumph Thunderbird, 649cc overhead-valve pre-unit twin, swinging-arm frame, full-width front brake hub.
£3,800–4,200
$5,500–6,100 ⊞ PMo
For 1957, the tank motif was changed to allow the use of a two-tone tank colour scheme for the first time.

Miller's is a price GUIDE not a price LIST

1956 Triumph Speed Twin, 499cc overhead-valve twin, iron head and barrel, Amal Monobloc carburettor, single-sided front brake, completely original, unrestored.
£2,500–2,800
$3,600–4,000 ⊞ PM

1957 Triumph TRW, 499cc side-valve twin, 63 x 80mm bore and stroke, 25bhp at 4,500rpm, 4-speed foot-change gearbox.
£1,800–2,000
$2,600–2,900 ⊞ PMo
The TRW appeared in 1948 and mainly was intended for military use; subsequently, some examples reached the civilian market. The last user of the TRW was the Royal Air Force, where it continued in service until the 1970s.

1958 Triumph Twenty-One, 349cc unit twin, original tinware, unrestored,
£1,600–1,700
$2,300–2,450 ⊞ MAY
The Twenty-One was introduced in 1957 to celebrate the 21st birthday of the Triumph Engineering Company. By coincidence, in the USA, a 350cc class engine falls into the 21cu.in category.

1958 Triumph T20 Tiger Cub, 199cc overhead-valve unit single, 63 x 64mm bore and stroke, 4-speed gearbox, distributor ignition, restored.
£1,000–1,400
$1,500–2,000 ⊞ BLM
The Tiger Cub was developed from the smaller-engined Terrier. The swinging-arm frame replaced the plunger type from the 1957 model year onward.

1959 Triumph T20 Tiger Cub, 199cc overhead-valve unit construction single, Amal Monobloc carburettor, headlamp nacelle.
£750–1,000
$1,100–1,500 ⊞ BLM
For 1959, the Cub was given partial rear enclosure (often referred to as the 'bathtub'). However, unlike the twins, this left the rear wheel exposed, and there were cut-outs for the oil tank and toolbox.

1958 Triumph T110, 649cc overhead-valve pre-unit twin, alloy head, single Amal Monobloc carburettor, magneto/dynamo ignition, swinging-arm frame, recently restored to original condition.
£3,200–3,500
$4,650–5,000 ⚒ PS

c1959 Triumph Trophy Replica, 649cc overhead-valve pre-unit twin, swinging-arm frame, full-width front brake hub, 'as-new' condition.
£3,500–4,000
$5,000–5,800 ⊞ BLM
This machine was built as a replica of Triumph's famous Trophy dirt bike. It is fitted with a pre-unit T110-specification engine, alternator electrics, a BTH magneto, a high-level 2-into-1 exhaust, a Lucas chrome headlamp and fork gaiters.

1960 Triumph T20 Tiger Cub, 199cc overhead-valve unit single, 4-speed gearbox, telescopic forks, swinging-arm frame.
£900–1,100
$1,300–1,600 ✗ H&H
Introduced for the 1955 season, the Tiger Cub remained a popular machine until finally dropped in 1968, after giving many thousands of youngsters their first motorcycling experience.

1961 Triumph T120 Bonneville, 649cc overhead-valve pre-unit engine, twin Monobloc carburettors, 4-speed Slickshift gearbox, original tinware, standard specification apart from later twin-leading-shoe front brake and front forks.
£4,500–5,000
$6,500–7,250 ⊞ MAY

A known continuous history can add value to and enhance the enjoyment of a motorcycle.

1961 Triumph T120R Bonneville, 649cc overhead-valve pre-unit twin, alloy head, twin Amal Monobloc carburettors, full-width front brake hub, fork gaiters.
£6,600–7,800
$9,500–11,300 ✗ H&H
Together with the BSA 500 Gold Star Clubman, the Triumph Bonneville was at the top of the list of bikes almost every motorcycle enthusiast aspired to own during the early 1960s – it was certainly one of the fastest and most attractive production roadsters of the time.

◀ **1961 Triumph T21 Twenty-One,** 349cc overhead-valve unit twin, distributor ignition, 4-speed gearbox, headlamp nacelle, 'bathtub' rear enclosure.
£1,500–2,000
$2,175–2,900 ⊞ BLM
The T21 was the first of Triumph's new breed of unit-construction twins.

1962 Triumph T100SS, 490cc overhead-valve unit twin, 69 x 65.6mm bore and stroke, siamesed exhaust, fork gaiters, Lucas chrome headlamp, 2-tone tank colours, dualseat.
£2,500–2,800
$3,600–4,000 ⊞ SiC
This T100SS has been nicely restored, but it lacks the correct 'half-bathtub' rear enclosure fitted that year.

Miller's is a price GUIDE not a price LIST

1966 Triumph T100C Tiger, 490cc overhead-valve unit twin, high handlebars, small chrome headlamp, side and centre stands.
£2,600–3,000
$3,800–4,400 ⊞ PMo
Originally, the T100C was built for the USA, but later it was sold in the home market. Designed for American enduro use, with energy-transfer ignition, it had a high-level exhaust as standard.

1962 Triumph T20 Cub, 199cc overhead-valve unit single, 63 x 64mm bore and stroke, 'half-bathtub' rear enclosure, 2-tone seat, restored to original specification.
£900–1,000
$1,300–1,500 ⊞ MAY
This was the last year of distributor ignition for the T20 model.

1967 Triumph T100SS, 490cc overhead-valve unit twin, alloy head, iron barrel, single carburettor, siamesed exhaust, standard specification.
£1,800–2,000
$2,600–2,900 ⊞ PM
The 1967 model was the final version of the T100SS, with all rear enclosure removed, points in the timing cover and revised front forks.

▶ **1967 Triumph Bonneville,** 649cc overhead-valve unit-construction twin, 4-speed foot-change gearbox, fitted later twin-leading-shoe front brake, otherwise standard specification, concours condition.
£5,000–5,500
$7,250–8,000 ⊞ PMo

Auction prices

Miller's only includes motorcycles declared sold. Our guide prices take into account the buyer's premium, VAT on the premium, and the extent of any published catalogue information relating to condition and provenance. Motorcycles sold at auction are identified by the ⤳ icon; full details of the auction house can be found on page 167.

1969 Triumph TR6 Trophy, 649cc overhead-valve unit twin, 40bhp at 6,500rpm, 4-speed gearbox, twin-leading-shoe front brake, Zenor diode under headlamp, non-standard horn, good condition.
£3,000–5,000
$4,400–7,250 ⊞ BLM
The 1969 Trophy featured revised front brake linkage and an exhaust balance pipe.

1970 Triumph T120 Bonneville, 649cc overhead-valve unit twin, twin-leading-shoe front brake, concours condition.
£5,000–5,500
$7,250–8,000 ⊞ PMo
This was the final year before the introduction of the new (and largely unpopular) model from the Umberslade Hall design team, which included an oil-bearing frame.

1969 Triumph Bonneville, 649cc, US export model.
£4,000–5,000
$5,800–7,250 ⚒ COYS
Following its launch in 1959, the Triumph Bonneville soon established a reputation as the fastest motorbike available – no other manufacturer produced a machine that could match its performance on road or track. Its name had been chosen in recognition of the 214mph World Speed Record set in 1954 by Johnny Allen, at Bonneville Salt Flats in Utah, aboard a modified 650cc Triumph Thunderbird. The standard 650cc twin-cylinder engine produced a very impressive 48bhp, sufficient for a 120mph top speed via a four-speed gearbox, while the twin-downtube frame offered excellent roadholding. In 1963, a unit-construction frame was adopted. This had a single downtube, the engine and transmission being mounted as a stressed member.

1970 Triumph TR25W Trophy, 247cc overhead-valve unit single, 67 x 70mm bore and stroke, trials exhaust, twin-leading-shoe front brake, conical brake hubs, aluminium tank, chrome oil tank.
£1,800–2000
$2,600–2,900 ⊞ MAY

1970 Triumph T100C Tiger, 490cc overhead-valve unit-construction twin, high-level exhaust, speedometer/rev-counter, side and centre stands, standard specification, unrestored, in need of cosmetic attention.
£2,000–2,400
$2,900–3,500 ⊞ BLM

Miller's is a price GUIDE not a price LIST

1971/72 Triumph Trail Blazer, 247cc overhead-valve unit single, twin-leading-shoe front brake, indicators, wiring in need of attention.
£600–750
$870–1,100 ⊞ MAY
The Trail Blazer was essentially a badge-engineered BSA.

1972 Triumph 250 Trophy, 247cc overhead-valve unit single, high-level exhaust, conical brake hubs, chrome headlamp, small tank, indicators, dualseat.
£600–800
$870–1,150 ⊞ MAY
This was the final version of the BSA/Triumph 250 unit range, modelled on similar lines to Triumph's 500 Adventurer twin.

► **1971 Triumph T100SS,** 490cc overhead-valve twin, single carburettor, 7in twin-leading-shoe front brake, US market model with high handlebars and side reflectors.
£2,000–2,800
$2,900–4,000
⊞ BLM

1972 Triumph T100C, 490cc overhead-valve twin, single Amal Concentric carburettor, high-level exhaust, 12 volt electrics, direction indicators, small chrome headlamp, original, unrestored, good condition.
£2,750–3,250
$4,100–4,700 ⊞ BLM

► **1973 Triumph TR5T Adventurer,** 490cc overhead-valve unit twin, 2-into-1 exhaust, 12 volt electrics, conical brake hubs, aluminium fuel tank, indicators, standard specification, excellent condition.
£3,000–3,250
$4,400–4,700 ⊞ SiC
The TR5T Adventurer was introduced for 1973 in trail-bike format.

Restored values

The cost of a professional restoration will have an influence on, but no direct relation to, a motorcycle's market value. A restored motorcycle can have a market value lower than the cost of its restoration.

1972 Triumph T100R, 490cc overhead-valve unit twin, twin carburettors, 12 volt electrics, 8in front brake, European model, one of last T100R models built in 1971, but not registered until 1972.
£2,200–2,600
$3,200–3,800 ⚲ AH
The T100R was similar to the T100T, but had rubber-mounted instruments, direction indicators and a rubber-mounted headlamp.

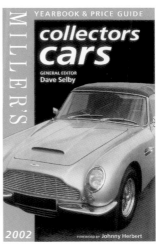

1973 Triumph X75 Hurricane, 740cc overhead-valve 3-cylinder engine, 67 x 70mm bore and stroke, 2,700 miles from new, original, unrestored.
£5,000–5,500
$7,250–8,000 ↗ BKS
Introduced at the 1972 Earls Court show, the X75 was a specially-styled variant of the Triumph/BSA triple. Although badged as a Triumph, it utilised the inclined-cylinder BSA variant of the overhead-valve engine. This was housed in a standard frame that was clothed with a stylish fibreglass seat and tank unit. The front forks were extended, increasing the wheelbase to 60in and adding to the 'Chopper-like' styling. However, the exhaust system was the most striking feature, three silencers being stacked upon each other on the right side of the motorcycle. Retailing for £895 – compared to a Honda CB750 at £761 – it was a prestige model, a position it maintains to this day. The X75 was only offered in 1973.

▶ **1974 Triumph T150V,** 740cc overhead-valve unit-construction 3-cylinder engine, disc front/drum rear brakes, original, unrestored.
£2,700–3,000
$3,900–4,400 ⊞ BLM
The original T150 (as opposed to the Trident of 1968–70) was offered with a disc front brake and four-speed gearbox between 1970 and 1972. The T150V (the 'V' stood for a five-speed gearbox) arrived in 1972 and ran through to 1975.

1975 Triumph T160 Slippery Sam No. 2, 740cc overhead-valve 3-cylinder engine, 67 x 70mm bore and stroke, rebuilt in production racing guise.
£6,200–7,000
$6,300–10,200 ⊞ PMo
At the end of 1971, Triumph was forced out of racing, but 'Slippery Sam' was still raced until as late as 1975. The famous 'Slippery Sam' series came about in no small part through the efforts of Les Williams. Race victories in the Isle of Man TT were secured by the likes of Roy Pickrell, Dave Croxford, Mick Grant and Alex George.

Miller's is a price GUIDE not a price LIST

1976 Triumph T140V, 744cc overhead-valve unit twin, 76 x 82mm bore and stroke, 5-speed gearbox, disc brakes front and rear, export model, original, unrestored.
£2,400–2,600
$3,500–3,800 ⊞ BLM

1980 Triumph T140V Executive, 744cc overhead-valve unit twin, 5-speed gearbox, front and rear disc brakes, direction indicators, lacking top box, panniers and fairing, needing some work, including recovering seat.
£1,200–1,500
$1,750–2,170 ⊞ BLM
This machine is one of the limited-edition Executive models built by the Meriden Workers' Co-operative.

1983 Triumph T140 E/S, 744cc overhead-valve unit twin, 5-speed gearbox, fitted with larger SU carburettor, non-standard rear carrier, unrestored, one of last Meriden-made Triumphs.
£2,300–2,700
$3,350–3,900 ⊞ BLM
This is the rare electric-start model, which was offered from 1980 onward, but the starter was seen by many simply as excess weight.

1983 Triumph T140V Executive, 744cc overhead-valve unit-construction twin, 5-speed gearbox, original and complete with fairing, top box and panniers, excellent overall condition.
£2,500–2,800
$3,600–4,000 ⊞ BLM

► **1995 Triumph Trident,** 900cc double-overhead-camshaft liquid-cooled 3-cylinder engine, electric start, telescopic front forks, monoshock rear suspension, triple disc brakes, completely original specification.
£3,000–3,700
$4,400–5,400 ⊞ BLM
This is one of the new John Bloor Hinkley factory models, and in this 'naked' guise it is popular with classic bike enthusiasts, offering the best of both worlds – a traditional appearance with modern technology.

◄ **1985 Triumph Bonneville 750,** 744cc overhead-valve twin, Mikuni carburettors, 5-speed gearbox, front and rear disc brakes, Marzocchi suspension.
£3,500–3,800
$5,000–5,500 ⊞ VER
This is one of the Harris-built Triumphs, utilising a combination of British, Italian and Japanese components.

TWN *(German 1903–57)*

1954 TWN Boss, 344cc 2-stroke split single, 2 x 53 x 78mm bore and stroke, alloy heads, chrome-plated alloy cylinders, twin exhausts, telescopic forks, plunger frame, hydraulic rear brake, complete but in need of cosmetic restoration.
£1,500–2,000
$2,150–2,900 ⊞ VICO
Although known as TWN in Germany's export markets – to avoid confusion with the British Triumph – in many ways the German Triumph marque had as much claim to the name as its British counterpart. In fact, it had been two Germans, Siegfried Bettman and Maurice Schultz, who founded the British company in Coventry during 1897. The German branch opened in 1903 and, at first, it used engines and other components supplied by the Coventry works. This arrangement continued until 1929, when the two companies went their separate ways.

Velocette *(British 1904–71)*

◀ **1936 Velocette MAC,** 349cc overhead-valve single, 68 x 96mm bore and stroke, rear-mounted magneto, 4-speed foot-change gearbox, girder forks, rigid frame, good original example.
£2,750–3,250
$4,000–4,700 ⊞ BLM
Velocette's overhead-valve family of singles began with the MOV 250 in 1933. The MAC arrived in 1934, followed by the MSS 500 in 1935.

▶ **c1937 Velocette MAC,** 349cc overhead-valve single, 68 x 96mm bore and stroke, 4-speed foot-change gearbox, front-wheel-driven speedometer, sprung saddle, pillion pad, large toolbox, restored to concours condition.
£3,500–4,000
$5,000–5,800
⊞ AtMC

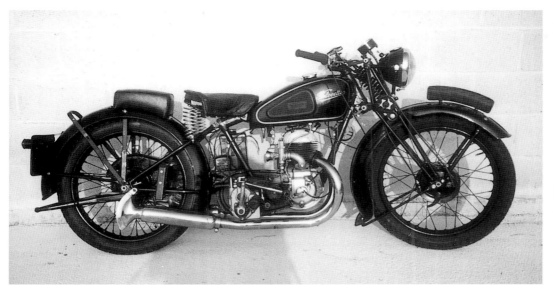

1939 Velocette GTP, 249cc piston-port 2-stroke single, twin-port exhaust, 4-speed foot-change gearbox, girder forks, rigid frame, unrestored.
£1,800–2,000
$2,600–2,900 ⊞ BLM
Compared with other two-strokes, the GTP's engine was both smooth and torquey – the latter helped by an outside flywheel. It also benefited from a throttle-controlled oil pump.

► **1940s Velocette KTS,** 350cc overhead-camshaft single, 4-speed foot-change gearbox, rigid frame, original, unrestored, good running order.
£4,400–4,900
$6,400–7,200 ⊞ AtMC
The KTS entered production in 1932 and was superseded post-war by the KSS. Both featured girder front forks.

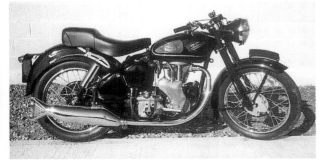

◄ **1953 Velocette MAC,** 349cc overhead-valve single, 68 x 96mm bore and stroke, alloy cylinder head, enclosed valve gear, 4-speed foot-change gearbox, standard specification.
£2,400–2,800
$3,500–4,000 ⊞ BLM
For the 1953 model year, the MAC gained a sprung frame, which joined the Dowty oleomatic telescopic front forks that had arrived in 1948. The responsibility for updating the MAC was given to Charles Udall.

► **1954 Velocette LE,** 149cc water-cooled side-valve horizontally-opposed twin, hand-lever starting, 3-speed gearbox, shaft final drive, monocoque frame, period side bags, original specification.
£1,000–1,150
$1,500–1,675 ⊞ PMo
The LE was introduced in 1949. It was not only a very quiet-running machine, but it also offered good weather protection. In many ways, it was a cross between a conventional motorcycle and a scooter, but its high cost reduced sales.

◀ **1956 Velocette MAC,** 349cc overhead-valve single, 4-speed foot-change gearbox, dualseat, supplied new with optional chrome fuel tank, pillion footrests and stop light, fewer than 4,000 miles from new, original, unrestored.
£2,000–2,400
$2,900–3,500 ⚲ **CGC**

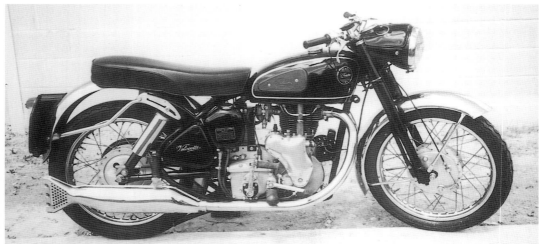

1956 Velocette Venom, 499cc overhead-valve single, 86 x 86mm bore and stroke, 7½in front/7in rear full-width drum brakes, chrome mudguards, deep headlamp shell with integral instruments, concours condition.
£3,000–4,000
$4,400–5,800 ⊞ **BLM**
The 350 Viper and 500 Venom were new for 1956. They were high-performance sports models with several other improvements over their touring brothers, the MAC and MSS.

▶ **1956 Velocette MAC,** 349cc overhead-valve single.
£2,500–2,800
$3,600–4,000 ⊞ **BLM**
For 1956, the MAC was updated to share several components with the new Viper sportster, including the silencer, tank, seat and headlamp. However, it still retained its long-stroke engine and single-sided brakes.

◀ **1957 Velocette Viper,** 349cc overhead-valve single, 72 x 86mm bore and stroke, full-width hubs, chrome mudguards, standard apart from aftermarket finned pushrod tube.
£2,600–2,950
$3,800–4,350 ⊞ **PM**
The Viper had a shorter-stroke, tuned version of the MAC engine. This power unit was also fitted to the limited-production Scrambler model.

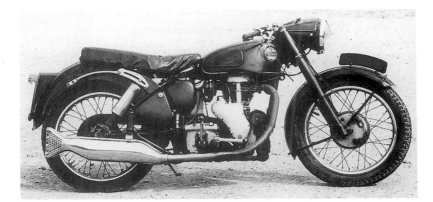

1958 Velocette MAC, 349cc overhead-valve single, 1 owner and fewer than 11,000 miles from new, in need of cosmetic restoration.
£1,700–2,000
$2,450–2,900 ✗ AG

◄ **1960 Velocette Venom,** 499cc overhead-valve single, 4-speed gearbox, telescopic forks, swinging-arm frame, Brooklands fishtail exhaust, standard specification.
£3,500–4,000
$5,000–5,800 ⊞ BB
The Venom could exceed 105mph and was often the first choice of those looking for a sporty roadster single; more so after the BSA Gold Star departed at the end of 1962.

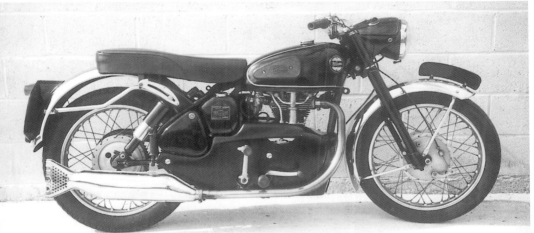

1960 Velocette Viper Special, 349cc overhead-valve single, 72 x 86mm bore and stroke, dry-sump lubrication, 4-speed foot-change gearbox, full-width brake hubs, fishtail silencer.
£3,000–3,500
$4,400–5,000 ⊞ BLM
The Special featured a factory-fitted fibreglass enclosure for the bottom end of the engine and the transmission. It was very much a case of fashion winning over practicality.

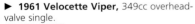

► **1961 Velocette Viper,** 349cc overhead-valve single.
£2,500–3,000
$3,600–4,400 ✗ H&H
Capable of over 85mph, the Viper was the quality sporting option for those wanting a heavyweight British single during the 1960s.

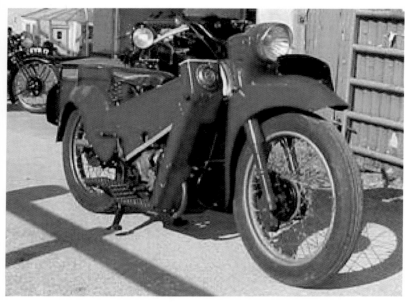

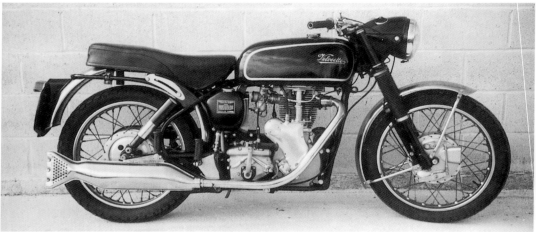

◀ **1963 Velocette LE Mk III,** 192cc water-cooled side-valve flat-twin.
£580–650
$850–950 ⊞ BB
The Mk III LE had the four-speed gearbox from the Valiant with foot-change and kick starter. In addition, the speedometer, ammeter and light switch were moved to the headlamp shell.

1965 Velocette Venom Clubman, 499cc overhead-valve single, 4-speed gearbox, sweptback exhaust pipe, fishtail silencer, twin-leading-shoe front brake, rearset foot controls, flat handlebars, fork gaiters.
£4,000–4,500
$5,800–6,500 ⊞ BLM

▶ **1967 Velocette Thruxton,** 499cc overhead-valve single, 86 x 86mm bore and stroke, big-valve cylinder head, 4-speed close-ratio gearbox, original specification, excellent condition.
£8,500–9,000
$12,300–13,000 ⊞ VER
The Thruxton specification included a chrome headlamp, dual racing saddle, oil tank with built-in heat shield, sweptback exhaust pipe, clip-ons, rearsets, a special tank and an Amal GP carburettor. Braking was improved by the fitment of a twin-leading-shoe front brake. The Thruxton ran from 1965 until 1970.

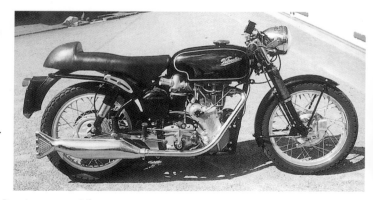

◀ **1967 Velocette Thruxton,** 499cc overhead-valve single, GP carburettor, twin-leading-shoe front brake, alloy rims, special oil tank, full Thruxton specification.
£9,000–11,000
$13,000–16,000 ➶ H&H
This example of the Thruxton is fitted with the optional Avon fairing; often used by riders who raced the Thruxton in long-distance production events, including the famous annual Thruxton 500-miler.

Vincent-HRD *(British 1928–55)*

Between them, Philip Vincent and Phil Irving created what many still be regard as one of the greatest motorcycles of all time, the Vincent-HRD V-twin series. And when you start to probe the reasoning behind this very special range of bikes, it's not unusual for even the most disinterested to sit up and take notice.

The Vincent-HRD was truly a marque that created genuine enthusiasm among its ownership. The pre-war model was not a particularly clean design, but Vincent and his chief engineer spent the last two years of WWII creating what they saw as the ultimate Grand Touring motorcycle. The result was the Rapide, a 998cc overhead-valve V-twin, introduced in 1946 as the Series B. Vincent's machine was a very different animal from the pre-war crop of big V-twins, which had mainly been of the side-valve variety and intended largely for sidecar work.

The Rapide was a very compact bike for its engine size, being hardly any bulkier than a 500 single. The major feature was the engine, which was built in unit with the gearbox to provide a single rigid structure. In fact, it was so rigid that there was very little conventional frame at all, the rear fork being the major part, and even this was attached to the rear of the engine structure.

The remainder of the frame comprised a beam over the engine, which had the steering head at its forward end and also doubled as the oil tank for the dry-sump lubrication system. To the rear was an early form of cantilever suspension, while at the front was a set of Brampton girder forks – retained because both Vincent and Irving had little faith in the ability of conventional telescopic forks to carry out both solo and sidecar roles successfully.

The engine was a 50-degree V-twin with overhead valves, and alloy heads and barrels. These were mounted to a massive crankcase casting, which was split vertically on the centre-line between the two cylinders. These were offset to each other.

Thus it was a relatively simple task to create the 499cc Comet single, effectively by using the front cylinder from the V-twin and a suitably modified crankcase assembly. However, this was not a very cost-effective creation, either for the customer or the company. And this was Vincent's dilemma: how to make a profit from such a project. On one hand, he and Irving sought to build the best-quality bikes possible; on the other, doing so put the machines' cost out of the reach of all but the most well-heeled. This resulted in the demise of the company as a bike manufacturer during the mid-1950s; the first major post-war failure of the British motorcycle industry.

1950 Vincent-HRD Rapide, 998cc V-twin.
£8,000–13,000
$11,600–18,850 ✗ BKS
The Series C Vincents entered the range alongside the Series B models in 1949, before displacing them during 1950. The most obvious differences between the two versions were to be found in the suspension. The Brampton girder forks that had graced the Series B variants were replaced with Girdraulic items designed in-house. The new design was intended to incorporate the best feature of the telescopic design – smooth damping control – with the rigidity of girders. The rear suspension was also improved with hydraulic damping. The other noticeable change concerned the name on the tank and engine covers. The 'HRD' element was dropped from the title, supposedly because some potential American buyers thought it related to a link with Harley-Davidson.

Restored values
The cost of a professional restoration will have an influence on, but no direct relation to, a motorcycle's market value. A restored motorcycle can have a market value lower than the cost of its restoration.

1951 Vincent-HRD Rapide, 998cc overhead-valve V-twin engine, 84 x 90mm bore and stroke, 45bhp at 5,300rpm, 115mph top speed, polished engine outer casings, large 150mph speedometer, correct specification, excellent condition.
£12,000–14,000
$17,400–20,300 ⚡ VER

1951 Vincent-HRD Comet, 499cc overhead-valve single, 4-speed foot-change gearbox, original specification.
£4,500–6,000
$6,500–8,000 ⚡ COYS
The Comet shared almost all of its running gear with the V-twin Black Shadow machines, for which the marque was renowned. In effect, the only difference between the two was the lack of the rear cylinder of the Irving-designed engine and its replacement with a cast aluminium frame member. The Comet was a much higher-quality machine than most other contemporary singles, and it earned a reputation for fine handling and an enthusiastic engine. Although it cost as much as a small car when new, the model sold well, and today it represents a more realistically priced alternative to its big brother.

◀ **1954 Vincent-HRD Rapide Series D,** 998cc overhead-valve twin.
£12,000–16,000
$17,400–23,200 ⊞ MW
The open Series D Black Shadow was built as a stop-gap with a tubular sub-frame, but somehow it lacked the superb lines of the Series C range. However, in terms of rarity, it was produced in far fewer numbers.

1952 Vincent-HRD Black Shadow Series C, 998cc overhead-valve V-twin, 84 x 90mm bore and stroke, 4-speed foot-change gearbox, concours condition.
£18,000–22,000
$26,000–32,000 ⚡ BKS
When introduced, the Black Shadow was the fastest and most expensive motorcycle produced. By the end of the 1940s, a special version of the Vincent Rapide, called 'Gunga Din', was being campaigned so effectively by George and Cliff Brown that some refused to race against it, such was its power. This encouraged Phil Vincent to produce the ultimate road machine, capable of an assured 120mph. The first example was seen at the 1948 Earls Court show, and its black-painted engine gave rise to the Black Shadow name. Identical in appearance to the Rapide engine, the power unit featured specially selected internals, including polished and raised cam profiles, and improved carburation. The heads were ported and polished, and although only 72-octane fuel was available – limiting compression to 7.3:1 – bhp rose to 55 at 5,700rpm. Thus the required performance was obtained. The raised speedometer and improved braking were additional features which, to this day, mark this machine as arguably the greatest of all classic motorcycles.

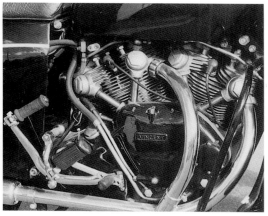

1955 Vincent-HRD Black Knight, 998cc overhead-valve
V-twin, fully enclosed engine and rear of machine, screen
and hand protection, black outer engine casings.
£12,000–15,000
$17,400–21,750 ✗ BKS

Since the Series A's arrival in 1937, the Vincent V-twin had been synonymous with design innovation,
engineering excellence, and high performance. So, in September 1955, when it was revealed that production of
the machines would cease, the news stunned the motorcycling world. It had been decided that the firm's
future lay in more profitable lines of manufacture. By the time its demise was announced, the Series D had
been in production for just six months. It had been Philip Vincent's belief that provision of ample weather
protection, combined with enclosure of engine and gearbox, would make the Series D the ultimate
'gentleman's motorcycle'. However, delayed delivery of the fibreglass panels – plus continuing demand for
traditionally-styled models – resulted in over half the the production leaving the factory in unenclosed form.
The enclosed Rapide and Black Shadow were known as Black Knight and Black Prince respectively. Other Series
D innovations included a new frame and rear suspension, a user-friendly centre stand, plus many
improvements to the V-twin engine. When production ceased in December 1955, around 460 Series D machines
had been built, some 200 of which were enclosed models.

Werner *(French 1897–1908)*

c1902 Werner 2hp, 4-stroke single-cylinder engine, vertical cylinder, pedal cycle-type frame, in need of full restoration.
£6,500–7,500
$9,400–10,800 ✗ BKS

The Werner motorcycle was conceived by two Russian brothers who settled in France at the end of the 19th
century. They built their first machine in 1896, followed by another in 1897 with an engine attached to the
steering head, which drove the front wheel by a belt. Although the front-wheel drive and high centre of
gravity made the machine unstable, 300 machines were sold during 1898. Following the sale of British rights to
their design to the British Motor Manufacturing Company, the brothers were able to increase production to
500 machines a year by 1899. In 1901, a model was introduced with its engine mounted as an integral part of
the bottom of the frame. With its lower centre of gravity, this new machine was one of the first to
demonstrate a new wave of thinking in motorcycle manufacture. It was an immediate success, and since BMMC
had only purchased the rights to the old Werner design, this resulted in the formation of a new British
company, Werner Motors Limited.

Yamaha *(Japanese 1954–)*

◀ **1967 Yamaha YR2,** 348cc piston-port 2-stroke twin, 61 x 59.6mm bore and stroke, full-width aluminium drum brakes with twin-leading-shoe operation on front wheel, full duplex frame.
£2,250–2,500
$3,300–3,600 ⊞ PMo
The YDS series of 250 twins and the 350 YR1 and YR2 were the first true high-performance Yamaha street bikes.

1978 Yamaha XS 650 Special, 649cc double-overhead-camshaft parallel twin, US custom version.
£1,000–1,400
$1,500–2,000 ⊞ MAY

1986 Yamaha XT600 Tenere, 600cc double-overhead-camshaft single, electric start, disc front brake, 21in front wheel, high-level exhaust, front and rear carriers.
£1,800–2,000
$2,600–2,900 ⊞ RWHS

1979 Yamaha XS1100, 1100cc double-overhead-camshaft across-the-frame 4-cylinder engine, 5-speed gearbox, shaft final drive, triple disc brakes, cast alloy wheels, original specification.
£1,800–2,000
$2,600–2,900 ⊞ RWHS

Colour Review

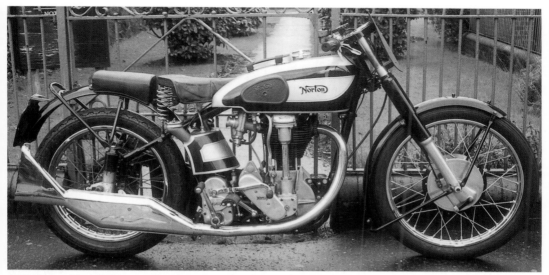

1949 Norton Model 30 International, 490cc overhead-camshaft single, iron head and barrel, Amal TT-type carburettor, 4-speed foot-change gearbox, telescopic front forks, large front brake, 'Brooklands can' exhaust, Manx-style tanks.
£6,500–7,500
$9,500–11,000 ⊞ VER
This Model 30 International is an early post-war machine with the 'Garden Gate' plunger frame.

1957 Norton Dominator 99, 597cc overhead-valve twin, 68 x 82mm bore and stroke, restored.
£4,000–5,500
$5,800–8,000 ⊞ PM
The larger-engined Dominator, the 99, was introduced for 1956. Essentially it was the same as the 88, which meant Featherbed frame, Roadholder forks and full-width hubs for 1957.

c1968 Norton Atlas, 745cc overhead-valve pre-unit parallel twin, 4-speed gearbox, full-width hubs, Roadholder forks, chrome mudguards, slimline Featherbed frame, concours condition.
£6,000–7,000
$9,000–10,000 ⊞ AtMC

1975 Norton 850 Commando Roadster Mk III, 829cc overhead-valve twin, front and rear disc brakes.
£3,500–4,000
$5,000–5,800 ⊞ BLM
This electric-start model is one of the rarer examples in the distinctive JPS colour scheme.

1961 Royal Enfield Constellation, 692cc overhead-valve semi-unit twin, 70 x 90mm bore and stroke, siamesed exhaust, chrome tank, painted mudguards, rear crashbars, restored, excellent condition.
£5,400–6,000
$8,000–8,700 ⊞ PM

1938 Rudge Sports Special, 493cc overhead-valve twin-port single, 84.5 x 88mm bore and stroke, 4-speed gearbox, chrome tank, girder forks rigid frame, fully restored, concours condition.
£7,200–8,000
$10,000–11,600 ⊞ PM

1950 Sunbeam S7, 489cc overhead-camshaft inline twin, 70 x 63.5mm bore and stroke, 4-speed gearbox, shaft final drive, 16in wheels, telescopic front forks, plunger frame, original specification, very good condition.
£2,500–2,800
$3,600–4,000 ⊞ VER

1954 Sunbeam S8, 489cc overhead-camshaft inline twin, 4-speed foot-change gearbox, shaft final drive, non-standard air filter.
£2,000–2,500
$2,900–3,500 ⊞ **BLM**
The S8 was lighter than the S7, thanks to BSA forks and narrower wheels (the front one also BSA).

1911 Triumph Touring, 499cc side-valve single, pedals, belt final drive, complete with period lighting equipment, carrier and leather side bags.
£5,750–6,500
$8,400–9,400 ⊞ **VER**
The Touring utilised Triumph's own design of twin-choke carburettor.

1949 Triumph Tiger 100, 498.8cc overhead-valve pre-unit twin, 63 x 80mm bore and stroke, iron head and barrel, telescopic forks, rigid frame, chrome tank, headlamp nacelle, tank-top parcel grid, fully restored, concours condition.
£4,400–4,600
$6,400–6,700 ⊞ **VER**

1955 Triumph 5T Speed Twin, 498.8cc overhead-valve pre-unit twin, fully restored to concours condition.
£4,500–4,800
$6,500–7,000 ⊞ **VER**
The Tiger 100 and new Tiger 110 models were the first Triumphs to receive a swinging-arm frame for the 1954 season. The other twins were given this improvement the following year, consigning the sprung hub to the history books.

1959 Triumph 5TA Speed Twin, 490cc overhead-valve unit twin, 69 x 65.5mm bore and stroke, 27bhp at 6,500rpm.
£1,800–2,100
$2,600–3,000 ⊞ BLM
The 3TA 350 was the first of the Triumph unit twins when it appeared in 1957; the 5TA Speed Twin was added for 1959. Like the 3TA, it had full 'bath-tub' rear enclosure, a distributor and headlamp nacelle.

1961 Triumph T120R Bonneville, 649cc overhead-valve pre-unit twin, twin carburettors, rev-counter, fork gaiters, twin silencers, chrome headlamp.
£5,200–5,800
$7,500–8,400 ⊞ PM
This is an example of the famous powder-blue and silver 1961 Bonneville – probably the finest of its genre.

1970 Triumph TR6 Trophy, 649cc overhead-valve unit-construction twin, 40bhp, 109mph top speed, American export model with 9-stud head, single Amal Concentric Mk I carburettor, high-level exhaust system, exhaust shields, twin-leading-shoe front brake, side reflectors, chrome headlamp, original specification.
£4,750–5,000
$6,900–7,200 ⊞ VER

1979 Triumph T140V Bonneville, 744cc overhead-valve unit twin, 5-speed gearbox, disc front brake, megaphone-type silencers, US specification, seat padding altered for shorter rider.
£2,700–3,300
$3,900–4,800 ⊞ BLM

◄ **c1940 Moto Guzzi Alce,** 498.4cc inlet-over-exhaust horizontal single, 88 x 82mm bore and stroke, 13.2bhp at 4,000rpm, 4-speed hand-change gearbox, fully rebuilt, North African 'sand' finish.
£5,200–5,800
$7,750–8,500 ⊞ AtMC
The Alce was the most widely used Italian military motorcycle of WWII. Today, these 500cc bikes are very rare.

1941 Matchless G3L, 348cc overhead-valve single, 4-speed foot-change gearbox, AMC Teledraulic front forks, rigid frame, sprung saddle, pillion pad, pannier cases.
£2,500–3,000
$3,600–4,400 ⊞ VER

1926 Moto Guzzi Corsa 4V, 498.4cc overhead-camshaft horizontal single, 88 x 82mm bore and stroke, 22bhp at 5,500rpm, 3-speed hand-change gearbox, concours condition.
£27,000–30,000
$39,000–43,500 ⊞ AtMC

1936 Excelsior Manxman, 250cc overhead-camshaft single, foot-change close-ratio gearbox, wrap-around oil tank, girder forks, rigid frame.
£4,200–5,000
$6,000–7,000 ⚒ H&H
In the British short circuit racing events immediately prior to WWII, the Excelsior Manxman was often the machine to beat.

c1948 Gilera San Remo, 499cc overhead-valve semi-unit single, wet-sump lubrication, 4-speed close-ratio gearbox.
£13,500–15,000
$19,600–21,750 ⊞ AtMC
Named after the famous Italian Riviera resort (and race circuit of the era), the San Remo was a full-blown racing version of the Saturno roadster.

c1946 Norton Manx, 348cc shaft-and-bevel-driven overhead-camshaft single, rev-counter, alloy rims, telescopic front forks, 'Garden Gate' plunger frame, restored to concours condition.
£10,000–12,000
$14,500–17,500 ⊞ AtMC

◀ **c1948 Moto Morini 125 Competizione,** 124cc, piston-port 2-stroke single, 4-speed close-ratio gearbox, blade girder forks, plunger frame, fully restored, excellent condition, very rare.
£4,500–5,000
$6,500–7,200 ⊞ AtMC
Alfonso Morini's first racing motorcycle took its inspiration from the German DKW RT125. It was raced by the works and sold, in small numbers, to privateers.

◄ **c1948 Moto Guzzi Works 500**, 494.8cc overhead-camshaft 120° V-twin, foot-change close-ratio 4-speed gearbox, girder forks, sprung frame, genuine ex-works Grand Prix bike.
£150,000–165,000
$218,000–240,000 ⊞ AtMC
In 1935, Stanley Woods created history on an earlier version of Guzzi's V-twin. Not only did he record the first Isle of Man TT win by a foreign make (500cc) since the American Indian firm took the Senior in 1911, but also it was the first TT victory by a sprung-framed machine.

1953 MV Augusta 125 Competizione, 124cc, overhead-camshaft single.
£8,000–11,000
$11,600–16,000 ⊞ MW
Built in small numbers from 1953 until 1956, the 125C production racer was essentially a single-overhead-camshaft version of Cecil Sandford's works double-overhead-cam, 1952 125cc World Championship winning machine.

1960s Norton 40M Manx, 348cc double-overhead-camshaft single, assembled from spares 1990–91, 1961-specification engine built by George Beale, Summerfield crankcases and barrel, original head and cambox, Quife 5-speed gearbox, Featherbed frame, Roadholder forks, twin-leading-shoe front brake, fly screen, alloy tanks.
£10,000+
$14,500+ ⊞ MW

c1965 Honda CR93, 124cc double-overhead-camshaft twin, Keihin carburettors, 6-speed gearbox, double-sided front brake, alloy fairing, standard specification, very rare, excellent condition.
£25,000–28,000
$36,250–40,500 ⊞ AtMC
The CR93 was a purpose-built racing machine that dominated 125cc-class racing at privateer level during the mid-1960s. Riders included Bill Ivy and Rod Scivyer.

1898 Clément De Dion et Bouton 2.25hp Tricycle and Trailer, single-cylinder De Dion engine, restored to original condition.
£12,000–14,000
$17,500–20,500 ✗ BKS
Famed pioneer motorcyclist and motorist Adolphe Clément became involved with motorised vehicles through the manufacture of bicycles and the acquisition of the French patent rights to the Dunlop pneumatic tyre.

c1950 Nimbus Four and Sidecar, 750cc 4-cylinder inline engine, high-level exhaust, separate rider and pillion saddles, single-seat Steib sidecar, near concours condition.
£9,500–11,000
$13,750–16,000 ⊞ AtMC
This machine was built in Denmark.

1923 Harley-Davidson 1000 V-Twin and Sidecar,
1000cc inlet-over-exhaust V-twin, sprung forks, rigid frame, tank-mounted instruments, separate rider and pillion saddles, sidecar with period hood and windscreen.
£15,000–18,000
$21,750–26,000 ⊞ VER

> A known continuous history can add value to and enhance the enjoyment of a motorcycle.

1970 Moto Guzzi Nuovo Falcone and Sidecar, 498cc overhead-valve unit-construction single, 88 x 82mm bore and stroke, 4-speed gearbox, 18in wheels, concours condition.
£3,000–3,500
$4,400–5,000 ⊞ MW

An 8th International Motorcycle Road Race Meeting programme, Thruxton Circuit, 1957, 8½ x 5½in (21.5 x 14cm).
£3–5
$5–8 ⊞ TiC

A TT Races programme, 1955, 9 x 6in (23 x 15cm).
£6–8
$10–12 ⊞ COB

Dirt Bikes

c1936 Velocette Grass Track Special, 348cc KSS overhead-camshaft single-cylinder engine, alloy cylinder head, 4-speed foot-change gearbox, AMC forks and front wheel, rigid frame, knobbly tyres.
£1,500–1,800
$2,150–2,600 ⚒ BKS
This machine was modified during the early post-war period.

1937 AJS R10, 498cc overhead-camshaft single, 79 x 101mm bore and stroke, 4-speed gearbox, unrestored.
£4,600–5,500
$6,650–8,000 ⚒ BKS
The overhead-camshaft R10 was dropped from the 1932 AJS catalogue, but it returned in 1933 in revised form. Although it retained the chain-driven camshaft of the original model, it was different in many other respects. The magneto was sited at the rear of the cylinder and was driven by a vernier coupling.

1950 BSA ZB32 Works Trials, 348cc overhead-valve single, 71 x 88mm bore and stroke, iron head and barrel, telescopic forks, rigid frame.
£2,250–2,500
$3,300–3,600 ⊞ PMo

1952 Triumph Trophy, 499cc overhead-valve pre-unit single, 63 x 80mm bore and stroke, alloy head and barrel, siamesed exhaust, sprung rear hub, rigid frame, chrome tank, original specification.
£3,900–4,500
$5,650–6,500 ⊞ MAY

1952 Matchless G3LC Competition, 348cc overhead-valve single, 69 x 93mm bore and stroke, 16bhp at 5,600rpm, 4-speed wide-ratio gearbox, oil-bath chain case, Teledraulic front forks, AMC 'jampot' rear suspension units, excellent condition.
£2,450–2,750
$3,600–4,000 ⊞ OBMS
This model was one of the most popular long-stroke heavyweight British trials mounts.

1954 BSA B34 Trials Replica, 499cc overhead-valve single, 85 x 88mm bore and stroke, 4-speed gearbox, 21in front wheel, concours condition.
£2,500–3,200
$3,600–4,650 ⋟ TEN
Built regardless of cost, this machine is a replica of the swinging-arm Gold Star Trials. It utilises the pukka GS engine in lightened B33 cycle parts. A Lyta alloy tank, alloy rims and high-level exhaust complete the picture.

1959 Dot Trials, 246cc Villiers 32A 2-stroke single-cylinder engine, Armstrong leading-link front forks, swinging-arm frame.
£1,100–1,250
$1,600–1,800 ⊞ PMo
In the main, Dot concentrated on building competition machines, and it was one of the oldest companies in the business. It began producing bikes in 1903, and the founder won a TT in 1908. Motorcycles were not built between 1932 and 1949. During the 1950s and 1960s, the company used mainly Villiers engines.

Dealer prices

Miller's guide prices for dealer motorcycles take into account the value of any guarantees or warranties that may be included in the purchase. Dealers must also observe additional statutory consumer regulations, which do not apply to private sellers. This is factored into our dealer guide prices. Dealer motorcycles are identified by the ⊞ icon; full details of the dealer can be found on page 167.

1957 Matchless Works Trials, 348cc overhead-valve single, 4-speed gearbox, telescopic front forks, swinging-arm frame.
£2,650–3,000
$3,850–4,400 ⋟ BKS
During the 1950s and 1960s, British manufacturers viewed success in trials competitions as an essential component in the marketing of their motorcycles. Thanks to its position as one of the largest manufacturers, AMC was able to attract riders of the highest calibre, including Hugh Viney, Artie Rathcliffe and Gordon Jackson who, between them, secured nine victories in the Scottish Six-Day Trial between 1947 and 1961, with Gordon Jackson accounting for four of them. This machine was ridden by works rider Dave Curtis and later by well-known competitor, photographer, author and authority on trials motorcycles Don Morley.

1957 Hagon JAP Speedway, 499cc JAP 2-valve pushrod engine, engine recently rebuilt and fitted with new Mahle piston.
£1,150–1,400
$1,700–2,000 ⋟ BKS
Before the arrival of the Jawa engine in the 1960s, the JAP dominated speedway racing. Alf Hagon, a famous dirt-bike competitor (and sprinter), developed a successful business manufacturing and selling speedway and grass-track frames.

1959 BSA Gold Star Scrambler, 499cc overhead-valve single, 4-speed gearbox, open-pipe exhaust, 21in front wheel, alloy fuel tank.
£5,200–6,200
$7,500–9,000 ⚹ BKS
By 1959, the Gold Star was listed in two versions and with the 350cc engine as an option. The two variants, the Clubmans and Scrambler, shared such items as the frame, forks and engine, but otherwise were equipped according to their particular role. The Clubmans had a close-ratio gearbox, clip-ons, rearsets and a sweptback exhaust, while the Scrambler was offered with a wide-ratio gearbox, the option of a central oil tank and a more conventional silencer, which was usually discarded and replaced by an open exhaust pipe. The front brakes differed, too, the Scrambler utilising a 7in item, and the Clubmans a standard 8in unit.

1958 Greeves Scottish Trials, 246cc Villiers 32A 2-stroke engine, 4-speed wide-ratio gearbox, aluminium beam front frame sections, leading-link front forks.
£1,000–1,200
$1,500–1,750 ⚹ CGC
Founded by Bert Greeves and assisted by the wheelchair-bound Derry Preston Cobb, the Thundersley, Essex, Greeves concern rose to premier position as builders of off-road motorcycles in the 1950s and 1960s.

A known continuous history can add value to and enhance the enjoyment of a motorcycle.

1959 Royal Enfield Scrambler, 692cc overhead-valve parallel twin, alloy rims, fork gaiters, knobbly tyres, braced handlebars.
£3,500–3,800
$5,000–5,500 ⊞ PMo
This Royal Enfield Constellation has been professionally converted to full motocross specification.

1960 BSA Gold Star, 499cc overhead-valve single, 4-speed gearbox, special head and barrel, kick-starter, 8in front brake, single saddle, concours condition.
£8,500–9,500
$12,300–13,800 ⊞ PMo
This ISDT machine has full lighting equipment, a silencer and other road-legal features.

◄ **1960 BSA Gold Star Competition,** 348cc overhead-valve single, alloy head and barrel, 6:1 compression-ratio piston, Amal Monobloc carburettor, chrome chainguard, centre stand.
£3,700–4,500
$5,300–6,500 ⚹ PS
This machine has been totally rebuilt in Scrambler guise, but all the parts are available to allow conversion to Clubmans racing trim.

1960s Gilera 98 Sei Giorni, 98cc overhead-valve unit single, parallel valves, wet-sump lubrication, high-level exhaust, 4-speed gearbox, standard specification, excellent condition.
£1,750–2,500
$2,500–3,600 ⊞ OBMS
By the mid-1950s, Gilera's off-road efforts were being chanelled away from its traditional big singles and into its new range of small unit-construction, overhead-valve singles. The first, the 175, debuted at the 1956 ISDT, but by the early 1960s, the Sei Giorni (Six Days) bikes also included 124 and 98cc versions.

1960s Triumph ISDT Replica, 490cc overhead-valve twin, 4-speed gearbox, high-level exhaust, knobbly tyres, concours condition.
£2,500–3,600
$3,600–5,200 ⊞ OBMS
During the 1960s, riders such as Ken Heanes, Johnny Giles and Roy Peplow all made an impact on the trials world, both in one-day and six-day events, on the 500 unit Triumph twin. This machine is a faithful replica of the type they rode.

1963 Dot Demon Scrambler, 246cc Villiers 34A 2-stroke engine, light-alloy barrel, 4-speed gearbox, square-tube swinging-arm, alloy tanks.
£1,500–1,800
$2,150–2,600 ⚒ H&H

1960s Moto Morini Corsaro Regolarita, 124cc overhead-valve unit-construction single, wet-sump lubrication, 4-speed gearbox, almost complete, in need of full restoration.
£600–720
$870–1,050 ⊞ NLM
This machine is an example of the genuine Moto Morini Six Days enduro bike; now very rare.

c1964 Triumph Tiger Cub Trials Replica, 199cc overhead-valve unit single, dry-sump lubrication, high-level exhaust, 4-speed gearbox, pan seat, trials bars, fork gaiters and other off-road features.
£900–1,200
$1,300–1,750 ⊞ BLM
This machine is a very neatly crafted replica and has a late-type points-in-timing-cover engine.

1969 Greeves Challenger 36MX4, 362cc piston-port 2-stroke engine, twin exhaust pipes, Ceriani front forks.
£800–960
$1,150–1,500 ⚒ H&H
The 362cc engine had the same stroke as the 24MX5 motocross unit.

1972 Bultaco Sherpa, 244cc 2-stroke single, 72 x 60mm bore and stroke, 20bhp at 6,500rpm, original, unrestored.
£500–700
$720–1,000 ⊞ BLM
The Spanish Bultaco Sherpa and Montesa Cota were the top names in the trials world of the early 1970s.

1975 Ducati 125 Regolarita, 124cc piston-port 2-stroke single, 54 x 54mm bore and stroke, alloy head and barrel, 22bhp at 9,000rpm, 6-speed gearbox, conical hubs, Marzocchi forks, gas rear shocks, Megura controls, restored with original factory parts.
£2,700–3,200
$3,900–4,650 ⊞ MW
This machine was ridden by Pat Slinn in the 1975 ISDT.

1970s Triumph Enduro Special, 490cc T100SS-specification overhead-valve unit twin, 1971-type forks and front wheel, alloy wheel rims, aluminium fuel tank, abbreviated side panels, chrome instruments, small carrier, concours condition.
£5,000–6,000
$7,250–8,700 ⊞ OBMS
This machine was built specially for a European customer.

1973 Triumph Adventer, 490cc overhead-valve unit twin, 59 x 65.5mm bore and stroke, conical wheel hubs, underslung siamesed exhaust system, aluminium fuel tank, original specification.
£2,000–2,500
$2,900–3,600 ⊞ MAY

◄ **1979 SWM 125 Motocross,** 124cc piston-port 2-stroke single, 6-speed gearbox.
£900–1,100
$1,300–1,600 ⚒ H&H
Founded in Italy in 1971, SWM (Speedy Working Motors) specialised in off-road competition bikes. Many of its early models used German Sachs two-stroke engines. The marque gained many successes, including victory in the 1981 World Trials Championship, but the mid-1980s saw the company's closure due to financial problems.

Military Bikes

◀ **1941 Matchless G3L,** 348cc overhead-valve single, 69 x 93mm bore and stroke.
£1,400–2,800
$2,000–4,000 ⚲ BKS
Developed from the girder-fork G3 overhead-valve single, the G3L offered despatch riders the luxury of telescopic forks. This, combined with relatively high performance compared to rival manufacturers' side-valve models, made it the most popular choice with 'Don Rs'.

1942 Indian 640, 500cc side-valve V-twin, hand-change gearbox, 18in wheels, girder forks, rigid frame, screen, panniers, sprung saddle, footboards.
£4,500–5,000
$6,500–7,250 ⊞ AtMC
The Harley-Davidson and Indian V-twins made up the majority of American wartime motorcycles. Today, Indians are highly prized.

1943 BMW R75 Combination, 745cc overhead-valve flat-twin, 78 x 78mm bore and stroke, 4-speed-and-reverse gearbox, 16in wheels, Steib Nürnberg sidecar.
£10,000–12,000
$14,500–17,400 ⚲ BKS
The BMW R75 sidecar outfit used by the German armed forces during WWII was not simply a motorcycle and sidecar, but a purpose-built off-road vehicle. Allied engineers concluded that it cost more to produce than the Jeep, which performed similar tasks. It was designed by engineer/racing driver Alex von Falkenhausen and powered by a 750cc flat-twin engine. The key to the model's off-road capability lay in the transmission system, which incorporated a high-/low-ratio gearbox acting on the four forward and single reverse gears in the main gearbox. This effectively provided eight forward and two reverse gears. Drive, by shaft, was transmitted to both the sidecar and rear wheel, a lockable differential being provided for when extreme conditions were encountered. Capable of carrying three fully-equipped combat troops at speeds approaching 55mph and weighing 900lb unladen, it was fitted with a hydraulic braking system.

◀ **1946 Royal Enfield Model CO,** 346cc overhead-valve single, iron head and barrel, 4-speed foot-change gearbox, speedometer.
£1,350–1,800
$1,900–2,600 ⊞ BLM
Although built for wartime duties, this Model CO was not registered until 1946, it being one of thousands of former military motorcyles that were sold off for civilian use at the end of hostilities. Since the war, it has been housed in a museum.

▶ **1946 Moto Guzzi Superalce,** 498cc overhead-valve single, 88 x 82mm bore and stroke, 18.5hp, 4-speed foot-change gearbox, 19in wheels, unrestored.
£3,350–4,000
$4,800–5,800 ⊞ NLM
The Superalce entered production in 1946 and replaced the Alce, which had been built from 1939 to 1945. The main difference between the two was that the former had overhead valves instead of an inlet-over-exhaust arrangement.

◀ **1958 Bianchi MT61,** 500cc overhead-valve unit-construction single, 4-speed foot-change gearbox, telescopic front forks, swinging-arm frame, 75mph top speed.
£1,475–1,775
$2,150–2,600 ⊞ NLM
The MT61 saw service with the Italian forces until well into the 1960s. It proved robust and reliable in service.

1960s Triumph TRW, 493cc side-valve twin, alloy head, iron barrel, telescopic front forks, rigid frame, sprung rider's seat, pillion pad, carrier.
£2,200–2,450
$3,200–3,600 ⊞ CotC
In general, the TRW was a reliable, smooth-running bike, which could reach 80mph when pushed. However, its need to continue running was more important than outright speed, hence the side-valve engine rather than an overhead-valve unit.

Monkey Bikes

1975 Moto Zodiaco Tuareg, 250cc Rockwell fan-cooled 4-stroke engine, full duplex frame, balloon tyres, matching speedometer and rev-counter.
£770–860
$1,120–1,250 ⊞ VICO

1975 Honda ST70, 71.8cc overhead-camshaft horizontal single, 47 x 41.4mm, bore and stroke, only 25 miles from new, museum displayed for some time.
£1,150–1,400
$1,600–2,000 ↗ CGC

1971 Honda Z50A, 49cc overhead-camshaft horizontal single, 41 x 49.5mm bore and stroke, 2.5 bhp, 6,000rpm, fully restored.
£1,350–1,625
$1,900–2,300 ↗ CGC

1971 Honda Z50A Mini Trials, 49cc overhead-camshaft horizontal single, high-level exhaust, U-shape frame, telescopic front forks, 12in wheels, fold-down handlebars.
£1,450–1,750
$2,000–2,500 ↗ CGC

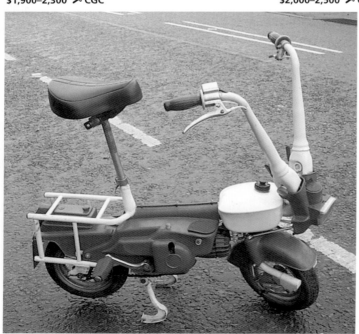

Auction prices

Miller's only includes motorcycles declared sold. Our guide prices take into account the buyer's premium, VAT on the premium, and the extent of any published catalogue information relating to condition and provenance. Motorcycles sold at auction are identified by the ↗ icon; full details of the auction house can be found on page 167.

◄ **1979 Carnielli Graziella,** 49cc piston-port 2-stroke horizontal single, single-speed automatic transmission, fold-down handlebars.
£695–850
$1,000–1,250 ⊞ NLM

Mopeds

1938 Raynal Autocycle, 98cc Villiers 2-stroke engine.
£675–750
$975–1,100 ⊞ PMo
Raynal entered the motorcycle scene late in 1937 with a production version of the prototype Jones autocycle. This was very much a pedal cycle type of machine with an engine slotted in. In 1950, Raynal was acquired by Raleigh Industries.

1950 Ducati Cucciolo, 49cc pull-rod 4-stroke single, 2-speed foot-change gearbox.
£1,600–1,925
$2,300–2,750 ⊞ NLM
This is one of the many Cucciolos that found their way into conventional pedal cycles. Ducati also sold the engine to other companies for them to build into new machines.

◀ **1951 Bown Autocycle,** 98cc Villiers 2F 2-stroke engine, fully restored.
£250–275
$360–400 🚲 NAC
This name from the 1920s was revived in 1950 and used by the Welsh firm for its autocycle, which had been marketed previously under the Aberdale brand name.

A known continuous history can add value to and enhance the enjoyment of a motorcycle.

▶ **1955 Ducati 55E,** 49cc overhead-valve single, wet-sump lubrication, 1.35bhp at 5,500rpm, 2-speed gearbox, leading-link front forks, swinging-arm frame.
£800–1,000
$1,150–1,500 ⊞ MW
The 55E was offered between 1955 and 1957, and together with the German NSU quickly was one of the first really modern mopeds. The engine had been developed from the pull-rod Cucciolo.

1964 Mobylette Moped, 49cc 2-stroke single.
£500–600
$720–870 ⊞ CotC
This popular French moped sold by the hundreds of thousand on the domestic market. It was also exported to other European countries, notably Great Britain.

1978 Vespa Ciao Moped, 49cc 2-stroke horizontal single, leading-link forks, rigid frame.
£150–200
$220–290 ⊞ MAY
The Ciao was popular in Italy, but less so elsewhere.

Police Bikes

1965 BMW R50/2, 494cc overhead-valve twin, 68 x 68mm bore and stroke, 26bhp at 5,800rpm, shaft final drive, 92mph top speed, ex-French police, restored, concours condition.
£5,000–5,500
$7,250–8,000 🚲 BMWC

1964 Velocette LE Series 3, 192cc side-valve flat-twin, kickstarter, foot-change gearbox, 12 volt electrics, restored.
£700–900
$1,000–1,300 ⊞ MAY

1972 Norton Commando Interpol, 745cc overhead-valve pre-unit twin, 73 x 89mm bore and stroke, 4-speed foot-change gearbox, disc front brake, fully restored to original police specification apart from early Interstate exhaust pipes, complete with radio equipment, panniers and fairing.
£4,000–5,500
$5,800–8,000 ⊞ MW
This machine was supplied new to Lancashire Constabulary.

1984 Ducati 600TL Pantah Police, 583cc belt-driven overhead-camshaft V-twin, 80 x 80mm bore and stroke, desmodromic valve gear, 5-speed gearbox, fairing, panniers, crashbars, baton carrier, concours condition.
£2,000–2,500
$2,900–3,600 ⊞ MW

1986 Moto Guzzi 850 T5 Police, 844cc overhead-valve V-twin, 83 x 78mm bore and stroke, shaft final drive, fairing, panniers and crashbars, centre and side stands, ex-Italian police.
£1,600–1,800
$2,300–2,600 ⊞ MAY

Racing Bikes

Among motorcycle sports, road-racing has always headed the field, with its unique combination of speed and glamour – and the high cost of taking part. Today, matching the rise in interest in veteran, vintage and classic road bikes, has come a similar explosion in road-racing for older bikes.

Historic motorcycle racing is an integral part of the world road-racing scene. And in contrast to years past, when a racer became outdated and was simply retired, this trend has been reversed, large numbers of previously unwanted 'old warhorses' being put back into action.

At first, it was simply a case of original bikes being raced again, often by their original riders, but with the huge increases in values toward the end of the 1980s, many of these bikes changed hands, and a substantial quantity were exported, notably to Japan. With the fall in prices at the beginning of the 1990s, a new breed of classic racing arrived, both bikes and riders being new to the sport.

The interest in racing older machines also has led to the formation of new clubs and classes

within The Forgotten Era organisation, the latter being open to bikes that previously had been excluded by the classic regulations (for example, post-1968 two-strokes and post-1972 four-strokes). This let in a flood of machines, such as the Yamaha TZ, Suzuki RG500, Honda RS125/250 and several makes powered by the Austrian Rotax inline twin-cylinder engine.

Currently, for example, the famous annual Mallory Park Post-TT meeting has races for both Classic and Forgotten Era bikes. Even the CRMC (Classic Racing Motorcycle Club) allows several types of Forgotten Era-category bikes.

Another recent innovation is the Landsdowne Cup series, named after James Landsdowne Norton, which was inspired by the first Goodwood Revival meeting in 1998 and aims to re-create, as far as possible, the spirit and spectacle of racing from the immediate post-WWII period until the mid-1960s. Besides the Manx Norton, eligible machinery includes the Matchless G50 and G45 twin, and the 7R AJS.

c1916 Indian Model H, 8-valve narrow-angle V-twin, front-mounted magneto, chain primary and final drive, pedalling gear, one of only 5 known to exist, fully restored, concours condition.
£63,000–70,000
$90,000–101,500 ⊞ AtMC
Credit for the design of these engines has been attributed to both Charles Gustafson Senior and Charles B. Franklin; the controversy remains.

► **1924 Moto Guzzi Corsa 2V,** 498.4cc overhead-valve horizontal single, 17bhp at 4,200rpm, 3-speed hand-change gearbox.
£22,500–25,000
$32,500–36,250 ⊞ AtMC
The Corsa 2V (two-valve), Guzzi's first racing design, employed an overhead-valve arrangement and achieved good results in long-distance events. By 1925, however, it was becoming outdated.

1926 Moto Guzzi Corsa 2V, 498.4cc overhead-valve single, 88 x 82mm bore and stroke, 3-speed gearbox, girder forks, rigid frame, caliper front brakes, 26in wheels.
£27,000–32,500
$39,000–47,000 ⊞ NLM

1928 Velocette KTT Mk I, 348cc single, drum brakes, girder forks, rigid frame.
£5,000–6,200
$7,250–8,800 ↗ BKS
By the early 1920s, it was becoming apparent that Veloce needed a more upmarket machine to supplement its existing two-strokes, and compete with the overhead-valve and overhead-cam models being released by their rivals. In 1924, therefore, the Percy Goodman-designed Model K overhead-cam single was released. The retention of the existing frame and transmission design determined the use of a narrow crankcase, which offered the benefit of a stiff crankshaft assembly. Following a dismal 1925 TT, where the three works entries failed due to inadequate lubrication, the engine was redesigned with a dry-sump system. The Model K returned to the island the following year and, in Alec Bennett's hands, secured a memorable victory in the Junior, ten minutes ahead of the nearest rival. Subsequent victories in 1927 and 1928 ensured a healthy demand for 'cammy' Velos and prompted the launch of the KTT production racer at Olympia in 1928.

1930s Cotton Racer, 499cc overhead-valve JAP single-cylinder engine, foot-change gearbox, drum front brake, Brooklands exhaust.
£4,500–5,000
$6,500–7,250 ⊞ AtMC
These JAP-engined bikes are rare and very fast in race trim. This 500cc sprint version is ready to go.

> **Cross Reference**
> See Colour Review (pages 126)

▶ **1931 Ariel Brooklands Square Four,** 498cc overhead-camshaft 4-cylinder engine, 51 x 61mm bore and stroke, girder forks, rigid frame.
£14,000–15,500
$20,300–22,500 ⊞ PMo
The Square Four made a great impact when it made its public debut at London's Olympia show in late 1930. This very special machine took part at Brooklands during the early 1930s.

◀ **1934 Sunbeam Little 95 250 Racer,** 246cc overhead-valve single, 59 x 90mm bore and stroke, hairpin valve springs, girder forks, rigid frame, concours condition.
£10,000–11,000
$14,500–16,000 ⊞ PMo
The Little 95 was only built in 1936, and today is very rare.

c1939 Gilera VTGS, 498.76cc overhead-valve single, 84 x 90mm bore and stroke, 7:1 compression ratio, Dell'Orto 28.5mm carburettor, 24bhp at 4,800rpm, 4-speed foot-change gearbox, lighting set, 92mph top speed.
£15,000–16,000
$21,750–23,200 ⊞ AtMC
The Gilera marque was founded in Milan by Guiseppe Gilera in 1908, its first production motorcycle being a 317cc single with inlet-over-exhaust valve configuration. Gilera soon became involved in racing to demonstrate the capability of his machines, gaining his first victory in 1912. The 1920s brought more recognition, particularly in long-distance trials. In 1939, Gilera gained the European Championship crown following the arrival of a four-cylinder racing engine. This particular model is the rarest of all pre-war Gileras, the VT tipo Milano-Taranto. The push-rod overhead-valve single was designed to compete in the gruelling motorcycle equivalent of the Mille Miglia, and the engine still bears the Milan-Taranto stamp. To cope with the less than ideal road conditions, the motorcycle featured Gilera's own version of rear suspension, which was adopted on later road-going machines. At the front, sprung girder forks were used with friction dampers. The option of lighting was available for those who wanted to compete at night.

c1948 Triumph T100 Grand Prix Replica, 499cc overhead-valve twin, 63 x 80mm bore and stroke, 4-speed foot-change gearbox.
£4,200–5,000
$6,100–7,250 ⚲ BKS
The very first post-war Manx Grand Prix was won in 1946 by Ernie Lyons on a Tiger 100 model. This had a silicone-aluminium-alloy cylinder head and barrel adapted from a wartime aircraft auxiliary power unit. In addition to a variety of competition extras, the machine featured an unusual rear springing system designed by Edward Turner: the springs were contained within the oversize hub of the rear wheel. This 'sprung hub' would soon become a feature of Triumph's road bikes. Thereafter named the GP, the new Triumph racer was developed progressively until it became a team entry for the 1948 Senior TT, although all failed due to various problems. In all, 175 of these machines were assembled, and it is thought that a further 20 engines were made available. This Replica was built from a mixture of genuine GP components and an early T100 sprung-hub model.

Cross Reference
See Colour Review (page 126)

1950 FB Mondial World 125 Grand Prix, 124cc double-overhead-camshaft single, alloy head and barrel, 5-speed close-ratio gearbox, blade girder forks, plunger rear suspension, original, unrestored.
£27,000–30,000
$39,000–43,500 ⊞ AtMC
FB Mondial created history by winning the first three 125cc World Championship titles, in 1949, 1950 and 1951. This machine is one of a very small number of machines that were built to achieve this feat.

Miller's is a price GUIDE not a price LIST

1949 Triumph Grand Prix, 499cc overhead-valve pre-unit twin, 63 x 80mm bore and stroke, alloy head and barrel, parallel-mounted twin carburettors, telescopic forks, sprung-hub rear suspension, concours condition.
£14,750–16,500
$22,850–24,000 ⊞ PMo

1950 AJS 7R, 349cc chain-driven overhead-camshaft single, 4-speed close-ratio foot-change gearbox, engine rebuilt by George Beale Motorcycles, 1949 specification in most respects, apart from later gearbox, very good condition throughout.
£8,500–10,500
$12,300–15,250 ⋌ BKS
Associated Motor Cycles introduced the 7R during 1948, and over the course of the ensuing 15-year production run – and beyond – it became one of the most successful over-the-counter racers of all time. Although the engine was a fresh design by Phil Walker, the chain-driven overhead-cam layout was reminiscent of the pre-war 'cammy Ajays'. The Teledraulic forks remained constants during the model's production life, but the rear suspension units were subject to revision, the early 'candlesticks' giving way to 'jampots', then Girling items. The engine also came in for upgrades, with a progressive reduction in valve angle and, in 1956, a change from the early long-stroke dimensions of 74 x 90mm to a shorter-stroke configuration of 75.8 x 78mm.

◀ **1950 AJS 7R,** 348cc overhead-camshaft single, 74 x 81mm bore and stroke, magnesium engine castings, dry-sump lubrication, Burman 4-speed close-ratio gearbox.
£10,000–12,000
$14,500–17,400 ⊞ PMo
An AJS competed in the TT as early as 1911, when a pair of 350s finished 15th and 16th in the Junior race. This was some two years after AJS (Albert John Stevens) began trading as a limited company in Wolverhampton. During the 1920s, AJS enjoyed considerable racing success. In 1930 came the R7 'over-the-counter' racer – the forerunner of the post-war 7R. AJS became part of AMC in 1931.

◄ **1950 Moto Guzzi Gambalunghino,** 246.8cc overhead-camshaft single, 68 x 68mm bore and stroke, 25bhp at 8,000rpm, 4-speed close-ratio gearbox, leading-link front forks, sprung rear suspension, 109mph top speed.
£40,000–48,000
$58,000–69,600 ⊞ NLM
The Gambalunghino (Little Long Leg) was built in small numbers between 1949 and 1952.

1951 Moto Guzzi Gambalunga Tipo Falenza, 498.4cc overhead-valve horizontal single, 88 x 82mm bore and stroke, 34bhp at 5,500rpm, 118mph top speed, concours condition.
£35,000–42,000
$50,750–60,000 ⊞ NLM

1952 MV Agusta Works Twin Cam Single, 124cc double-overhead-camshaft unit-construction single, 5-speed gearbox, full-width brake hubs, Earles front forks, swinging-arm frame, fairing as used at some faster circuits.
£45,000–54,000
$65,250–79,500 ⊞ NLM
The type of MV was used by Cecil Sandford to win the marque's first World Championship title, the 1952 125cc.

1952 Rumi Competizione SS52 Gobbetto, 124.68cc piston-port 2-stroke horizontal twin, 10.8:1 compression ratio, leading-link front forks, plunger frame, full-width hubs.
£22,000–26,500
$32,000–38,000 ⊞ NLM
Rumi's first pukka racing model was the Gobbetto. Production began in late 1951.

1953 MV Agusta 125, 124cc overhead-camshaft single, 53 x 56.4mm bore and stroke, 4-speed gearbox, telescopic front forks.
£10,500–12,500
$15,250–18,150 ⚒ BKS
Introduced in 1953, MV's overhead-cam 124cc racing motorcycle was intended to provide privateers with a competitive mount at reasonable cost. The telescopic forks with central spring unit, brakes and frame were all clearly derived from the works twin-cam 125s. Producing a nominal 16bhp at 10,300rpm and weighing 75kg dry, the model was instantly successful. Provision was made for a lighting kit, and a full set of road-legal equipment was available, enabling it to be used in the long-distance road races that were popular in Italy at the time. Production continued until 1956. This example was imported into the UK in 1953 by Bill Webster and competed in the 1953, 1954 and 1955 TTs. It was also ridden by Mike Hailwood in his first road race during 1957.

◄ **1953 Norton International Manx Special,** 348cc overhead-camshaft 40 International engine, Featherbed frame, Roadholder forks, International hubs, Manx cycle parts, Isle of Man 5-gallon fuel tank.
£7,000–9,000
$10,200–13,000 ⊞ PMo
This attractive machine has been neatly crafted from a mixture of International and Manx components.

1954 Jawa Works Twin, 498cc double-overhead-camshaft twin, 65.76 x 73.6mm bore and stroke, twin Amal carburettors, duplex cradle frame, telescopic forks, swinging-arm rear suspension, concours condition.
£36,000–40,000
$51,000–58,000 ⊞ AtMC

1955 AJS 7R, 347cc chain-driven overhead-camshaft single, magnesium engine castings, 4-speed close-ratio gearbox, dry clutch, chain primary drive.
£10,000–11,000
$14,500–16,000 ⊞ MW

1955/61 AJS 7R, 1955 engine and Burman gearbox, 1961 chassis, fully rebuilt, unused for 30 years.
£6,500–7,500
$9,400–10,875 ⋋ BKS
The 7R's successes on the circuits, particularly at club level, are legendary, and a developed 7R even took Bill Nilsson to victory in the World Moto-Cross Championships of 1957. Almost all of Britain's road race stars of the 1950s and 1960s rode a 7R at some stage of their careers, and the model remains a major force in classic racing.

> ## Restored values
> The cost of a professional restoration will have an influence on, but no direct relation to, a motorcycle's market value. A restored motorcycle can have a market value lower than the cost of its restoration.

1955 Norton 40M Manx, 348cc double-overhead-camshaft single.
£10,000–12,000
$14,500–17,400 ⊞ MW
This machine was originally supplied through Harold Daniell to Alan Trow at the beginning of 1955; subsequently, he raced it to ninth position in the 1955 Junior Manx GP that September. Two days later, Trow took fourth place in the Senior TT on his 499cc machine. Those finishes gained him the Newcomer's Award. In the following month, he finished second to John Surtees at Brands Hatch, then was signed by Jock West of AMC to race Nortons the following year.

◀ **1956 AJS 7R,** 349cc overhead-camshaft single, 75.5 x 78mm bore and stroke, Burman gearbox, excellent condition.
£12,000–14,000
$17,400–20,300 ⊞ PMo
This was the first year of the revised bore-and-stroke dimensions, and also minor changes, such as a double timing-side main bearing, reverse-cone megaphone silencer and modified AMC 'jampot' rear suspension units.

▶ **c1957 Moto Morini Settebello,** 172cc overhead-valve single, magnesium brakes, alloy rims, works F3 fuel tank.
£6,200–7,000
$9,000–10,200 ⊞ AtMC
The Settebello was the fastest of the overhead-valve Morinis of the late 1950s. It was intended for fast road work and Formula 3-type Italian racing events.

1959 Norton 40M Manx, 348cc double-overhead-camshaft single, 76 x 85mm bore and stroke, AMC gearbox, twin-leading-shoe front brake, alloy wheel rims, basically standard specification apart from high-level exhaust and unpainted rear mudguard.
£10,000–11,000
$14,500–16,000 ⊞ VER

1960 Ducati Elite Racer, 204cc bevel-driven overhead-camshaft unit-construction single, 67 x 57.8mm bore and stroke, Dell'Orto SS1 carburettor, 20bhp at 8,000rpm, 4-speed gearbox, Vic Camp Milano twin-leading-shoe front brake conversion, 96mph top speed.
£1,800–2,100
$2,600–3,000 ⊞ MW

1959 Ducati 175 F3, 174cc overhead-camshaft single, 62 x 57.8mm bore and stroke, wet sump lubrication, 4-speed close-ratio gearbox.
£5,500–8,000
$8,000–11,600 ⚲ BKS
In 175cc form, the Ducati F3 racing motorcycle produced 16bhp at 9,000rpm. Introduced in 1958, it was assembled in limited numbers, total production of the two variants – 125 and 175 – amounting to about 100 machines. Of these, half were 175s. The mechanics drew heavily on experience gained with the previous Gran Sport models. Sand-cast crankcases, straight-cut level and primary-drive gears, a longer, lower and lighter frame, and a unique fuel tank all help identify the F3. However, the most obvious features are the Amadoro front and rear vented brakes, as used on the factory desmo racers. This particular machine and a 125 Desmo GP model were taken to Portugal by Ducati in 1959. The Desmo was raced by Francesco Villa at Lisbon, this machine being ridden by local star Angelo Driniz, who finished second behind Villa. The Formula 3 remained in Portugal for the next 40 years.

1962 Aermacchi Ala d'Oro, 246cc overhead-camshaft unit-construction single, wet-sump lubrication, 4-speed gearbox, updated with later components including bodywork and non-standard Grimeca 4-leading-shoe front brake, restored in Italy 1998, excellent condition.
£4,000–6,000
$5,800–8,700 ⚲ BKS
The origins of Aermacchi's successful horizontal, single-cylinder, overhead-valve 250 and 350cc road-racers can be traced back to an unsuccessful road-going single introduced in 1956 – the Chimera. This machine was an attempt to create an 'everyman's motorcycle'. Although well received, it met with very little commercial success, even when the capacity was increased to 250cc from the original 175. A hasty redesign occurred during 1957, which resulted in the Ala D'Oro models. These lacked the Chimera's enclosing bodywork, had conventional twin-shock rear suspension in place of the previous machine's monoshock system, and received some tuning to the engine. Equipped in typically Italian sporting style, the new models were an instant success and soon appeared on the race track. In 1961, the first 250cc 'over-the-counter' racers were offered. By 1964, a 344cc racing variant had been introduced.

1965 Moto Morini Corsarino Competizione, 49cc overhead-valve unit single, Dell'Orto carburettor, dry clutch, close-ratio gearbox, Fontana double-sided front brake, alloy rims, works-style tank, concours condition.
£4,000+
$5,800+ ⊞ MW

Dealer prices

Miller's guide prices for dealer motorcycles take into account the value of any guarantees or warranties that may be included in the purchase. Dealers must also observe additional statutory consumer regulations, which do not apply to private sellers. This is factored into our dealer guide prices. Dealer motorcycles are identified by the ⊞ icon; full details of the dealer can be found on page 167.

c1966 Aermacchi Ala d'Oro, 344cc overhead-valve single.
£4,600–5,500
$6,650–8,000 ⚒ BKS

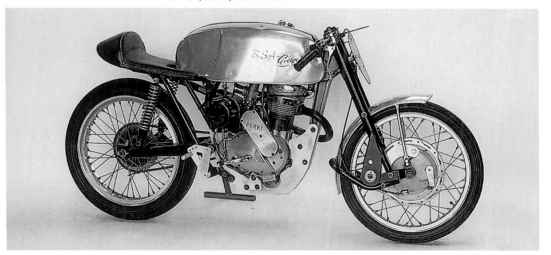

1966 BSA/Greeves Special, Perry-tuned overhead-valve BSA B40 unit engine, Amal GP carburettor, magneto ignition, one-off engine mounting plates, modified Greeves frame, large front brake.
£1,400–1,600
$2,000–2,300 ⚒ TEN
This machine was raced between 1966 and 1970, mainly in Scotland by Newcastle upon Tyne rider Stan Pennel.

◄ **c1968 Aermacchi Ala d'Oro,** 248cc overhead-valve unit single, Ceriani GP forks, Girling rear shocks, Ceriani 4-leading-shoe front brake, Fontana rear brake.
£16,200–18,000
$23,500–26,000 ⊞ AtMC
This machine has the short-stroke, dry-clutch engine and is reputed to have been an official Team Lawton bike.

► **1970s Spondon Kreidler,** 49cc air-cooled 2-stroke horizontal single, 5-speed gearbox, Spondon Engineering frame, Yamaha full-width drum brakes, aluminium fuel tank.
£1,800–2,000
$2,600–2,900 ⊞ MW
This machine was designed by the late two-stroke specialist and tuner, Brian Wooley. The original prototype, with a six-speed one-off gearbox and Itom-based engine, was intended for Bill Ivy, but later it was raced by George Ashton.

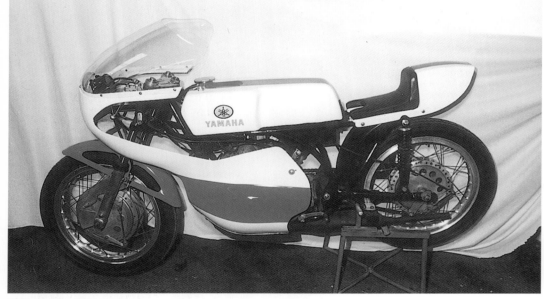

1970 Yamaha TD2B, 247cc air-cooled 2-stroke twin, 6-speed gearbox, drum brakes, twin-shock rear suspension, standard specification apart from Grimeca 4-leading-shoe front drum brake, unrestored.
£1,800–2,000
$2,600–2,900 ⊞ MW

► **1972 Aermacchi Works Model Ala d'Oro,** 349cc overhead-valve single, 5-speed gearbox, outside flywheel, dry clutch, Fontana brakes, Ceriani GP forks.
£15,000–18,000
$21,750–26,000 ⊞ NLM

◀ **1972/74 Ducati 450,** tuned 436cc Mark 3 overhead-camshaft valve-spring engine, Mikuni carburettor, high-level exhaust, 5-speed gearbox, wet clutch, twin-leading-shoe front brake, alloy rims, camshaft-driven rev-counter.
£2,200–2,500
$3,200–3,600 ⊞ MW

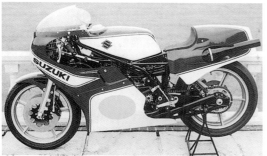

1978 Laverda 500 Formula, 496.7cc double-overhead-camshaft parallel twin, 4 valves per cylinder, 10:3:1 pistons, 6-speed gearbox, triple disc brakes, cast alloy wheels, original, concours condition.
£6,000–7,200
$8,700–10,500 ⊞ NLM
Some 150 examples of the 500 Formula were built in two batches. Based on the Alpino roadster, it was intended for an Italian one-model race series.

1979 Suzuki RG500 Mk V, 494.69cc liquid-cooled 2-stroke square-4, 54 x 54mm bore and stroke, 96bhp at 11,200rpm, 6-speed gearbox, dry clutch, triple disc brakes, cast alloy wheels, hydraulic steering damper.
£9,200–11,000
$13,000–16,000 ⚒ BKS

▶ **1981 Honda CB1100R,** 1062cc air-cooled double-overhead-camshaft 4-cylinder engine, 70 x 69mm bore and stroke, 16-valve cylinder head, four 33mm carburettors, 120bhp at 9,000rpm, 5-speed gearbox.
£9,000–10,000
$13,000–14,500 ⊞ PMo
This is reputed to have been one of the CB1100Rs ridden by Ron Haslam to victory in the 1981 British Streetbike racing series.

1994 Norton Rotary Duckhams Racer, 588cc.
£18,000–21,000
$26,000–30,500 ⚒ BKS
During the 1987 August Bank Holiday meeting at Darley Moor, one of the greatest names in British motorcycle history returned to the tracks. The new machine was a Norton Rotary, built by development engineer Brian Crighton and mechanic Dave Evans, in their own time and with their own money. By the beginning of the 1988 season, a three-man team had been announced, the success of which attracted sponsorship from John Player for 1989. For the next three years, the team was a major force in British Superbike racing, securing numerous wins, including Hislop's 1992 victory in the Isle of Man, two British Superbike Championships and the British Formula 1 title. At the end of 1992, the team withdrew from racing, then came news that Team Crighton Norton had secured sponsorship from GSE (Groundwork South East) and Duckhams. Over the course of the next two and a half seasons, the team achieved a total of 86 rostrum finishes, 53 during 1994, when Ian Simpson won the British Superbike Championship on this particular machine. In fact, the pairing gained 25 victories in 1994. Unfortunately, at the end of that season, the British governing body ruled that the Norton would not be eligible for the following year.

Scooters

1958 Lambretta 125LD, 124cc piston-port 2-stroke single, twist-grip gearchange, rider and pillion saddles, carrier, spare wheel, original condition.
£750–850
$1,100–1,250 ⚡ BKS
A total of 44,665 125LDs were built between December 1956 and July 1958. The 150 version was even more popular.

1958 Lambretta 125LD, 124cc air-cooled 2-stroke single.
£650–750
$950–1,100 ⊞ MAY
This French-market model has slightly different styling to versions imported into Britain.

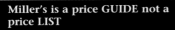

Miller's is a price GUIDE not a price LIST

▶ **1964 Triumph Tigress TS1,** 175cc 2-stroke single 4-speed foot-change gearbox, fully restored, concours condition.
£1,000–1,200
$1,500–1,750 ⊞ CotC
The Tigress TS1 did not reach the public until 1960. By then, much of the scooter boom was over and, together with the larger overhead-valve twin-cylinder-engined TW2, it proved a poor seller.

1973 Simson Schwalde, 49cc 2-stroke horizontal single, Earles forks, swinging-arm rear suspension, dualseat, enclosed engine.
£300–360
$440–500 ⚡ Bri
In 1973, Simson returned to the scooter fold with its Schwalde range of 49cc models.

1963 Moto Guzzi Galletto, 192cc overhead-valve single, 65 x 58mm bore and stroke, 7.7bhp at 5,200rpm, 4-speed gearbox, 17in wheels.
£1,300–1,500
$1,900–2,150 ⊞ NLM
The Galletto 192 with electric start was manufactured betweeen 1961 and 1966. It was the last in the series that had begun with the 160 model in 1950.

1957 TWN Contessa, 197cc 2-stroke split-single, 4-speed gearbox, electric start, 12 volt electrics, 10in wheels, totally restored 1994, unused since.
£1,200–1,500
$1,750–2,150 ⚒ H&H
The Contessa's engine was based on that of the Cornet motorcycle.

▶ **1967 Lambretta 125J,** 125cc piston-port 2-stroke single, 4-speed gearbox, twist-grip gearchange, dualseat.
£500–600
$720–870 ⊞ MAY
The 125J was produced from May 1966 until April 1969, a total of 16,052 four-speed models being built. There was also an early three-speed version.

1966 Ducati Brio 100, 94cc fan-cooled piston-port 2-stroke single, 51 x 46mm bore and stroke, 6bhp at 5,200rpm, 3-speed gearbox, 8in wheels, dualseat.
£700–800
$1,000–1,150 ⊞ MAY

1960 Triumph Tigress, 249cc overhead-valve 4-stroke twin, restoration project.
£100–200
$145–290 ⊞ MAY

1970 Vespa 90, 90cc 2-stroke single, split steel wheels, dualseat, original specification, very good condition.
£500–600
$720–870 ⊞ MAY
The Vespa 90 series was sold between 1964 and 1971. There was also a higher-performance Super Sprint model. In this latter version, the spare wheel was fitted centrally between the rider's legs and capped by a motorcycle-type fuel tank.

Dealer prices

Miller's guide prices for dealer motor-cycles take into account the value of any guarantees or warranties that may be included in the purchase. Dealers must also observe additional statutory consumer regulations, which do not apply to private sellers. This is factored into our dealer guide prices. Dealer motorcycles are identified by the ⊞ icon; full details of the dealer can be found on page 167.

1964 Vespa 150 Standard, 150cc fan-cooled 2-stroke single.
£500–600
$720–870 ⊞ MAY
From 1961, the 150 Standard had four instead of three speeds and could touch 56mph.

Sidecars

► **1914 Sunbeam and Sunbeam-made Sidecar,** 498cc side-valve single, 3-speed hand-change gearbox, oil-bath chain guards.
£12,000–12,500
$17,400–18,150 ⚒ BKS
The first Sunbeam motorcycle made its appearance in 1912. It was stunning, with a mostly black, deep-gloss finish enhanced by lettering and lining reputed to be genuine gold leaf. Thereafter, it became known as the Gentleman's Motorbicycle. Within two years, the factory had entered the competition world, and in the 1914 Tourist Trophy race a young Howard Richard Davis finished an equal second to Oliver Godfrey who was riding an Indian.

Restored values
The cost of a professional restoration will have an influence on, but no direct relation to, a motorcycle's market value. A restored motorcycle can have a market value lower than the cost of its restoration.

◄ **c1917 Motorsacoche and Torpedo Sidecar,** 770cc MAG side-valve V-twin engine, chain final drive, caliper brakes, flat tank, footboards, made in Switzerland.
£18,000–20,000
$26,000–29,000 ⊞ AtMC

► **1921 Matchless Model H and Sidecar,** 996cc MAG V-twin engine, fitted with a Matchless child-and-adult sidecar.
£5,800–7,000
$8,400–10,200
⚒ H&H

◀ **1924 New Imperial Model 7 and Sidecar,** 980cc JAP V-twin engine, 3-speed Sturmey-Archer gearbox.
£6,000–7,200
$8,700–10,500 ✗ H&H
The New Imperial concern used as its slogan, 'Perfect Dependability'. It offered no less than ten models for 1924.

1925 Triumph with Folding Sidecar, 392cc side-valve single, hand-change gearbox, chain final drive, caliper rear brake, stored since late 1950s.
£2,800–3,400
$4,000–4,800 ✗ BKS
This machine is fitted with a collapsible sidecar chassis, which enables the combination to be pushed through alley-ways between houses and in confined spaces.

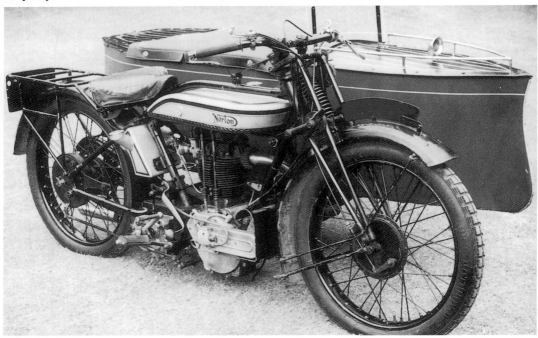

1927 Norton Model 18 and Sidecar, 490cc overhead-valve single.
£7,000–8,500
$10,200–12,300 ✗ BKS
At the beginning of the Brooklands season in March 1922, Norton introduced its new Model 18 fitted with a 490cc overhead-valve engine. Rex Judd immediately used it to raise the 500cc kilometre record to 89.92mph, and the mile to 88.39mph. The Model 18 went on sale shortly after and remained largely unchanged until 1927, during which time it gained many race wins. For 1928, it received a long-overdue redesigned saddle, tank and cradle frame.

▶ **1931 Ariel VB31 and Sidecar,** 557cc side-valve single, 86.4 x 95mm bore and stroke, one of only 2 such machines known to exist.
£2,400–2,800
$3,500–4,000 ✗ H&H

> A known continuous history can add value to and enhance the enjoyment of a motorcycle.

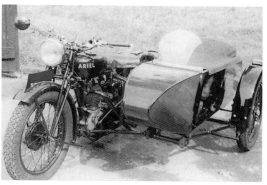

1947 Vincent Series B Rapide and Steib S500 Sidecar, 998cc overhead-valve V-twin, uprated to Black Shadow specification with correct pistons, carburettors, brakes and speedometer, 12 volt electrics, alternator.
£14,000–17,000
$20,300–24,650 ✗ BKS

Vincent-HRD unleashed its post-war twin on an austere world during 1946. It proved capable of speeds well in excess of 110mph on the low-grade pool petrol of the day. Innovative design features abounded, including alternative sprockets on the rear wheel (enabling a rapid change of final-drive ratio), the absence of a traditional frame, pivoted-fork suspension and an all-alloy engine with the gearbox built in unit. Known as the Series B Rapide, it was followed in 1948 by the even quicker Black Shadow, which benefited from an increase in compression ratio and larger carburettors, combined with ribbed brakes and a 5in 150mph speedometer on top of the forks. The two twins became popular with sidecar enthusiasts, who recognised their potential when combined with a suitable 'chair', such as the luxury Steib S500 fitted to this example.

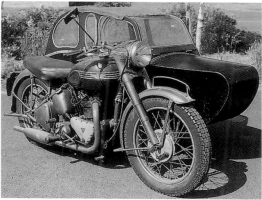

1950 Triumph 6T Thunderbird and Watsonian Child/Adult Sidecar, 649cc overhead-valve pre-unit twin, iron head and barrel, sprung rear hub, dualseat, unused since 1992, in need of cosmetic restoration.
£1,300–1,400
$1,900–2,000 ✗ TEN

1953 Ariel 4G Mk II and Watsonian Sidecar, 998cc overhead-valve 4-cylinder all-alloy engine, 40bhp at 5,600rpm, plunger frame, telescopic front forks.
£3,000–3,500
$4,400–5,000 ✗ H&H

By 1953, the Ariel Square Four had reached the zenith of its development. It was relaunched at the 1952 London show as the 4G Mk II, with modified induction and four exhaust pipes.

1955 Triumph Tiger 100 and Watsonian Sidecar, 499cc overhead-valve pre-unit parallel twin, swinging-arm frame.
£4,500–5,500
$6,500–8,000 ✗ BKS

1960 BSA M21 and AA Patrol Sidecar, 596cc side-valve single, legshields, fairing, box sidecar, restored to original condition.
£4,000–5,000
$5,800–7,250 ✗ PS
This machine was delivered new to the Automobile Association.

◄ **1960 Royal Enfield Super Meteor and Watsonian Sports Sidecar,** 692cc overhead-valve parallel twin, standard specification including 2-into-1 exhaust for sidecar use.
£3,900–4,200
$5,650–6,100 ⊞ MAY

1964 Butler-Greeves Trials Outfit, 246cc Villiers 2-stroke engine.
£2,500–2,800
$3,600–4,000 ⊞ PMo
Built by Butler Mouldings of Essex (near the Greeves Thundersley plant), the Butler-Greeves Trials Outfit is now extremely rare.

1974 Yamaha-Wasp Off-Road Outfit, Yamaha 649cc XS650 double-overhead-camshaft parallel twin, Wasp forks, chassis and sidecar.
£700–850
$1,000–1,250 ✗ PS
The Wasp company was run by the Rhind-Tutt family and specialised in off-road competition sidecar outfits.

Specials

1932/52 Ariel Square-Four Special, 1932 600cc overhead-camshaft 4-cylinder engine, 1952 plunger frame.
£8,000–9,000
$11,600–13,000 ⊞ PMo
This very neatly executed special provides the best of two eras.

1946 Matchless/Benelli Special, 348cc Matchless G3L overhead-valve engine, plunger frame and telescopic front forks, built in Italy.
£3,000–3,500
$4,400–5,000 ⊞ PMo

1950 Moto Guzzi Guzzino Special, 73cc overhead-valve conversion of original 2-stroke engine, fully enclosed valves, new lubrication system actuated by gear-type feed and return pump, very rare, concours condition.
£2,500–2,800
$3,600–4,000 ⊞ MW

◄ **1956 Triton Special,** 499cc Triumph pre-unit engine, laid-down Norton gearbox.
£2,600–3,000
$3,800–4,400 ⚒ BKS
Motorcycling folklore suggests that the first Tritons came about as a result of Formula 3 car racing. Norton was not willing to supply Manx engines to the racing-car fraternity, forcing the builders of Formula 3 cars to purchase complete Manx machines, from which the engines were removed. In so doing, they released numbers of race-proven rolling motorcycle chassis on to the market. It was readily apparent that the Featherbed frame was capable of accommodating almost any motorcycle engine and gearbox. The Triumph twin in its various forms was considered the strongest, and thus the Triton was born.

► **1959 Tribsa Special,**
649cc Triumph Thunderbird overhead-valve pre-unit engine, 4-speed foot-change gearbox, BSA frame, Ariel full-width alloy brake hubs.
£3,800–4,200
$5,500–6,100 ⊞ CotC

◄ **c1959 BSA A10 Chopper,** 646cc pre-unit twin.
£800–1,000
$1,150–1,500 ⊞ BLM
Many British motorcycles were 'chopped' following the release of the film *Easy Rider* at the beginning of the 1970s. This machine uses a BSA A10 Golden Flash engine as its base.

► **1960 Triumph T100A Café Racer,** tuned 490cc overhead-valve unit-construction twin, twin Amal 626 Concentric carburettors, high-level exhaust, racing seat and tank, fairing, rearsets, clip-ons, alloy mudguards, alloy rims.
£1,900–2,100
$2,750–3,000 ⊞ MAY

◄ **1960 Norton 99 Café Racer,** 596cc twin-cylinder engine, sweptback exhaust pipes, megaphone-type silencers, slimline frame, clip-ons, rearsets, alloy rims, racing tank and seat, central oil tank with built in battery holder.
£1,800–2,200
$2,600–3,200 ⊞ MAY

► **1960s Triton,** 750cc unit-construction Triumph engine enlarged to 780cc with big-bore kit, nickel-plated Norton wideline frame, 1970-type BSA/Triumph conical hubs, twin-leading-shoe front brake, alloy rims, racing tank, seat and fairing.
£2,200–2,500
$3,200–3,600 ⊞ TSG

◄ **1960s Triton,** 499cc pre-unit Tiger 100 engine, AMC gearbox, twin-leading-shoe front brake, alloy tanks, racing seat, alloy rims, clip-ons, rearsets.
£7,500–9,000
$10,875–13,000 ⊞ OBMS

1960s Dresda Triton 650, 649cc pre-unit Triumph Trophy engine, sweptback exhaust pipes, Norton wideline frame, combined fuel and oil tanks, racing dualseat, alloy rims, clip-ons, matching Smiths speedometer and rev-counter, Lucas chrome headlamp.
£3,000–3,200
$4,400–4,650 ⊞ MAY

1960s Norton Special, 745cc Atlas engine, 88 wideline frame, twin-leading-shoe front brake, alloy wheel rims, matching Smiths instruments, central oil tank, Manx 5 gallon fuel tank, Chuck-type short megaphone silencers.
£3,500–4,000
$5,000–5,800 ⊞ MW

1977 Jasuki Special Café Racer, 400cc Suzuki GS overhead-camshaft twin-cylinder engine, Jawa frame, one-off tank and seat, chrome headlamp,
£600–700
$870–1,000 ⊞ MAY

1962 Aermacchi Ala Verda Café Racer, 246cc overhead-valve engine, 4-speed gearbox, wet clutch, Ala d'Oro bodywork, indicators.
£1,800–2,000
$2,600–2,900 ⊞ MW

1970s/1990s Magni AFI GP500, 498cc double-overhead-camshaft across-the-frame 4-cylinder engine, 4-pipe exhaust, 4-leading-shoe front brake, alloy rims.
£30,000–36,000
$43,500–52,250 ⊞ NLM
This machine was built as a replica of MV's 500 Grand Prix racer, which ruled from the late 1950s onward.

◀ **1982 Moto Morini Valentini Special,** 498cc overhead-valve 72° V-twin, Heron heads, parallel valves, 6-speed gearbox.
£1,800–2,100
$2,600–3,000 ⊞ VICO
Valentini was a small tuning company that specialised in building Morinis with a difference. This example has a tuned 6-speed 500 engine, special bodywork and other Valentini goodies, including exhaust, rearsets and fairing.

1983 Ducati 900S2 Special, 864cc 900S2 overhead-camshaft bevel V-twin engine, electric start, Hailwood tank and seat, 2-into-1 exhaust.
£2,500–3,000
$3,600–4,400 ⊞ MW

1985 Harris Ducati TT F2 Replica, 600cc V-twin, belt-driven camshafts, desmodromic valve gear.
£2,400–3,200
$3,500–4,650 ⊞ MW
During the mid-1980s, there were many variations of the TT F2 'Rutter' Replica, as a result of Tony Rutter's record-breaking four TT F2 world titles for Ducati. These bikes were usually built either by specialist dealers or by enthusiasts, and they used a number of different frames. The most popular were the British Harris and Italian Verlicchi.

1990 Spondon Sports M/LS Ducati, 904cc Ducati 90° V-twin engine, 2 valves per cylinder, desmodromic valve gear, 6-speed gearbox, Comstar riveted wheels, floating disc brakes, Marzocchi front forks.
£3,000–3,500
$4,400–5,000 ⊞ MW

2001 Triton, 649cc overhead-valve pre-unit Triumph T120R engine, Triumph gearbox, Norton Dominator wideline frame, twin-leading-shoe front brake, alloy wheel rims, racing tank, central oil tank, matching Smiths speedometer and rev-counter.
£10,000–12,000
$14,500–17,400 ⊞ OBMS

> A known continuous history can add value to and enhance the enjoyment of a motorcycle.

◀ **2001 Triton,** 649cc pre-unit Triumph Bonneville engine, Amal Concentric Mk I carburettors, Gold Star black silencers, sweptback exhaust pipes, one of 10 recently built.
£7,500–9,000
$10,875–13,000 ⊞ OBMS

Memorabilia

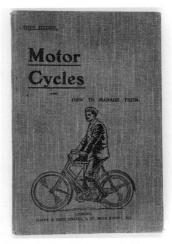

Donington Park Motor Cycle Races Programme, 1939, 9 x 6in (23 x 15cm).
£8–10
$10–15 ⊞ COB

Motor Cycles And How To Manage Them, 5th Edition, 1902, 9 x 6in (23 x 15cm).
£32–35
$45–50 ⊞ DM

Triumph Replacement Parts Catalogue for Speed Twin, Thunderbird, Tiger 100, Trophy, 1951, 9 x 6in (23 x 15cm).
£18–20
$25–30 ⊞ DM

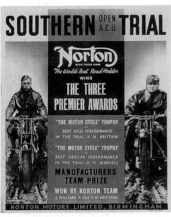

Motor Cycling, Volume 21, in publisher's green bindings, 1919–20.
£150–170
$220–250 ⋏ BKS

Norton celebration and advertising posters, 42 x 27in (106.5 x 68.5cm).
£120–140
$175–200 ⋏ BKS

Norton celebration and advertising posters, 47 x 30in (119.5 x 76cm).
£120–140
$175–200 ⋏ BKS

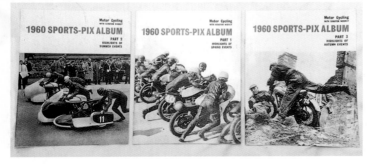

◀ *Sports-Pix Album*, Parts 1, 2 and 3, 1960, 10 x 7in (25.5 x 18cm).
£3–5 each
$2–7 ⊞ TIC

◀ **c1950 Triumph 5T Speed Twin fuel tank.**
£25–30
$35–45 ⋏ GAZE

▶ **1948 Triumph 3T twin-cylinder crankcases.**
£15–18
$20–25 ⋏ GAZE

1950 BSA B31 swinging-arm frame assembly.
£100–110
$145–160 ✦ GAZE

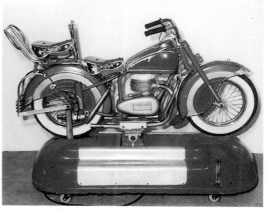

A Lenaerts Children's Ride, in the form of a lightweight motorcycle, finished in blue and silver, capable of carrying two children, made in Brussels, believed in working order, 1950s.
£630–760
$880–1,000 ✦ BKS

◀ A cast aluminium fairground motorcycle, 1950s, 11¾in (30cm) high.
£160–180
$230–260 ⊞ TRA

▶ A cast aluminium fairground motorcycle, 1950s, 23in (58.5cm) high.
£225–275
$320–400 ⊞ JUN

A signed black and white photograph of Geoff Duke, Isle of Man TT, 1951, 9 x 8in (23 x 20.5cm).
£50–75
$75–110 ⊞ SMW

A Motocyclette Rochet poster, after P. Chapellier, depicting a motorcycle racing a goods train, laid on linen, stretched on a wooden frame, wide green tape to create an enhanced border, c1904, 33 x 47in (83.5 x 119.5cm).
£400–460
$580–660 ✦ BKS

166

Key to Illustrations

Each illustration and descriptive caption is accompanied by a letter code.
By referring to the following list of Auctioneers (denoted by *), dealers (•), Clubs, Museums and Trusts (§), the source of any item may be immediately determined. Inclusion in this edition no way constitutes or implies a contract or binding offer on the part of any of our contributors to supply or sell the goods illustrated, or similar articles, at the prices stated. Advertisers in this year's directory are denoted by †.
If you require a valuation, it is advisable to check whether the dealer or specialist will carry out this service and if there is a charge. Please mention *Miller's* when making an enquiry. A valuation by telephone is not possible. Most dealers are willing to help you with your enquiry; however, they are very busy people and consideration of the above points would be welcomed.

AG * Anderson & Garland (Auctioneers), Marlborough House, Marlborough Crescent, Newcastle-upon-Tyne, Tyne & Wear NE1 4EE Tel: 0191 232 6278

AH * Andrew Hartley, Victoria Hall Salerooms, Little Lane, Ilkley, Yorkshire LS29 8EA Tel: 01943 816363 ahartley.finearts@talk21.com

AMOC § AJS & Matchless Owners Club

AOC/AOM § Ariel Owners Motor Cycle Club, Andy Hemingway, 80 Pasture Lane, Clayton, Bradford, Yorkshire BD14 6LN

AtMC •† Atlantic Motorcycles, 20 Station Road, Twyford, Berkshire RG10 9NT Tel: 0118 9342266 www.classicbikesatlantic.co.uk

BB • www.britishbikes.co.uk, PO Box 1, Northwich, Cheshire CW8 2RD Tel: 01928 788500 bikes@motorcycle-classics.co.uk

BKS *† Bonhams & Brooks, Montpelier Street, Knightsbridge, London SW7 1HH Tel: 020 7393 3900 www.bonhams.com

BLM •† Bill Little Motorcycles, Oak Farm, Braydon, Swindon, Wiltshire SN5 0AG Tel: 01666 860577

BMWC § The BMW Club, Bowbury House, Kirk Langley, Derbyshire DE6 5NJ

Bri * Bristol Auction Rooms, St John's Place, Apsley Road, Clifton, Bristol, Gloucestershire BS8 2ST Tel: 0117 973 7201 www.bristolauctionrooms.co.uk

CGC * Cheffins, 2 Clifton Road, Cambridge CB2 4BW Tel: 01223 213343 www.chefins.co.uk

COB • Cobwebs, 78–80 Northam Road, Southampton, Hampshire SO14 0PB Tel: 023 8022 7458 www.cobwebs.uk.com

CotC •† Cotswold Classics, Ullenwood Court, Leckhampton, Nr Cheltenham, Gloucestershire GL53 9QS Tel: 01242 228622 Mobile: 07974 224383

COYS * Coys of Kensington, 2–4 Queens Gate Mews, London SW7 5QJ Tel: 020 7584 7444

CStC •† Cake Street Classics, Bellview, Cake Street, Laxfield, Nr Woodbridge, Suffolk IP13 8EW Tel: 01986 798504

CYA • Courtyard Antiques, 108A Causewayside, Edinburgh, Scotland EH9 1PU Tel: 0131 662 9008

DM • Don Mitchell & Company, 132 Saffron Road, Wigston, Leicestershire LE18 4UP Tel: 0116 277 7669

DOC * David Dockree, Cheadle Hulme Business Centre, Clemence House, Mellor Road, Cheadle Hulme, Cheshire SK7 1BD Tel: 0161 485 1258

DSCM § Derbyshire and Staffordshire Classic Motorcycle Club, 51 Westwood Park, Newhall, Swadlincote, Derbyshire DE11 0R5 Tel: 01283 214542

GAZE * Thomas Wm Gaze & Son, 10 Market Hill, Diss, Norfolk IP22 3JZ Tel: 01379 651931 www.twgaze.com

GSO § Gold Star Owners Club, Maurice Evans, 211 Station Road, Mickleover, Derby DE3 5FE

H&H * H & H Classic Auctions Ltd, Whitegate Farm, Hatton Lane, Hatton, Warrington, Cheshire WA4 4BZ Tel: 01925 730630 www.classic-auctions.co.uk

JUN • Junktion, The Old Railway Station, New Bolingbroke, Boston, Lincolnshire PE22 7LB Tel: 01205 480068/480087

MAY •† Mayfair Motors, PO Box 66, Lymington, Hampshire SO41 0XE Tel: 01590 644476

MW •† Mick Walker, 10 Barton Road, Wisbech, Cambridgeshire PE13 1LB Tel: 01945 461914 www.mickwalker.co.uk

NAC § National Autocycle & Cyclemotor Club, Rob Harknett, 1 Parkfields, Roydon, Harlow, Essex CM19 5JA Tel: 01279 792329

NLM •† North Leicester Motorcycles, Whitehill Road, Ellistown, Leicestershire LE67 1EL Tel: 01530 263381 stuart@motomorini.demon.co.uk

OBMS • The Old British Motorcycle Shop, Unit 13 Southwold Business Centre, St Edmunds Road, Southwold, Suffolk IP18 6BZ Tel: 01502 724488

PM •† Pollard's Motorcycles, The Garage, Clarence Street, Dinnington, Sheffield, Yorkshire S25 7NA Tel: 01909 563310

PMo •† Planet Motorcycles, 44–45 Tamworth Road, Croydon, Surrey CRO 1XU Tel: 020 86865650

PS *† Palmer Snell, 65 Cheap Street, Sherbourne, Dorset DT9 3BA Tel: 01935 812218

RSS § Raleigh Safety Seven and Early Reliant Owners Club, incorporating Historic Raleigh Motorcycle Club, Mick Sleap, 17 Courtland Avenue, Chingford, London E4 6DU Tel: 020 8524 6310

RWHS • www.classicbikes.co.uk, RWHS Classic Bikes, Hales Farm, Nr Market Drayton, Shropshire TF9 2PP Tel: 01630 657156 enquiries@classicbikes.co.uk

SiC • Silverstone Classic Cars Tel: 01933 622484 classiccarsales@lineone.net www.classiccarsales.net

SMW • Sporting Memorabilia of Warwick, 13 Market Place, Warwick CV34 4FS Tel: 01926 410600 Mobile: 07860 269340 sales@sportsantiques.com www.sportsantiques.com

SOC § Suzuki Owners Club, P.O. Box 7, Egremont, Cumbria CA22 2GE

TEN * Tennants, 34 Montpellier Parade, Harrogate, Yorkshire HG1 2TG Tel: 01423 531661

TIC • Tickers, 37 Old Northam Road, Southampton, Hampshire SO14 0NZ Tel: 02380 234431

TRA • Tramps, Tuxford Hall, Lincoln Road, Tuxford, Newark, Nottinghamshire NG22 0HR Tel: 01777 872 543 info@trampsuk.com

TSG • The School Garage, 47 Buxton Road, Whaley Bridge, High Peak, Derbyshire SK23 7HX Tel: 01663 733209 www.classiccarshop.co.uk

VER •† Verralls (Handcross) Ltd, Caffyns Row, High Street, Handcross, Haywards Heath, West Sussex RH17 6BJ Tel: 01444 400678

VICO • Toni Vico, Reg. Tre Rivi 40, 12040 Monteu Rodero(CN), Piedmont, Italy Tel: 00 39 173 90121

WbC • Woodbridge Classic Cars, Blomvyle Hall Garage, Easton Road, Hacheston, Suffolk IP13 0DY Tel: 01728 746413 sales@tr6.com www.tr6.com

WI • David Winstone, Bartlett Street Antique Centre, 5–10 Bartlett Street, Bath, Somerset BA1 2QZ Tel: 01225 466689 Mobile: 07979 506415 winstampok@netscapeonline.co.uk

YEST •† Yesterday's, V.O.F. Yesterday's, Maaseikerweg 202, 6006 AD Weert, The Netherlands Tel: 0475 531207

Glossary

We have attempted to define some of the terms that you will come across in this book. If there are any other terms or technicalities you would like explained or you feel should be included in future editions, please let us know.

ACU – Auto Cycle Union, which controls a large part of British motorcycle sport.

Advanced ignition – Ignition timing set to cause firing before the piston reaches centre top, variation is now automatic.

Air-cooling – Most motorcycle engines rely on air-cooling, their cylinder barrels and heads being finned to dissipate heat.

Air intake – The carburettor port that admits air to mix with fuel from the float chamber.

AMCA – Amateur Motor Cycle Association, promoters of British off-road events.

APMC – The Association of Pioneer Motor Cyclists.

Auto Cycle Club – Formed in 1903, this was the original governing body of motorcycle sport. In 1907 it became the Auto Cycle Union.

Automatic inlet valve – Activated by the engine suction; forerunner of the mechanically-operated valve.

Balloon tyres – Wide-section, low-pressure tyres, fitted to tourers for comfort.

Beaded-edge tyres – Encased rubber beads in channels on wheel rim.

Belt drive – A leather or fabric belt running from the engine or gearbox to the rear wheel.

BHP – A measure of engine output; the amount of power required to lift 33,000lb to a height of 1ft in a minute equals 1bhp.

BMCRC – British Motor Cycle Racing Club, formed in 1909.

BMF – British Motorcycle Federation.

Bore/stroke ratio – The ratio of an engine's cylinder diameter to its piston stroke.

Caliper – A clamping device containing hydraulically-operated pistons that forms part of a disc brake.

Cam – Device for opening and closing a valve.

Camshaft – The mounting shaft for the cam; can be in low, high or overhead position.

Carburettor – Used to produce the air/fuel mixture required by the engine.

Chain drive – Primary form of drive from engine to gearbox and secondary gearbox to rear wheel.

Combustion chamber – Area where the fuel/air mixture is compressed and ignited, between the piston and cylinder head.

Compression ratio – The amount by which the fuel/air mixture is compressed by the piston in the combustion chamber.

Crankcase – The casing enclosing the crankshaft and its attachments.

Crankshaft – The shaft that converts the vertical motion of the piston into a rotary movement.

Cylinder – Contains the piston and is capped by the cylinder head. Upper portion forms the combustion chamber where the fuel/air mixture is compressed and burnt to provide power.

Cylinder head – Caps the top of the cylinder. In a four-stroke engine, it usually carries the valves and, in some cases, the camshaft(s).

Damper – Fitted to slow the movement in the suspension system, or as a crankshaft balance.

Displacement – The engine capacity or amount of volume displaced by the movement of the piston from bottom dead centre to top dead centre.

Distributor – A gear-driven contact that sends high-tension current to the spark plugs.

DOHC – Double overhead camshaft.

Dry sump – An engine lubrication system in which the oil is contained in a separate reservoir and pumped to and from the engine by a pair of pumps.

Earles forks – A front fork design incorporating long leading links connected by a rigid pivot behind the front wheel.

Featherbed – A Norton frame, designed by Rex and Crommie McCandless, of Belfast, used for racing machines from 1950; road machines from 1953.

FIM – Federation Internationale Motorcycliste, controls motorcycle sport worldwide.

Flat-twin – An engine featuring two horizontally-opposed cylinders.

Float – A plastic or brass box that floats upon the fuel in a float chamber and operates the needle valve controlling the fuel flow.

Flywheel – Attached to the crankshaft, this heavy wheel smooths intermittent firing impulses and helps slow running.

Friction drive – An early form of drive using discs in contact instead of chains and gears.

Gearbox – Cased trains of pinion wheels that can be moved to provide alternative ratios.

Gear ratios – Differential rates of speed between sets of pinions to provide faster or slower rotation of the rear wheel in relation to the engine speed.

GP – Grand Prix, an international race to a fixed formula.

High camshaft – Mounted high up in the engine to shorten the pushrods in an ohv arrangement.

IOE – Inlet over exhaust, a common arrangement with an overhead inlet valve and side exhaust valve.

Leaf spring – Metal blades clamped and bolted together, used in early suspension systems.

Magneto – A high-tension dynamo that produces current for the ignition spark; superseded by coil ignition.

Main bearings – Bearings in which the crankshaft runs.

Manifold – Collection of pipes supplying fuel/air mixture or removing exhaust gases.

MCC – The Motor Cycling Club, which runs sporting events; formed in 1902.

Moped – A light motorcycle of under 50cc with pedals attached.

OHC – See Overhead camshaft.

Overhead camshaft – An engine design in which the camshaft (or camshafts) is carried in the cylinder head.

OHV – See Overhead valve.

Overhead valve – A valve mounted in the cylinder head.

Pinking – A distinctive noise produced by an engine with over-advanced ignition or inferior fuel.

Piston – Moves up and down the cylinder, drawing in fuel/air mixture, compressing it, being driven down by combustion and forcing spent gases out.

Post-vintage – A motorcycle made after December 31, 1930, and before January 1, 1945.

Pressure plate – The plate against which the clutch springs react to load the friction plates.

Pushrods – Operating rods for overhead valves, working from cams below the cylinder.

Rotary valve – A valve driven from the camshaft for inlet or exhaust and usually of a disc or cylindrical shape; for either two- or four-stroke engines.

SACU – Scottish Auto Cycle Union, which controls motorcycle sport in Scotland.

SAE – Society of Automotive Engineers. Used in a system of classifying engine oils such as SAE30, l0W/50, etc.

Shock absorber – A damper, used to control vertical movement of suspension, or to cushion a drive train.

Silencer – Device fitted to the exhaust system of an engine in which the pressure of the exhaust gases is reduced to lessen noise.

Swinging arm – Rear suspension by radius arms, which carry the wheel and are attached to the frame at their forward ends.

Torque – Twisting force in a shaft; can be measured to determine at what speed an engine develops most torque.

Index to Advertisers

Antiques Magazine 166
Atlantic Motorcycles 117
Len Baker 159
Keith Benton 166
Peter Best Insurance Services Ltd . . . . *front endpaper*
Bonhams & Brooks . . . . *back endpaper, back cover*
Boyer-Bransden Electronics Ltd . . . . *front endpaper*
Cake Street Classics 165
Classic & Motorcycle Mechanics 164
Classic Bike Guide 170
The Classic Motor Cycle 164
Classic Racer . . . . *back endpaper*
Cotswold Classics 4
Devitt DA 6
Elk Engineering 39
The Finishing Touch 166
Footman James & Co Ltd . . . . *front endpaper*
Bill Little Motorcycles 17

Christopher Marshall 79
Mayfair Motors 151
Miller's Club 165
Miller's Publications 109, 168
Moto Guzzi Club 67
North Leicester Motorcycles 71
Old Bike Mart 164
Oxney Motorcycles 29
Palmer Snell 165
Planet Motorcycles . . . . *front endpaper*
Pollard's Motorcycles 81
Pooks Motor Bookshop 163
Peter Smith Motorcycles 59
Verralls (Handcross) Ltd 95
The Vintage Motor Cycle Club 173
Mick Walker 141
George Yeoman's Motor Cycle Spares 6
Yesterday's 155

Bibliography

Bacon, Roy; *British Motorcycles of the 1930s*, Osprey, 1986
Bacon, Roy; *Honda The Early Classic Motorcycles*, Osprey, 1985
Bacon, Roy; *BSA Twins & Triples*, Osprey, 1980
Davis, Ivor; *It's a Triumph*, Haynes, 1980
Tragatsch, Erwin, ed; *The New Illustrated Encyclopaedia of Motorcycles*, Grange Books, 1993
Vanhouse, Norman; *BSA Competition History*, Haynes, 1986
Walker, Mick; *BMW Twins The Complete Story*, Crowood, 1998
Walker, Mick; *Laverda Twins & Triples The Complete Story*, Crowood, 1999
Walker, Mick; *Moto Guzzi Twins The Complete Story*, Crowood, 1998

Walker, Mick; *MV Agusta Fours The Complete Story*, Crowood, 2000
Walker, Mick; *Gilera The Complete Story*, Crowood, 2000
Walker, Mick; *Ducati, Fabio Taglioni and his World Beating Motorcycles*, Sutton, 2000
Walker, Mick; *British Racing Motorcycles*, Redline, 1998
Walker, Mick; *Italian Racing Motorcycles*, Redline, 1999
Walker, Mick; *German Racing Motorcycles*, Redline, 1999
Walker, Mick; *European Racing Motorcycles*, Redline, 2000
Walker, Mick; *Manx Norton*, Redline, 2000
Walker, Mick; *Hamlyn History of Motorcycling*, Hamlyn, 1997
Webster, Mike; *Classic Scooters*, Parragon, 1997
Woollett, Mick; *Norton*, Osprey, 1992

Directory of Museums

ARE Classic Bike Collection, 285 Worplesdon Road, Guildford, Surrey GU2 6XN Tel: 01483 232006
50 bikes & memorabilia. Open Mon & Fri 9am–1pm, Tues & Thurs 9am–5pm.

Atwell-Wilson Motor Museum, Downside, Stockley Lane, Calne, Wiltshire SN11 0NF Tel: 01249 813119
Over 60 cars & vintage, post vintage and classic motorcycles. Open Mon–Thurs & Sun Apr–Oct 11–5pm, Nov–Mar & Good Friday 11–4pm.

Automobilia Motor Museum, The Old Mill, Terras Road, St Stephen, St Austell, Cornwall PL26 7RX Tel: 01726 823092
Around 50 vehicles 1900–66 & motorcycles. Open daily 10–4pm except Saturday in Apr, May & Oct, daily June–Sept 10–5pm.

Battlesbridge Motorcycle Museum, Muggeridge Farm, Maltings Road, Battlesbridge, Essex SS11 7RF Tel: 01268 769392
Collection of classic motorcycles & scooters. Open Sun 10.30–4pm.

Bradford Industrial Museum, Moorside Mills, Moorside Road, Bradford, Yorkshire BD2 3HP Tel: 01274 631756
General industrial museum including Jowett cars & Panther and Scott motorcycles. Open Tues–Fri & Bank Holidays, 10–5pm.

Bristol Industrial Museum, Prince's Wharf, City Docks, Bristol, BS1 4RN Tel: 0117 925 1470
Douglas machines, including the only surviving V4 of 1908 and a 1972 Quasar. Open Tues–Sun 10–1pm & 2–5pm. Closed Thurs & Fri, also Good Friday, December 25–27 & January 1.

Brooklands Museum, Brooklands Road, Weybridge, Surrey KT13 0QN Tel: 01932 857381
Motorsport and aviation museum. Around 20 motorcycles pre WWII. Open daily except Mon, Good Friday & Christmas 10–5 in Summer, 10–4 in Winter.

Caister Castle Car Collection, Caister-on-Sea, Nr Great Yarmouth, Norfolk Tel: 01572 787251
Cars & motorcycles from 1893. Open daily mid-May–end Sept, closed Sat.

The Combe Martin Motorcycle Collection, Cross Street, Combe Martin, Ilfracombe, Devon EX34 0DH Tel: 01271 882346
Around 100 classic and British motorcycles. Open daily May–Oct 10–5pm.

Cotswold Motoring Museum & Toy Collection, Sherbourne Street, Bourton-on-the-Water, Nr Cheltenham, Gloucestershire GL54 2BY Tel: 01451 821 255
Collection of advertising signs, toys and motorcycles. Home of the Brough Superior Co and "Brum", the small open 1920s car that has a television series. Open daily Feb–Nov, 10–6pm.

Craven Collection of Classic Motorcycles, Brockfield Villa, Stockton-on-the-Forest, Yorkshire YO3 9UE Tel: 01904 488461/400493
Over 200 vintage & post-war motorcycles. Open first Sun of every month & Bank Holiday Mon 10–4pm. Club visits & private parties arranged.

Foulkes-Halbard of Filching, Filching Manor, Jevington Road, Wannock, Polegate, East Sussex BN26 5QA Tel: 01323 487838
About 100 cars 1893–1993 & 30 motorcycles including American pre-1940s ex Steve McQueen. Open Easter–Oct, Thurs–Sun, 10.30–4pm.

Geeson Bros. Motorcycle Museum and Workshop, South Witham, Grantham, Lincolnshire Tel: 01572 767280/768195
Over 80 motorcycles restored since 1965 by the Geeson brothers.

Grampian Transport Museum, Alford, Aberdeenshire, Scotland AB33 8AE Tel: 019755 62292 info@gtm.org.uk
Displays and working exhibits tracing the history of travel and transport in the locality. Open Apr 2–Oct 31, 10–5pm.

Haynes Sparkford Motor Museum, Sparkford, Yeovil, Somerset BA22 7LH Tel: 01963 440804
Haynes Publishing Company museum with collection of vintage, veteran & classic cars & motorcycles. Cafe, shop. Open daily Summer 9.30–5.30pm, Winter 10–4pm, except Dec 25–26 and Jan 1.

Historic Vehicles Collection of C. M. Booth, Falstaff Antiques, 63–67 High Street, Rolvenden, Kent TN17 4LP Tel: 01580 241234
Morgan three-wheelers, some motorbikes and memorabilia. Open Mon–Sat, 10–6pm.

Lakeland Motor Museum, Holker Hall & Gardens, Cark-in-Cartmel, Grange-over-Sands, South Lakeland, Cumbria LA11 7PL
150 classic and vintage cars, tractors, cycles and engines including about 40 motorcycles. Open end Mar–end Oct, Sun–Fri 10.30–4.45pm, closed Sat.

Llangollen Motor Museum, Pentrefelin, Llangollen, Wales LL20 8EE Tel: 01978 860324
Over 20 cars, 10 motorcycles, signs, tools & parts. Open daily 10–5pm, Easter–Sept.

London Motorcycle Museum, Ravenor Farm, 29 Oldfield Lane South, Greenford, Middlesex UB6 9LB Tel: 020 8579 1248/020 8575 6644 thelmm@hotmail.com www.motorcycle-uk.com/lmm.htm
Collection of around 50 British motorcycles. Open weekends.

Madog Cars & Motorcycle Museum, Snowdon Street, Porthmadog, Wales LL49 9DF Tel: 01758 713618
15 cars and nearly 70 motorcycles plus memorabilia. Open Mon–Sat 10–5pm, May–Sept.

Midland Motor Museum, Stanmore Hall, Stourbridge Road, Bridgnorth, Shropshire WV15 6DT Tel: 01746 762992
Collection of 60 cars and 30 motorcycles. Open daily 10.30–5pm except December 25–26.

Sammy Miller Museum, Bashley Manor, Bashley Cross Roads, New Milton, Hampshire BH25 6TF Tel: 01425 620777
Around 200 bikes plus artefacts and memorabilia. Open daily 10–4pm.

Moray Motor Museum, Bridge Street, Elgin, Scotland IV30 2DE Tel: 01343 544933
Cars & motorcycles plus memorabilia and diecast models. Open daily Easter–Oct, 11–5pm.

Mouldsworth Motor Museum, Smithy Lane, Mouldsworth, Chester, Cheshire CH3 8AR Tel: 01928 731781
Over 60 cars, motorcycles and early bicycles housed in 1937 art deco building. Open Sun March–end Nov 12–5pm inc all bank holidays & weekends, also Weds in July & Aug 1–5pm.

Murray's Motorcycle Museum, Bungalow Corner, Mountain Road, Snaefell, Isle of Man Tel: 01624 861719
140 machines, including Mike Hailwood's 250cc Mondial and Honda 125cc. Open May–Sept 10–5pm.

Museum of British Road Transport, St. Agnes Lane, Hales Street, Coventry, Warwickshire CV1 1PN Tel: 024 7683 2425 museum@mbrt.co.uk www.mbrt.co.uk
Around 100 motorcycles. Open daily 10–5pm except Dec 24–26.

Museum of Transport, Kelvin Hall, 1 Bunhouse Road, Glasgow, Scotland G3 8DP Tel: 0141 357 2656/2720
A museum devoted to the history of transport on the land. Open daily 10–5pm, Sunday 11–5 except Dec 25 & Jan 1.

Myreton Motor Museum, Aberlady, Longniddry, East Lothian, Scotland EH32 0PZ Tel: 01875 870288
Cars, motorcycles, commercials and WWII military vehicles. Open daily from 10am except Dec 25. Parties & coaches welcome.

National Motor Museum, Brockenhurst, Beaulieu, Hampshire SO42 7ZN Tel: 01590 612123/612345
Over 200 cars, 60 motorcycles and memorabilia. Open daily from 10am except Dec 25.

National Motorcycle Museum, Coventry Road, Bickenhill, Solihull, West Midlands B92 0EJ Tel: 01675 443311
Over 650 restored machines. Open daily 10–6pm except Dec 25–26.

National Museum of Scotland, The Granton Centre, 242 West Granton Road, Edinburgh, Scotland EH1 1JF Tel: 0131 551 4106
Small display of engines and complete machines including the world's first 4-cylinder motorcycle, an 1895 Holden. Tours available, telephone to book in advance.

Newburn Hall Motor Museum, 35 Townfield Gardens, Newburn, Tyne & Wear NE15 8PY Tel: 0191 264 2977
About 50 cars and 10 motorcycles. Open daily 10–6pm except Mon.

Norfolk Motorcycle Museum, Station Approach, North Walsham, Norfolk NR28 0DS Tel: 01692 406266
100 motorcycles 1920s to 1960s. Open daily 10–4.30pm, closed Sun in Winter.

Ramsgate Motor Museum, West Cliff Hall, Ramsgate, Kent CT11 9JX Tel: 01843 581948
Open Apr–Nov, 10.30–5.30pm. Winter Sun, 10–5pm.

Shuttleworth Collection, Old Warden Aerodrome, Nr Biggleswade, Bedfordshire SG18 9EP Tel: 01767 627288
Collection of flying pre-1940 aircraft and veteran and vintage vehicles including 15 motorcycles.

Stanford Hall Motorcycle Museum, Stanford Hall, Lutterworth, Leicestershire LE17 6DH Tel: 01788 860250
A collection of older machines and racers. Open Sat, Sun, Bank Holiday Mon and Tues, Easter–Sept, 2.30–5.30pm. (12 noon–6pm when a special event is taking place.).

Stondon Museum, Station Road, Lower Stondon, Henlow, Bedfordshire SG16 6JN Tel: 01462 850339
Over 320 transport exhibits including Bentleys and over 30 motorcycles. Open daily 10–5pm.

Ulster Folk & Transport Museum, Cultra, Holywood, Co. Down, Northern Ireland BT18 0EU Tel: 028 90 428 428
Includes 70–100 motorcycles. Open all year round 10.30–5/6.00pm, Sundays 12 noon–6.00pm, except Christmas.

Western Lakes Motor Museum, The Maltings, Brewery Lane, Cockermouth, Cumbria Tel: 01900 824448
Some 45 cars and 17 motorcycles from Vintage to Formula 3. Open daily 10–5pm Mar–Oct, closed Jan, other dates weekends only.

Whitewebbs Museum of Transport, Whitewebbs Road, Enfield, Middlesex EN2 9HW Tel: 020 8367 1898
Collection of commercial vehicles, cars and 20–30 motorcycles. Telephone for opening times.

Directory of Motorcycle Clubs

If you wish to be included in next year's directory, or if you have a change of address or telephone number, please inform us by 27 April 2002.

ABC Owners' Club, D A Hales, The Hedgerows, Sutton St Nicholas, Hereford HR1 3BU

Aircooled RD Club, Susan Gregory (Membership Secretary), 6 Baldwin Rd, Burnage, Greater Manchester M19 1LY

AMC Owners' Club, c/o Terry Corley, 12 Chilworth Gardens, Sutton, Surrey SM1 3SP

Amicale du Tour du Dauphine, 82 rue de la Chapelle, 38150 Roussillon, France

Ariel Owners' Motor Cycle Club, Andy Hemingway, 80 Pasture Lane, Clayton, Bradford, Yorkshire BD14 6LN

Association of Pioneer Motorcyclists, Mrs J MacBeath (Secretary), 'Heatherbank', May Close, Headley, Nr Bordon, Hampshire GU35 8LR

Bantam Enthusiasts' Club, c/o Vic Salmon, 16 Oakhurst Close, Walderslade, Chatham, Kent ME5 9AN

Benelli Motobi Riders' Club, Steve Peace, 43 Sherrington Rd, Ipswich, Suffolk IP1 4HT

Best Feet Forward MCC, Paul Morris (Membership Secretary), 43 Finedon Rd, Irthlingborough, Northamptonshire NN9 5TY

The BMW Club, Bowbury House, Kirk Langley, Derbyshire DE6 5NJ

Bristol & District Sidecar Club, 158 Fairlyn Drive, Kingswood, Bristol BS15 4PZ

Bristol Genesis Motorcycle Club, Burrington, 1a Bampton Close, Headley Park, Bristol BS13 7QZ Tel: 0117 978 2584

British Motor Bike Owners' Club, c/o Ray Peacock, Crown Inn, Shelfanger, Diss, Norfolk IP22 2DL

British Motorcycle Association, Pete Reed, AMCA, 28 Mill Park, Hawks Green Lane, Cannock, Staffordshire WS11 2XT

British Motorcycle Club of Guernsey, c/o Ron Le Cras, East View, Village De Putron, St Peter Port, Guernsey, Channel Islands GY1

British Motorcycle Owners' Club, c/o Phil Coventry, 59 Mackenzie St, Bolton, Lancashire BL1 6QP

British Motorcycle Riders' Club, Geoff Ives, PO Box 2, Eynsham, Witney, Oxfordshire OX8 1RW

British Motorcyclists' Federation, Jack Wiley House, 129 Seaforth Ave, Motspur Park, New Malden, Surrey KT3 6JU

British Two-Stroke Club, Mrs Lynda Tanner (Membership Secretary), 259 Harlestone Rd, Duston, Northampton, Northamptonshire NN5 6DD Tel: 01604 581516

BSA Owners' Club, Chris Taylor, PO Box 436, Peterborough, Cambridgeshire PE4 7WD christaylor@natsecbsaoc.screaming.net

CBX Riders Club (United Kingdom), Mel Watkins, 9 Trem Y Mynydd, Abergele, Clwyd LL22 9YY

Christian Motorcyclists' Association, PO Box 113, Wokingham, Berkshire RG11 5UB cma-admin@bike.org.uk www.bike.org.uk/cma/

Classic Kawasaki Club (Formerly The Kawasaki Triples Club), PO Box 235, Nottingham NG8 6DT

Classic Racing Motorcycle Club Ltd, 6 Cladgate Grove, Wombourne, Wolverhampton, West Midlands WV5 8JS

Cossack Owners' Club, Alan Mottram (Membership Secretary), 19 The Villas, West End, Stoke on Trent, Staffordshire ST4 5AQ

Cotton Owners' Club, P. Turner, Coombehayes, Sidmouth Rd, Lyme Regis, Dorset DT7 3EQ

Derbyshire and Staffordshire Classic Motorcycle Club, 51 Westwood Park, Newhall, Swadlincote, Derbyshire DE11 0RS Tel: 01283 214542

Dot Motorcycle Club, c/o Chris Black, 115 Lincoln Ave, Clayton, Newcastle-under-Lyne ST5 3AR

Edge & District Vintage Motorcycle Club, 10 Long Lane, Larkton, Malpas, Cheshire SY14 8LP

Excelsior Talisman Enthusiasts, Ginger Hall, Village Way, Little Chalfont, Buckinghamshire HP7 9PU

Exeter British Motorcycle Club, c/o Bill Jones, 7 Parkens Cross Lane, Pinhoe, Exeter, Devon EX1 3TA

Exeter Classic Motorcycle Club, c/o Martin Hatcher, 11 Newcombe St, Heavitree, Exeter, Devon EX1 2TG

Federation of Sidecars, Jeff Reynard, 5 Ethel St, Beechcliffe, Keighley, Yorkshire BD20 6AN

Fellowship of Christian Motorcyclists, Phil Crow, 6 St Anne's Close, Formby, Liverpool, Merseyside L37 7AX

FJ Owners' Club, Lee & Mick Beck (Membership Secretaries), 1 Glen Crescent, Stamford, Lincolnshire PE9 1SW

Forgotten Racing Club, Mrs Chris Pinches, 73 High St, Morton, Bourne, Lincolnshire PE10 0NR

Francis Barnett Owners' Club, Sue Dorling (Club Secretary), Clouds Hill, 5 Blacklands Rd, Upper Bucklebury, Nr Reading, Berkshire RG7 6QP Tel: 01635 864256

Gold Star Owners' Club, Maurice Evans, 211 Station Rd, Mickleover, Derby DE3 5FE

Goldwing Owners' Club, 82 Farley Close, Little Stoke, Bristol BS12 6HG

Greeves Owners' Club, c/o Dave McGregor, 4 Longshaw Close, North Wingfield, Chesterfield, Derbyshire S42 5QR

Harley Davidson Riders' Club of Great Britain, SAE to The Membership Secretary, PO Box 62, Newton Abbott, Devon TQ12 2QE

Harley Davidson UK, The Bell Tower, High St, Brackley, Northamptonshire NN13 7DT Tel: 01280 700101 www.harley-davidson.co.uk www.harley-davidson.com

Harley Owners' Group, HOG UK, The Bell Tower, High St, Brackley, Northamptonshire NN13 7DT Tel: 01280 700101

Hedingham Sidecar Owners' Club, John Dean (Membership Secretary), Birchendale Farm, Fole Lane, Stoke-on-Trent, Staffordshire ST10 4HL

Hesketh Owners' Club, Peter White, 1 Northfield Rd, Soham, Cambridgeshire CB7 5UE

Honda Monkey Club, 28 Newdigate Rd, off Red Lane, Coventry, Warwickshire CV6 5ES

Honda Owners' Club (GB), The Membership Secretary, 61 Vicarage Rd, Ware, Hertfordshire SG12 7BE Tel: 01932 787111

Indian Motorcycle Club, c/o John Chatterton (Membership Secretary), 183 Buxton Rd, Newtown, Disley, Stockport, Cheshire SK12 2RA Tel: 01663 747106

International Laverda Owners' Club, c/o Alan Cudipp, 29 Claypath Rd, Hetton-le-Hole, Houghton-le-Spring, Tyne & Wear DH5 0EL

International Motorcyclists' Tour Club, James Clegg, 238 Methane Rd, Netherton, Huddersfield, Yorkshire HD4 7HL

Italian Motorcycle Owners' Club (GB), John Riches, 12 Wappenham Rd, Abthorpe, Towcester, Northamptonshire NN12 8QU

Jawa-CZ Owners' Club, John Blackburn, 39 Bignor Rd, Sheffield, Yorkshire S6 1JD

Kawasaki GT Club, D. Shucksmith (Club Secretary), Flat K, Lichfield Court, Lichfield Rd, Walsall, West Midlands WS4 2DX Tel: 01922 37441

Kawasaki Riders' Club, Gemma Court, 1 Concord House, Kirmington, Humberside DN39 6YP

The Kettle Club, Shaun Chandler, 66 Provene Gardens, Waltham Chase, Southampton, Hampshire SO32 2LE

Kickstart Club Torbay, c/o Eddie Hine, 12 Vale Rd, Kingskerswell, Newton Abbot, Devon TQ12 5AE

Laverda Owners' Club, c/o Ray Sheepwash, 8 Maple Close, Swanley, Kent BR8 7YN

Leader and Arrow Club, Stan Davies, 11 Hollins Lane, Tilstock, Whitchurch SY13 3NT

Leominster Classic MCC, Ron Moore, The Yew Tree, Gorsty, Pembridge, Herefordshire HR6 9JF

The London Douglas Motorcycle Club Ltd, Reg Holmes, 48 Standish Ave, Stoke Lodge, Patchway, Bristol BS34 6AG www.douglasmotorcycles.co.uk

London Sidecar Club, 107 Silverweed Rd, Walderslade, Chatham, Kent ME5 0RF

Maico Owners' Club, c/o Phil Hingston, 'No Elms', Goosey, Faringdon, Oxfordshire SN7 8PA Tel: 01367 710408

Marston Sunbeam Register, Ray Jones, 37 Sandhurst Drive, Penn, Wolverhampton, West Midlands WV4 5RJ
Morini Riders' Club, c/o Kevin Bennett, 1 Glebe Farm Cottages, Sutton Veny, Warminster, Wiltshire BA12 7AS Tel: 01985 840055
Moto Guzzi Club GB, Paulette Foyle (Membership Secretary), 43 Poplar Ave, Bedworth, Nuneaton, Warwickshire CV12 9EW
MV Agusta Owners' Club of GB, Liz Cornish, Station House, 57 Briar Close, Evesham, Worcestershire WR11 4JJ www.manxman.co.im/mvagusta
MVT, PO Box 6, Fleet, Hampshire GU52 6GE
National Association of Supertwins, Sue Beneke, 10A Queen's Rd, Evesham, Worcestershire
National Autocycle & Cyclemotor Club, Rob Harknett, 1 Parkfields, Roydon, Harlow, Essex CM19 5JA Tel: 01279 792329
National Sprint Association, Judith Sykes (Secretary), 10 Compton St, Clifton, York YO3 6LE
National Trailers Owners' Club (NaTo), 47c Uplands Ave, Rowley, Regis Warley, West Midlands B65 9PU
New Imperial Owners' Association, Mrs J E Jarvis, Lyndhurst House, Victoria Rd, Hayling Island, Hampshire PO11 0LU Tel: 023 9246 9098
North Devon British Motorcycle Owners' Club, D E Davies (Hon Secretary), 47 Old Town, Bideford, Devon EX39 3BH Tel: 01237 472237
Norton Owners' Club, Colin Coleman, 110 Skegby Rd, Annesley Woodhouse, Nottinghamshire NG17 9FF
Norton Owners' Club, c/o Philip Hill (Secretary), 11 Hammond Close, Thatcham, Newbury, Berkshire RG19 4FF
Norton Rotary Enthusiasts' Club, Alan Jones, 112 Fairfield Crescent, Newhall, Swadlingcote DE11 0TB
Panther Owners' Club, Graham & Julie Dibbins, Oakdene, 22 Oak St, Netherton, Dudley, West Midlands DY2 9LJ
Ponthir British Motorcycle Club, 44 Emerald St, Reath, Cardiff CF24 1QB
Racing 50 Enthusiasts' Club, Chris Alty, 14a Kestrel Park, Ashhurst, Skelmersdale, Lancashire WN8 6TB
Raleigh Safety Seven and Early Reliant Owners' Club incorporating Historic Raleigh Motorcycle Club, Mick Sleap, 17 Courtland Ave, Chingford, London E4 6DU Tel: 020 8524 6310
Rolls Royce Vintage & Classic Motorcycle Club, Ken Birch, 111 Havenbaulk Lane, Littleover, Derby DE23 7AD
Rotary Owners' Club, c/o David Cameron, Dunbar, Ingatestone Rd, Highwood, Chelmsford, Essex CM1 3QU rotaryoc@aol.com
Royal Automobile Club, PO Box 700, Bristol BS99 1RB
Royal Enfield Owners' Club, Sylvia and Mick Seager, 30/32 Causeway, Burgh-Le-Marsh, Skegness PE24 5LT
Rudge Enthusiasts' Club Ltd, Bloomsbury, 13 Lade Fort Crescent, Lydd-on-Sea, Romney Marsh, Kent TN29 9YG Tel: 01797 367029 www.rudge.ndirect.co.uk
Scott Owners' Club, Brian Marshall (Press Officer), Walnut Cottage, Abbey Lane, Aslockton, Nottingham NG13 9AE Tel: 01949 851027
Shrivenham Motorcycle Club, 12-14 Townsend Rd, Shrivenham, Swindon, Wiltshire SN6 8AS
Sidecar Register, c/o John Proctor, 112 Briarlyn Rd, Birchencliffe, Huddersfield, Yorkshire HD3 3NW
South Wales Sunbeam MCC, Kate Baxter, 17 Heol Gelynog, Beddau, Pontypridd, South Wales CF38 2SG
Street Specials Motorcycle Club inc Rickman O/C, Harris O/C & Featherbed O/C, c/o Dominic Dawson, 12 St Mark's Close, Gosport, Hampshire PO12 2DB
Sunbeam MCC Ltd, Ian McGill, 13 Victoria Rd, Horley, Surrey RH6 9BN. A club for all makes pre-1931
Sunbeam Owners' Club, Stewart Engineering, Church Terrace, Harbury, Leamington Spa, Warwickshire CV33 9HL
Sunbeam Owners' Fellowship, c/o Stewart Engineering, Church Terrace, Harbury, Nr Leamington Spa, Warwickshire CV33 9HL
Suzuki Owners' Club, PO Box 7, Egremont, Cumbria CA22 2GE
Tamworth & District Classic Motorcycle Club, Mrs Gemma Smith, 21 Tannery Close, Atherstone, Warwickshire CV9 1JS

Tiger Cub & Terrier Register, Mike Estall, 24 Main Rd, Edingale, Tamworth, Staffordshire B79 9HY Tel: 01827 383415
Tour du Dauphine en Petrolettes, 38550 St Maurice L'Exil, France
Trail Riders' Fellowship, Tony Stuart, 'Cambrea', Trebetherick, Wadebridge, Cornwall PL27 6SG
Trident and Rocket 3 Owners' Club, John Atkins, (Club Secretary), 47 Underhill Rd, Benfleet, Essex SS7 1EP
Triumph Motorcycle Club, 6 Hortham Lane, Almondsbury, Bristol BS12 4JH
Triumph Owners' MCC, Mrs M M Mellish (General Secretary), 4 Douglas Ave, Harold Wood, Romford, Essex RM3 0UT
Triumph Triples Club, H J Allen, 50 Sylmond Gardens, Rushden, Northamptonshire NN10 9EJ
Velocette Owners' Club, Vic Blackman (Secretary), 1 Mayfair, Tilehurst, Reading, Berkshire RG3 4RA
Veteran Grass Track Riders' Association (VGTRA), Carl Croucher, 4 Whitmore St, Maidstone ME16 9JU
Veteran Vespa Club, Ashley Lenton, 3 Vincent Rd, Croydon, Surrey CR0 6ED
Vincent HRD Owners' Club, c/o John Wilding (Information Officer), Little Wildings, Fairhazel, Piltdown, Uckfield, East Sussex TN22 3XB Tel: 01825 763529
Vintage Japanese Motorcycle Club, PO Box 515, Dartford, Kent DA1 3RE
Vintage Motor Cycle Club, Allen House, Wetmore Rd, Burton-on-Trent, Staffordshire DE14 1TR Tel: 01283 540557
Vintage Motor Scooter Club, c/o Ian Harrop, 11 Ivanhoe Ave, Lowton St Lukes, Nr Warrington, Cheshire WA3 2HX
Virago Owners' Club, John Bryning (President), River Green House, Great Sampford, Saffron Walden, Essex CB10 2RS
Vmax Club, H Doyle, 87 Honiton Rd, Wyken, Coventry, Warwickshire CV2 3EF
Yamaha Riders' Club, Alan Cheney, 11 Lodden Rd, Farnborough, Hampshire GU14 9NR
Z1 Owners' Club, c/o Jerry Humpage, 90 Delves Crescent, Walsall, West Midlands WS5 4LT
Zundapp Bella Enthusiasts' Club, Bill Dorling (Chairman), 5 Blacklands Rd, Upper Bucklebury, Reading, Berkshire RG7 6QP

Index

Italic numbers denote colour pages; **bold** numbers refer to information and pointer boxes

A

Aermacchi 11
  250 Ala Verde (1961) 11
  250 Sprint H (1965) 11
  350 Sprint SG (1971) 11
  Ala Azzurra (1961) 11
  Ala d'Oro (1962) 146;
  (c1966) 147; (c1968)
  148
  Ala Verda Café Racer
  (1962) 159
  Sprint (1966) 11
  SS350 (1973) 11; (1974)
  11
  Works Model Ala d'Oro
  (1972) 148
AJS 12–15
  7R (1950) 142; (1955)
  145; (1955/61) 145;
  (1956) 145
  500 (1928) 13
  Big Port (1926) 12;
  (1927) 12; (1928) 13
  Model 9 (1930) 13
  Model 14 CSR (1966) 15
  Model 16 (1959) 14
  Model 16M (1947) 13
  Model 16MS (1958) 14;
  16MS (1959) 14
  Model 20 (1960) 14
  Model 22 (1936) 13
  Model 31 (1960) 14, 15
  Model 185 (1951) 13
  Model D (1915) 12
  Model D1 (1924) 12
  R10 (1937) 129
  V-twin (1927) 12
Ambassador Supreme 2T
  (1958) 15
Ariel 16–19
  4G Mk II and Watsonian
  Sidecar (1953) 155
  4G Mk II Square Four
  (c1954) 18
  Arrow 200 (1964) 19
  Brooklands Square Four
  (1931) 140
  FH Huntmaster (1958) 19
  Golden Arrow Replica
  (1961) 19
  KH (1952) 17
  Leader (1958) 18;
  (1964) 49
  LH Colt (1957) 18
  NH (1957) 18
  NH Red Hunter (1951) 16
  NH350 Red Hunter
  (1953) 17; (1954) 17
  Square Four (1932) 16;
  (1950s) 18
  Square Four 4G Mk II
  (1953) 17
  Square-Four Special
  (1932/52) 157
  VB (1938) 16; (1956) 18
  VB31 and Sidecar (1931)
  155
  VH (1955) 49

VH350 (1951) 17
VH Red Hunter (1954) 17
automobilia 128, 162–3

B

BD 500 Single 19
Beardmore-Precision Model
  D (1923) 20
Benelli 20–1
  125 Leoncino 2T (1954)
  20
  250 Sport (1946) 20
  500 Quattro (1976) 21;
  (1977) 21
  750 SE1 (1975) 21
  Roadster (1934) 20
Berneg 150 Twin (1955) 21
Bianchi MT61 (1958) 135
Bimota SB8/R (2000) 22
BM Bonvicini BO (1958) 22
BMW 22–4
  R12 (1936) 23
  R35 (c1939) 23
  R50 (1960) 23
  R50/2 (1965) 138
  R51 (1938) 23
  R51/3 (1953) 23
  R60/2 (1960) 23
  R62 (1929) 22
  R75 Combination (1943)
  134
  R80 G/S (1981) 49
  R90S (1973) **24**
  R100CS (1981) 24
Bown Autocycle (1951) 137
Bradbury (1913) 24
Brough-Superior 25
  SS80 (1924) 25; (1935)
  25
  SS100 (1938) 25
BSA 26–32, 163
  A7 (1955) 28
  A7 Shooting Star (1954)
  50; (1955) 28; (1960) 29
  A7 Star Twin (1948) 27
  A7 Twin (1949) 27
  A10 Chopper (c1959)
  158
  A10 Golden Flash (1951)
  27; (1955) 27; (1961)
  29, 50
  A50 Royal Star (1970) 32
  A50/A65 (1962) **31**
  A65 Lightning (1965)
  30; (1966) 30; (1967) 31
  A65 Star (1965) 30
  A65T Thunderbolt (1967)
  31
  B20 (1937) 26
  B25 (1969) 32
  B31 (1946) 26, 49;
  (1954) 27
  B34 (1951) 27
  B34 Trials Replica (1954)
  130
  B40 (1962) 29
  B44 Shooting Star (1969)
  32

B50 Gold Star (1971) 32
Bantam D1 (1948) 26
Bantam D7 (1966) 30
Bantam D175 (1969) 51
Beagle (1963) 30
BSA/Greeves Special
  (1966) 147
C11G (1956) 29
C12 (1956) 28
C15 (1965) 30
C15 Star (1962) 29, 50
D10 Supreme (1967) 31
D14/4 (1968) 31
DB34 Gold Star (1956)
  50
Firebird (c1971) 32
G14 (1939) 26
Gold Star (1960) 131
Gold Star Competition
  (1960) 131
Gold Star Scrambler
  (1959) 131
J12 (1934) 26
M20 (1948) 26; (1955)
  50
M21 (1955) 28
M21 and AA Patrol
  Sidecar (1960) 156
Rocket Gold Star (1962)
  29, 30
Starfire (1969) 32;
  (1971) 32
Thunderbolt (1971) 32
ZB32 Works Trials (1950)
  129
Bultaco Sherpa (1972) 133
Butler-Greeves Trials Outfit
  (1964) 156

C

Cagiva 650GT Alazzura
  (1986) 33
Capriolo 33
  75 Sport (1953) 33
  75 TV (1962) 33
  Cento 50 (1955) 33
Carnielli Graziella (1979)
  136
Chater-Lea Single (1928)
  34
Cimatti 34
  Sport (1960) 34
Clément De Dion et Bouton
  2.25hp Tricycle and
  Trailer (1898) 128
Comet 35
  Twin (1955) 35
Cotton Racer (1930s) 140
Coventry Eagle F25 (1931)
  35

D

dirt bikes 129–33
DKW RT200VS (1958) 36
Dot
  Demon Scrambler (1963)
  132
  Trials (1959) 130

Douglas 36–7
  2-Speed (1914) 36
  2½hp (1914) 36
  Dragonfly (1957) 37, 51
  Model OB (1924) 37
  Model T6 (1930) 37
Dresda Triton 650 (1960s)
  159
Ducati 37–43
  55E (1955) 137
  125 Regolarita (1975)
  133
  125 Turismo (1959) 37
  175 F3 (1959) 146
  175 Sport (1958) 37
  175cc Turismo (1957)
  38
  200 TS (1960) 38
  250 Desmo Disc (1974)
  40
  250 Mk 3D (1970) 39
  350 Desmo (1974) 52
  350 Desmo Silver
  Shotgun (1972) 40
  350 GTV (1979) 42
  350 Mk 3D (1969/70) 39
  350 Scrambler (1971)
  52
  350 XL Pantah (1983) 43
  450 (1972/74) 149
  450 Mk 3 (1972) 40
  500 GTL (1977) 41
  500 Sport Desmo (1977)
  41
  600 SL Pantah (1982) 42
  600 TL Pantah Police
  (1984) 138
  750 F1 (1985) 43
  750 Sport (1972) 39;
  (1974) 41
  750GT (1973) 40;
  (1974) 40
  851 Monoposto (1989)
  43
  860 GT ES (1975) 41
  900 GTS (1978) 41
  900 S2 Special (1983)
  160
  900 SS (1978/80) 42;
  (1980) 42
  Brio 100 (1966) 152
  Cucciolo (1950) 137
  Elite Racer (1960) 146
  Mach 1 (1965) 51
  Mach 1 Replica (1960s)
  38
  MHR Mille (1985) 43
  Mike Hailwood Replica
  (1979) 42
  Monza (1966) 38;
  (1967) 38
  Pantah Special (1983) 43
Dunelt SD (1931) 44

E

Excelsior
  F10 Consort (1960) 44
  Manxman (1936) 126

F
FN 44
 (1912) 44
 Four (1911) 44
Francis-Barnett J43 Seagull
 (1939) 45

G
Gilera 45
 98 Sei Giorni (1960s) 132
 98 Turismo (1970) 45
 125 Turismo (1949) 45
 150 Turismo (1953) 45
 300B (1960) 45
 CX125 (1991) 45
 San Remo (c1948) *126*
 VTGS (c1939) 141
Greeves
 Challenger 36MX4
 (1969) 133
 Scottish Trials (1958) 131

H
Hagon JAP Speedway
 (1957) 130
Harley-Davidson 1000
 V-Twin and Sidecar
 (1923) *128*
Harris Ducati TT F2 Replica
 (1985) 160
Henderson Four (1925) 46
Hesketh 46
 V1000 (1982) 46;
 (1984) 46
Honda 47–8
 Ascot FT500 (1982) 48
 C92 (1964) 47
 CB400F (1977) 48
 CB450 (1966) 47;
 (c1965) 47
 CB500 Four (1971) 47
 CB750 K2 (1972) *52*
 CB750 K5 (1975) 48
 CB1100R (1981) 149
 CD200TB (1981) 48
 CL360 (1976) 48
 CR93 (c1965) *127*
 CX500 (1981) 48, *52*
 ST70 (1975) 136
 Super Dream Automatic
 (1980) 48
 Z50A (1971) 136
 Z50A Mini Trials (1971)
 136

I
Indian 57
 640 (1942) 134
 Four (1933) 57
 Model H (c1916) 139
 Scout Model 741 (1941)
 57
 Velo (1970) *53*
Iso 200 (1952) 57
Itom 58
 50 Competizione (1957)
 58
 Astor Sport (1961) 58

J
James 58
 Comet 1 (1950) 58
 Model B (1928) 58
Jasuki Special Café Racer

 (1977) 159
Jawa Works Twin (1954)
 144

K
Kawasaki 59–60
 250KH (1976) 59
 Z1 (1973) **60**
 Z1A (1974) 59
 Z1-R (1978) 60
 Z750 (1974) 59
 Z750 Turbo (1984) 60
 Z1100ST (1981) 60

L
Lambretta
 125J (1967) 151
 125LD (1958) 150
Laverda 61
 500 Formula (1978) 149
 750 SFC (1974) *53*
 Alpine S (1978) 61
 Montjuic Series 2 (1982)
 61
 SF1 (1972) 61
 SFC (1975) **61**
Levis 62
 (1913) 62
 Model A Special (1935)
 62
Lincoln Elk (1912) 62

M
Magni AFI GP500
 (1970s/1990s) 159
Malanca 50 Sport (1972)
 62
Maserati
 Competizione (1958) *53*
 Sport (1959) 63
Matchless 63–4
 Benelli Special (1946)
 157
 De Luxe (1960) 64
 G2 (1959) 64
 G3L (1941) *125*, 134
 G3LC Competition
 (1952) 129
 G3LS (1958) *53*
 G9 Spring Twin (1952)
 64
 G11 (1957) *53*
 G12 (1959) 64
 G12 CSR (1960) 64
 G80S (1955) 64; (1959)
 64
 Model H and Sidecar
 (1921) 153
 Model X4 (1934) 63
 Silver Arrow Model A
 (1930) 63
 Silver Hawk (c1948) 64
 Works Trials (1957) 130
memorabilia *128*, 162–3
Mi-Val 125 Sport (1954)
 65
military bikes *125*, 134–5
MM 250 Turismo (1955)
 65
Mobylette Moped (1964)
 137
Mondial 65
 50 Enduro (1969) 65
 175TV (1955) 65

World 125 Grand Prix
 (1950) 142
monkey bikes 136
mopeds 137
Moto Guzzi 66–9
 4V (1925) 66
 350 Imola (1981) 69
 500 Normale (1924) 66
 850 T5 Police (1986) 138
 Airone Sport (1951) 67
 Alce (c1940) *125*
 C4V (1924) **67**
 Cardellino (1961) 69
 Cardellino Lusso (1958)
 68
 Convert Automatic
 (1980) 69
 Corsa 2V (1924) 139;
 (1926) 140
 Corsa 4V (1926) *125*
 Falcone Sport (1951)
 54; (1955) 68
 Galletto (1963) 151
 Gambalunga Tipo
 Falenza (1951) 143
 Gambalunghino (1950)
 143
 GT 2VT Special (1928) *54*
 Guzzino Special (1950)
 157
 Le Mans (1977) 69
 Le Mans Series III (1982)
 69
 Lodola (1957) 68;
 (1961) *54*; (1962) 68
 Nuovo Falcone (1974) 69
 Nuovo Falcone and
 Sidecar (1970) *128*
 Superalce (1946) 135
 Tipo GT (1931) 66
 Tipo Sport 15 (1935) 67
 Works 500 (c1948) *127*
 Zigolo Series I (1957) 68
 Zigolo Series 2 (1960) 69
Moto Morini 70–2
 3½ Strada (1973) 70;
 (1981) 72
 3½ Strada Disc (1976)
 71; (1979) 71
 3½ Strada S1 (1974) 70
 125 Competizione
 (c1948) *126*
 125 Series II (1979) *55*
 125U Series 2 (1979) 71
 250T (1978) 71
 500 Camel (1983) 72
 500 Six Speed (1981) *55*
 500 Sport (1981) 72
 500 Touring (1979) 71
 500W Touring (1978) *54*
 501 Excalibur RLX (1992)
 72
 Briscola (1956) 70
 Camel Series 2 (1984) *55*
 Corsarino Competizione
 (1965) 147
 Corsaro Regolarita
 (1960s) 132
 Kanguro X (1983) *56*, 72
 Kanguro XI (1985) 72
 Sbarazzino (1956) 70
 Settebello (c1957) 145
 Valentini Special (1982)
 160

Moto Reve (1908) 73
Moto Zodiaco Tuareg
 (1975) 136
Motobi Sports Special
 (1971) 66
Motom Super Sport (1959)
 70
Motorsacoche and
 Torpedo Sidecar (c1917)
 153
MV Agusta 73–5
 125 (1953) 144
 125 Competizione
 (1953) *127*
 125 Sport (1970) *56*
 175 Turismo (1957) 73
 350B Elettronica (1971)
 74
 350S Elettronica (1973)
 74
 600 Four (1972) *56*
 750 America (1978) 75
 750GT (1973) *56*
 750S (1972) 74
 750 Super Sport (1972)
 75
 GP (1956) **74**
 Model 216 350 Sport
 (1976) 75
 Turismo Rapido (1957)
 73
 Works Twin Cam Single
 (1952) 143
MZ Super 5 (1980) 75

N
Neracar A2 (1922) 76
New Hudson 76
 2-Speed (1921) 76
 2½hp Semi Sports (1926)
 76
New Imperial
 Model 7 and Sidecar
 (1924) 154
 Semi Sports De Luxe
 (1927) 76
Nimbus Four and Sidecar
 (c1950) *128*
Norton 77–82, 162
 19S (1956) 79
 40M Manx (1955) 145;
 (1959) 146; (1960s) *127*
 99 Café Racer (1960) 158
 650SS (1962) 80; (1963)
 80
 850 Commando
 Interstate Mk3 (1977) 82
 850 Commando
 Roadster Mk III (1975)
 121
 Atlas (c1968) *121*
 CJ (1933) 77
 Commando (1971) 81;
 (1977) 82
 Commando Fastback
 (1971) 81
 Commando Interpol
 (1972) 138
 Commando Interstate
 (1973) 81
 Commando Roadster
 (1975) 82
 Commando S-Type
 (1969) 80

CS1 **77**; (1928) 77
Dominator 99 (1957)
121; (1961) 79
ES2 (1949) 78; (1951)
78; (1953) 78; (1962)
79
International (1938) 78
International Manx
Special (1953) 144
International Model 30
(1957) 79
JPS (1973) 81
Manx (c1946) *126*
Mercury (1969) 80, 81
Model 7 Dominator
(1951) 78
Model 18 (1931) 77
Model 18 and Sidecar
(1927) 154
Model 30 International
(1949) *121*; (1950) 78
Rotary Duckhams Racer
(1994) 149
Special (1960s) 159

O
OEC Model 34/8 (1934) 82

P
Panther 83
Model 10/4 (1962) 83
Model 20 (1938) 83
Model 100 (1956) 83
Redwing 90 (1930) 83
Parilla MSDS 175 (1957) 84
Peugeot 2hp Perfecta
(c1902) 84
police bikes 138
Premier 85
(1913) 85
Lightweight (1908) 85

Q
Quadrant 85
(1925) 85
4hp Tourer (1906) 85

R
racing bikes *126–7*,
139–49
Raleigh 86
250 (1925) 86
350 (1927) 86
Model 6 Sports (1924) 86
Model 12 De Luxe (1929)
86
Raynal Autocycle (1938)
137
Rickman-Kawasaki (1977)
87
Rover 87
3½hp (1914) 87
V-Twin (1917) 87
Royal Enfield 88–9
2½hp (1910) 88
2½hp Sports (1925) 88
350 Bullet (1961) 89
Bullet (1959) 89
Constellation (1961) *122*
Crusader Airflow (1958)
88
India (1991) 89
Interceptor (1970s) 89
J2 (1949) 89
Meteor Mini (1959) 89

Model 200 (1921) 88
Model CO (1946) 135
Scrambler (1959) 131
V-Twin (1914) 88
Rudge 90–1
250 Sports (1930) 90
Four (1925) 90
Multi (1919) 90
Radial (1931) 90
Special (1937) 91
Sports Special (1938) *122*
TT Multi (1921) 90
Rumi 91
125 Lusso (1954) 91
125 Sport (1954) 91
Competizione SS52
Gobbetto (1952) 143

S
scooters 150–2
Scott 92–3
Flying Squirrel (1930)
92; (1938) 92; (1947) 93
Squirrel (1928) 92
Two-Speed (1925) 92
Sertum 93
250 Turismo (1945) 93
sidecars *128*, 153–6
Simson Schwalde (1973)
150
specials 157–60
Spondon
Kreidler (1970s) 148
Sports M/LS Ducati
(1990) 160
Sun (1914) 93
Sunbeam 94–7
(1915) 94
(1916) 94
A29 Lion (1938) 97
Light Solo (1925) 94
Little 95 250 Racer
(1934) 140
Model 2 (1926) 94;
(1927) 94
Model 5 (1929) 96
Model 6 (1928) 94;
(1931) 96
Model 8 (1934) 96
Model 9 (1930) 96
S7 (1949) 97; (1950)
122
S8 (1949) 97; (1950)
97; (1952) 97; (1954)
123; (1956) 97
Sunbeam and Sunbeam
made Sidecar (1914) 153
Suzuki 98
GS850G (1979) 98
GS1000E (1980) 98
GT750L (1974) 98
RE5 Rotary Mark 1
(1975) 98
RG500 Mk V (1979)
149
T20 Super Six (1968) 98
T500 (1973) 98
XN 85 Turbo (1982) 98
SWM 125 Motocross
(1979) 133

T
Tribsa Special (1959) 157
Triton
(1960s) 158

(2001) 160
Special (1956) 157
Triumph 99–111, 162
3T (1951) 100
3½hp Model D (1911) 99
5T Speed Twin (1951)
101; (1953) 101; (1955)
102, *123*
5TA Speed Twin (1959)
124
6T Thunderbird (1952)
101; (1953) 101; (1954)
102; (1956) 102
6T Thunderbird and
Watsonian Child/Adult
Sidecar (1950) 155
250 Trophy (1972) 108
Adventer (1973) 133
Bonneville (1967) 106;
(1969) 107
Bonneville 750 (1985)
111
Enduro Special (1970s)
133
Grand Prix (1949) 142
ISDT Replica (1960s)
132
Model H (1923) 99
Model NSD (1930) 99
Speed Twin (1956) 103
T15 Terrier (1954) 101
T20 Cub (1962) 106
T20 Tiger Cub (1958)
104; (1959) 104; (1960)
105
T21 Twenty-One (1961)
105
T100 Grand Prix Replica
(c1948) 141
T100A Café Racer (1960)
158
T100C (1972) 109
T100C Tiger (1966) 106;
(1970) 108
T100R (1972) 109
T100SS (1962) 106;
(1967) 106; (1971) 108
T110 (1956) 102; (1958)
104
T120 Bonneville (1961)
105; (1970) 107
T120R Bonneville (1961)
105, *124*
T140 E/S (1983) 111
T140V (1976) 110
T140V Bonneville (1979)
124
T140V Executive (1980)
111; (1983) 111
T150V (1974) 110
T160 Slippery Sam No. 2
(1975) 110
Thunderbird (1957) 103
Tiger 80 (1937) 100;
(1938) 100
Tiger 100 (1947) 100;
(1949) 100, *123*; (1953)
101; (1956) 103
Tiger 100 and Watsonian
Sidecar (1955) 156
Tiger Cub Trials Replica
(c1964) 132
Tigress (1960) 152
Tigress TS1 (1964) 150
Touring (1911) *123*

TR5T Adventurer (1973)
109
TR6 Trophy (1969) 107;
(1970) *124*
TR25W Trophy (1970)
107
Trail Blazer (1971/72)
108
Trident (1995) 111
Trophy (1952) 129
Trophy Replica (c1959)
104
TRW (1957) 103;
(1960s) 135
Twenty-One (1958) 103
with Folding Sidecar
(1925) 154
X75 Hurricane (1973) 110
TWN
Boss (1954) 112
Contessa (1957) 151

V
Velocette 112–16
Grass Track Special
(c1936) 129
GTP (1939) 113
KTS (1940s) 113
KTT (1928) 140
LE (1954) 113
LE Mk III (1963) 116
LE Series 3 (1964) 138
MAC (1936) 112;
(c1937) 112; (1953)
113; (1956) 114; (1958)
115
Thruxton (1967) 116
Venom (1956) 114;
(1960) 115
Venom Clubman (1965)
116
Viper (1957) 114; (1961)
115
Viper Special (1960) 115
Vespa
90 (1970) 152
150 Standard (1964)
152
Ciao Moped (1978) 137
Vincent-HRD 117–19
Black Knight (1955) 119
Black Shadow Series C
(1952) 118
Comet (1951) 118
Rapide (1950) 117;
(1951) 118
Rapide Series D (1954)
118
Series B Rapide and Steib
S500 Sidecar (1947) 155

W
Werner 2hp (c1902) 119

Y
Yamaha 120
TD2B (1970) 148
Wasp Off-Road Outfit
(1974) 156
XS 650 Special (1978)
120
XS1100 (1979) 120
XT600 Tenere (1986)
120
YR2 (1967) 120

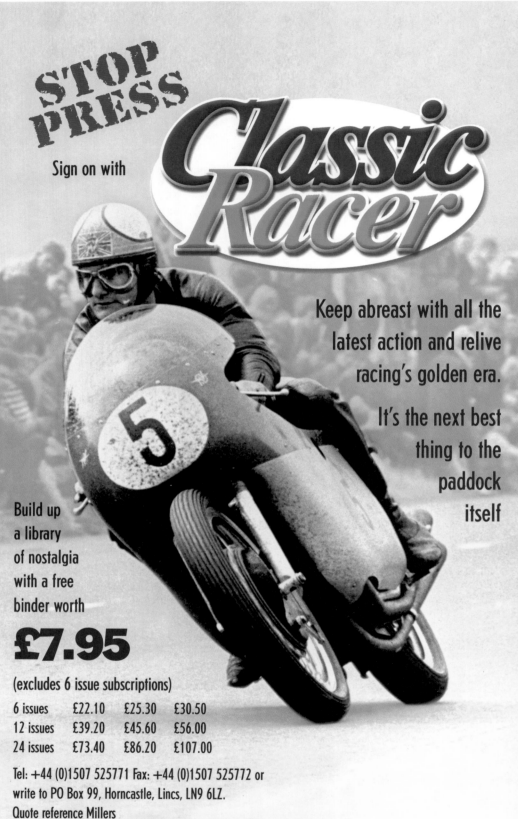

STOP PRESS

Sign on with

Classic Racer

Keep abreast with all the latest action and relive racing's golden era.

It's the next best thing to the paddock itself

Build up a library of nostalgia with a free binder worth

£7.95

(excludes 6 issue subscriptions)

6 issues	£22.10	£25.30	£30.50
12 issues	£39.20	£45.60	£56.00
24 issues	£73.40	£86.20	£107.00

Tel: +44 (0)1507 525771 Fax: +44 (0)1507 525772 or write to PO Box 99, Horncastle, Lincs, LN9 6LZ.
Quote reference Millers

From the people who bring you